ISAIAH

ISAIAH

Chronologically arranged, translated and interpreted

ELMER A. LESLIE

ABINGDON PRESS

NEW YORK   NASHVILLE

ISAIAH

Copyright © 1963 by Abingdon Press

Library of Congress Catalog Card Number: 63-7765

SET UP, PRINTED, AND BOUND BY THE
PARTHENON PRESS, AT NASHVILLE,
TENNESSEE, UNITED STATES OF AMERICA

DEDICATED TO

MY FORMER STUDENTS

of

Boston University School of Theology

Across thirty-six years

1921-1957

PREFACE

THE AIM OF THIS VOLUME IS TO MAKE THE READING OF THE ENTIRE BOOK OF ISAIAH AN INTELLIGIBLE, ENJOYABLE, INFORMING, AND INSPIRING experience. The distinctive feature which characterizes the present work is the attempted arrangement of the sixty-six chapters of the book on a chronological principle, so far as that can be discerned. This should help the reader to have an accurate sense of progress as he reads, and will make him sensitive to the probable historical background of each particular portion.

I have made my own translation of the entire book of Isaiah on the basis of the seventh edition (1951) of the late Rudolf Kittel's *Biblia Hebraica*, edited by Professors Albrecht Alt, Otto Eissfeldt, and Paul Kahle (Leipzig, Halle, and Oxford). I have worked directly from the Hebrew text in this latest edition and have availed myself of the critical apparatus which includes the most significant variant readings in the complete Hebrew manuscript of the book of Isaiah, which was discovered in 1947 in a cave near the northwest corner of the Dead Sea.

ELMER A. LESLIE

CONTENTS

INDEX TO ISAIAH

INTRODUCTION

The Nature of the Book of Isaiah

THE BOOK OF ISAIAH IS GENERALLY ACKNOWLEDGED TO BE THE GREAT-EST OF THE PROPHETIC BOOKS OF THE OLD TESTAMENT. UPON ITS SIXTY-SIX chapters there has been concentrated an amazing amount of scholarly research which has continued across many centuries and is now at white heat.

A. THE NUCLEUS OF THE BOOK OF ISAIAH

The nucleus of the Book of Isaiah is that portion the author of which is Isaiah, son of Amoz, whose prophetic ministry began in 742, the year of the death of King Uzziah of Judah, and lasted until 701. This nucleus is contained within chs. 1-39, although, as we shall see, there are several portions within this major section which do not come from this prophet. Just how this nucleus came to be so far as Isaiah's authorship is concerned, we learn from such passages as Isa. 30:8, wherein the prophet reports that he had received from the Lord an impulse regarding his activity as a prophet with a message for his rebellious people, to "go, write it before them on a tablet, and inscribe it in a book." Since they would not hear the Lord's instruction as uttered through him, to those who could read what he had written his message would be an enduring witness that the Lord was using Isaiah as his spokesman, his medium of communication to his people.

Early in Isaiah's ministry it was made clear to him by the Lord that when the king and the people of Judah rejected or ignored his prophetic message— the testimony as regards the Lord's will for them—he was to do something that would save that testimony for his people, the truth which the Lord, on their behalf, had revealed to him. He received a definite impulse from the Lord to "Bind up the testimony"—by which significant word is meant a solemn declaration made by a witness under oath as to the truth of what he was saying—and "seal the teaching among my disciples." It is his obedi-ence to such an impulse to which we owe the very existence of that nucleus of the Book of Isaiah which comes from Isaiah, son of Amoz.

All the prophetic messages to Judah and Israel in the Old Testament have come down to us in four major scrolls which are of approximately the same length. These are the books of Isaiah, Jeremiah, Ezekiel, and "the Twelve," by which latter term is designated the twelve relatively small prophetic books, respectively, Joel, Amos, Obadiah, Jonah, Micah, Nahum, Habakkuk, Zephaniah, Haggai, Zechariah, and Malachi.

Bernhard W. Anderson calls attention to the fact that as regards the book of Isaiah, "in many cases . . . the authorship of particular passages will never be known, since anonymous prophecies from various periods have clustered around great prophetic figures like Isaiah, Jeremiah, and Ezekiel." [1] Accordingly in the Old Testament scroll issued under the name of Isaiah we have what is really the depository not only of Isaiah's own oracles, but also of many others which he did not compose. This was due, as J. Philip Hyatt says, to "his prominence as a Jerusalem resident, and because he was concerned with hopes for the future more definitely than were former prophets." [2]

B. The Major Sections of the Book of Isaiah

There are three major sections of the Book of Isaiah.

1. The first major section is Isaiah 1-39. The opening verse is the title of this section and dates from *ca.* 701. It designates not only the beginning, but also the extent of the prophetic ministry of Isaiah, son of Amoz, so far as it has come down to us. This section includes all that we know of the life and teaching of Isaiah, son of Amoz.

Isa. 1:1 The vision of Isaiah, the Son of Amoz which he saw concerning Judah and Jerusalem in the days of Uzziah, Jotham, Ahaz, and Hezekiah, kings of Judah.

2. The second major section of the Book of Isaiah is Isaiah 40-55 and is designated Deutero-Isaiah or Second Isaiah. In comparing the authentic sections of Isaiah's poetry as found within Isa. 1-39 with that of Isa. 40-55, R. H. Pfeiffer says, "It is sufficient to say that the conciseness, variety, and concreteness of Isaiah's poetry contrast sharply with the eloquent verbosity, repetitiousness, and vagueness of Isa. 40-55. Isaiah belongs to the golden age of Hebrew literature, Isa. 40-55 to its silver age." [3] However, it is the

---

[1] *Understanding the Old Testament,* p. 257.

[2] *Prophetic Religion,* p. 21.

[3] *Introduction to the Old Testament,* pp. 462-63. Used by permission of Harper & Row, Publishers.

judgment of the late C. C. Torrey, that as a poet, the author of these chapters was "supreme and unrivalled among the great poets of the world." [4] Cyrus the Persian, twice mentioned by the poet-prophet (Isa. 44:28; 45:1), is on the march. Babylon is soon to fall. Pfeiffer summarized the message of the Second Isaiah as follows: "Monotheism and Israel's prophetic—nay, atoning—mission to mankind are the two cornerstones which the Second Isaiah provided as the basis of the three universal religions of salvation destined to spring eventually from his teaching, Judaism, Christianity and Islam." [5] The date of Isa. 40-55 is *ca.* 540.

3. The third major section of the Book of Isaiah is Isa. 56-66, and is designated Trito-Isaiah, or Third Isaiah. It was the pioneering research of Bernard Duhm, whose commentary on Isaiah in its fourth edition (1922) [6] has led to the separation of Isa. 56-66 from Isa. 40-55. Pfeiffer says there is "no proof that Isa. 56-66 could not have been written by a single writer." [7] However it is most likely that in this section we have to do not with a writer but with writers who are disciples of Second Isaiah. As James Muilenburg said:

Chapters 56-66 do not have the dominating coherence of Second Isaiah's eschatological poems. The writers are familiar with the work of their great leader, but the practical problems of restoration and reconstruction, the disappointment and discouragement of the people, the presence of alien influences corrupting their common life, all these press for immediate answer. . . . The prophecy as a whole gives us valuable insight into the conditions and religious life of Israel following 538 B.C. [8]

As H. H. Rowley says, "We are in the period between the return of the exiles from Babylon and the time of Nehemiah. It is unlikely that there is unity of authorship in this section, and the composition as a whole is ascribed to the period c. 520-450." [9]

C. THE DEAD SEA SCROLLS

A discovery of major importance which Professor William F. Albright considers to be "the greatest manuscript discovery of modern times," [10]

---

[4] *The Second Isaiah: A New Interpretation* (New York: Charles Scribner's Sons, 1928).
[5] Pfeiffer, *op. cit.,* p. 474.
[6] *Das Buch Jesaja* (Göttinger Handkommentar Zum Alten Testament) (4th ed.; Göttinger: Vandenhoeck und Ruprecht, 1922.)
[7] *Op. cit.,* p. 480.
[8] *Interpreter's Bible,* V, 414.
[9] *The Growth of the Old Testament,* p. 100.
[10] Millar Burrows, *The Dead Sea Scrolls,* p. 15. Used by permission of The Viking Press.

consists of eleven ancient scrolls or parts of scrolls found in 1947 in a cave in a cliff about five miles south of the northwest corner of the Dead Sea. This cave is within a mile of an old ruin named "Khirbet Qumran," or "Qumran ruin." Protruding from broken jars were eleven scrolls of leather wrapped in linen cloth. Two of these scrolls are of the greatest importance for rightly understanding the Book of Isaiah.

1. The St. Mark's Manuscript of Isaiah

The more significant one of the two for new insight into the book is now designated "the St. Mark's manuscript of Isaiah." [11] Millar Burrows describes it as a

scroll of leather made of strips sewed end to end. When unrolled it is about 1 foot wide and 24 feet long. It is remarkably well preserved, though considerably worn by much use. . . . The Hebrew text, written in fifty-four columns, is for the most part, still clearly legible.

. . . .

The forms of the letters in the Isaiah manuscript and the other Dead Sea Scrolls resemble those found in Palestinian inscriptions from about the last century before the birth of Christ.[12]

2. The Hebrew University Manuscript of Isaiah

The other Isaiah scroll is designated as the Hebrew University manuscript of Isaiah. It is composed of one large piece containing the last third of the Book of Isaiah from ch. 28 to the end, with some gaps. The smaller pieces contained parts of chs. 10, 13, 19-30, 35-40.[13] This scroll does not make so great a contribution to the study of the Hebrew text of Isaiah as the St. Mark's scroll does, not merely because of its incompleteness, but also because it agrees very closely with the Masoretic text of later manuscripts. It is the judgment of Millar Burrows as stated in his earliest article concerning the scroll that therein "lies its chief importance, supporting the fidelity of the Masoretic tradition." [14] The next basis of its importance is that emphasized by Paul Kahle. As Burrows interprets Kahle's view, "the most significant fact about the [St. Mark's] scroll is that it has a large number of real variant readings, which are elsewhere practically nonexistent in Hebrew manuscripts of the Old Testament." Burrows,

[11] *Ibid.,* pp. 19-20.
[12] *Ibid.*
[13] *Ibid.,* p. 21.
[14] *Ibid.,* p. 304.

however, views this as constituting not its first but "its second point of importance." [15]

Burrows calls attention to the fact that in the Revised Standard Version of the Bible (1952) "thirteen readings in which the [St. Mark's] manuscript departs from the traditional text were eventually adopted." [16]

3. The Distinctive Importance of the St. Mark's Isaiah Scroll

In reviewing these manuscript discoveries in his second book on the Dead Sea Scrolls, *More Light on the Dead Sea Scrolls,* looking back over the material of them Burrows says, "Some of the books—notably Deuteronomy, the Psalms, and Isaiah—appear in ten or more copies." He goes on to say:

> By far the most interesting and useful of all the Isaiah manuscripts for the study of the text is the complete St. Mark's Isaiah scroll—as it may still be called for convenience, although it is now in Israel. It, too, supports the accuracy, by and large, of the Masoretic text. . . . It presents, however, a more popular, less official form of the text than the other manuscripts. It was probably less carefully written and therefore contains a greater proportion of mistakes in copying, but it also preserves a number of ancient readings which were lost in the more orthodox tradition.[17]

D. THE PROPHETIC MINISTRY OF ISAIAH, SON OF AMOZ

The materials of the Book of Isaiah that come from or have to do with Isaiah, son of Amoz, comprise by far the largest block of material in the book. Their complexity and the importance of the historical background out of which they come warrant an additional word of introduction. While all such materials are contained within chs. 1 to 39, there are considerable portions within this major section which, as we shall see, are anonymous and date from periods later than Isaiah, son of Amoz. These portions will be dealt with in the order of their most likely chronology.

1. Chronology of the Kings of Judah and Israel During the Ministry of Isaiah, Son of Amoz

The prophetic ministry of Isaiah, son of Amoz, dates from 742, the year of the death of King Uzziah, to 701, the year when King Hezekiah of Judah, having seen forty-six of his fortified cities fall before Assyria's onslaught, "eventually decided to submit and pay tribute, so that Jerusalem escaped

[15] *Ibid.*
[16] *Ibid.,* p. 305.
[17] *More Light on the Dead Sea Scrolls,* p. 146.

destruction." [18] For the political background of the prophetic ministry of Isaiah, son of Amoz, it is essential to have before us the chronology of the kings of Judah, the Southern Kingdom, and of the kings of Israel, the Northern Kingdom, who ruled during his ministry. We shall follow the authoritative chronology as presented by George Barrois in *The Interpreter's Bible*. [19]

The Kingdom of Judah	*The Kingdom of Israel*
Uzziah, also called Azariah 783-742	Jeroboam 786-746
Jotham as regent for Uzziah 750-742	Zechariah 746-745
Jotham as king 742-735	(6 months)
Ahaz 735-715	Shallum 745
Hezekiah 715-687	(1 month)
	Menahem 745-738
	Pekahia 738-737
	Pekah 737-732
	Hoshea 732-724

2. Types of Literary Composition in Isa. 1-39

There are various types of literary composition in the first major section of the Book of Isaiah. The basic portion is composed of prophetic oracles which are messages of the Lord uttered by the prophet as the chosen human medium. There are memoirs spoken by the prophet to his hearers, often incorporating oracles. One of the most interesting and certainly most important of the types of writing is the public oracle usually preceded by "Thus says the Lord." There are a variety of moods which prophetic oracles may express—reproach, threat, exhortation, or promise. There are portions of prophetic biography, often in the third person, but sometimes, as in Isaiah's account of his call to be a prophet, we have an exceedingly significant autobiographical narrative.

In Isa. 36–39 we have a section of historical narrative which is primarily dependent upon the basic historical record in II Kings 18:13-20:19. This narrative in Kings clearly has priority over the version in the book of Isaiah as being the more objective and authentic source. While Isaiah plays a significant role in this narrative, the writer of Isa. 36-39 is dependent upon the source in the book of Kings, which is the fuller and more reliable account.

[18] So R. B. Y. Scott, *Interpreter's Bible*, V, 162.
[19] I, 146-47.

It is of human interest to know that Isaiah was married and had two sons. In speaking of his wife he calls her "the prophetess," which in this case merely means that she is the wife of a prophet (Isa. 8:3).

3. The Four Periods of the Prophetic Ministry of Isaiah

The prophetic ministry of Isaiah, son of Amoz, embraces the years from his call in 742 to *ca.* 701. It falls into four periods.

The earliest period dates from his call to 734. The prophet grapples with the moral and spiritual conditions in Judah and Jerusalem.

The second period dates from 734 to 715. The refusal by King Ahaz to give attention to Isaiah's counsel led Isaiah to withdraw to a considerable extent from public teaching. It would seem that he gave himself to writing down the prophetic messages he had proclaimed. He states in Isa. 8:16-18 his purpose in this period to "bind up" his preaching as to the will and purpose of God. He evidently withdrew from public proclamation and devoted himself to the more intimate and private teaching of his disciples.

The third period dates from 715 to 705. This begins with the ascent of Hezekiah to the Judean throne. He was a monarch of quite different stamp from Ahaz, and Isaiah now felt free to proclaim the Lord's message. His messages in this period are more definitely dated. He is very deeply concerned with the Lord's will in relation to the moving events which were transpiring in the international scene, more particularly the Egyptian antagonism to Assyria and the Judean reliance upon Egypt were uppermost in his concern.

The fourth and last period dates from 705 to 701. As regards the final date for Isaiah's prophetic career, some scholars would set it at 700.[20] In this phase of Isaiah's career he is deeply concerned with the political trend in Judah toward alliance with Egypt for support against Assyria.

---

[20] So Hyatt, *op. cit.*, p. 22: "his public ministry beginning in 742 and continuing to about 700."

CHAPTER I

The Earliest Period of the Ministry of Isaiah (742-734)

T HE FIRST PHASE OF ISAIAH'S MINISTRY (742-734) BEGINS WITH THE PROPH-
ET'S NARRATIVE OF HIS CALL TO THE PROPHETIC OFFICE.

A. ISAIAH'S ACCOUNT OF HIS CALL TO BE A PROPHET

In Isa. 6:1-13 a vivid and priceless autobiographical account is given of Isaiah's call to be a prophet and of his acceptance of that call. It came to him in a vision experience in the Temple at a strategic moment in Judean and Israelite history, "in the year that King Uzziah died," (ca. 742). The given name of this monarch was Azariah (II Kings 14:21), which means "the Lord is my helper," but Uzziah, which means "the Lord is my strength," was most likely the throne name given to Azariah when he became king. He mounted the throne at the age of sixteen and ruled over Judah for forty-one years.

Uzziah was a great king whose marked achievements gave strength to his reign. He was religious minded and was a vigorous leader of Judah with marked initiative. The features that made his reign memorable are summarized in II Chr. 26. He built Elath, a strategic commercial port situated on the northeast arm of the Red Sea. He fought victoriously against the Philistines, the Arabs, the Meunites—a people south of Canaan, and the Ammonites. He built and fortified towers at strategic points in Jerusalem and in the wilderness. In the lowlands west of the Judean mountains and in the plain he developed agriculture. As a lover of the soil he made cisterns for his herds and settled farmers and winedressers in the fertile Shephelah, the strip of land west of the Judean mountains. He developed an army of 307,500 fighting troops and equipped them for warfare. He created military machines to shoot arrows and hurl stones. Leprosy took the king in the end, however, and the Judean throne fell to his son Jotham.

In Isaiah's own firsthand account (Isa. 6) we learn how he became a prophet. A. B. Davidson, brilliant Scotch scholar of the Old Testament, suggestively interprets "in the year that King Uzziah died" as it relates to Isaiah's call.[1] He imaginatively pictures youthful Isaiah as joining the throng of Judeans passing through the palace to gaze upon the body of the deceased monarch, whose life leprosy had taken. From there Isaiah passed into the Temple, where, in a moving and heart-searching spiritual experience, he had a vision of the living King who never dies, the Lord of all mankind and of all human history. The account of the vision experience is autobiographical. He saw the Lord seated upon his throne, his royal robes seemingly filling the Temple. He penetrated behind the official ritual into those spiritual realities and their meaning that lie beyond physical vision.[2] Thus he describes the vision, giving its date and portraying the living movement of the worship. The seraphim, divine beings, as Scott says, "have the hands, faces, and voices of men, and stand upright; and they have three pairs of wings." [3] These six wings of each of the divine beings moved in perfect harmony and suggest mingled reverence and dread in the divine presence—two wings for covering the face, expressing awe, lest they see God and die; two for covering their nakedness; and two for flight. Youthful Isaiah hears, as it were, the anthem of the seraphs, in which the holiness and the glory of the Lord are two majestic themes. The smoke symbolizes the cloud of glory which, as we are told in Exod. 40:34, covered the tent of meeting in the wilderness.

Isa. 6:1 In the year of the death of King Uzziah, I saw the Lord seated upon a throne, high and exalted, with the skirts of his robe filling the Temple. 2 Seraphs were standing above him. Each had six wings. With two he covered his face and with two he covered his feet and with two he kept flying. 3 And one proclaimed unto the other and said:
"Holy, holy, holy is the Lord of Hosts;
  The whole earth is full of his glory."
4 And the foundations of the thresholds shook at the voice of the proclaimer, and the house began to fill with smoke.

Isaiah, keenly sensitive to the contrast between his own character and the purity of God, as implied in his response, utters a cry of humiliation and despair, yet of reverent awe. How vast is the gulf between the lofty spiritual being of God and mere man at his best! Sensitive, youthful Isaiah utters a cry in words of almost inexpressible woe. He has come to the vivid awareness that he is standing before the spiritual king of the entire

[1] *The Called of God*, pp. 189-91.
[2] In parts of this section I am indebted to Ivan Engnell, *The Call of Isaiah.*
[3] *Interpreter's Bible*, V, 208.

world, and never before has he felt his own inadequacy, his own uncleanness of life, and the uncleanness of his people as now.

6:5 "Woe to me, for I am ruined; for a man unclean of lips am I, and in the
midst of a people unclean of lips am I dwelling; for the king, the Lord of Hosts,
my eyes have seen!"

Then there begins, symbolically, the divine purification of the life of
him who was destined to become a great spokesman for the Holy God
(vss. 6-7). One of the seraphs, as though at divine order, flies to the altar
and with tongs takes from the altar fire a burning coal and applies it to
the lips of Isaiah. Then in spoken words the seraph gives him assurance of
the forgiveness of his sins and the removal of iniquity, wickedness, and un-
righteousness from his life. The reality here is the forgiving and cleansing
grace of God which fits him to be the Lord's spokesman. Thus his account
continues:

6:6 Then flew one of the seraphs to me, and in his hand a burning coal which
he had taken with the tongs from off the altar, 7 and he applied it to my mouth,
and said: "Behold, this has touched your lips; and your iniquity is removed, and
your sin atoned for."

Thus far the experience has been forgiveness and cleansing, both symbolic and actual. Then fast upon it comes his commission to be a prophet.
We sense the unwritten thought that forgiveness must precede mission. For
the first time in this profound inner experience he hears the voice of the
Lord speaking, as it were, for the entire heavenly host and pronouncing his
commission to prophesy, to proclaim, to preach as the messenger of God.
Without a moment's hesitation Isaiah offers himself to be sent by the Lord.

6:8 Then I heard the voice of the Lord, saying, "Whom shall I send, and who
will go for us?" Then I said, "Behold me! Send me!"

Then follows in some detail (vss. 9-10) the nature of this divine commission. His was not to be an easy mission, nor does the Lord seek to lighten it.
He is to preach and preach, with few hearing or heeding the prophetic
word. The hearts of the people generally are heavy and insensitive; the
ears of the people seemed clogged and unreceptive, their eyes dull and unsee-
ing. But Isaiah is to keep preaching. He will often feel that the more he proclaims the duller becomes his hearers' receptivity. The people of Judah do
not adequately see, hear, or understand spiritual things. It will often seem

that the more earnestly, intensively, and pertinently the prophet speaks the less attentive or responsive his hearers become. The prophet's words are so uttered that the result appears to be the Lord's intent. It is the social entity, the people of Israel and Judah, that is in the focus of the prophet's words. There is a glimpse here of the impervious nature of the Judean souls whom it was to be his mission to address. The Lord speaks:

> 6:9 And he said, "Go and say to this people:
> 'Hear, again and again, but you will not understand;
> And see, over and over, but you will not perceive.'
> 10 Make the heart of this people unreceptive,
> And make their eyes dull,
> And besmear their eyes,
> Lest they see with their eyes,
> And hear with their ears,
> And understand with their hearts,
> And turn and be healed."

The summons to a mission so difficult in its nature almost overwhelms inexperienced Isaiah. We can readily understand what is passing through his mind as, in a mood of deep lamentation, he utters to the Lord an implied protest, "Until when?" "How long?" It is Isaiah's remonstrance against the finality of the Lord's judgment upon his people, along with the seeming futility of his own now accepted commission. He feels that in all integrity the message of doom, and that alone, must be the burden of his preaching. The final sentence of vs. 13, "The holy seed is its stump," is missing in the Septuagint. It is rightly viewed as a late marginal comment and does not come from Isaiah. Scott calls attention to its close analogy with Ezra 9:2, where the people of Israel "the holy race has mixed itself with the peoples of the lands." [4] To Isaiah's protest in Isa. 6:11a regarding the duration of his now accepted commission comes the Lord's answer in 6:11b-13.

> 6:11a "Then I said, 'How long, O Lord?' and he said:
> 11b Until there shall have crashed into ruins
> Cities without inhabitant,
> And houses without men,
> And the land be left a desolation,
> 12 And the Lord sends men far away,
> And desolation in the midst of the land be great.
> 13 And although there remain in it a tenth,

[4] Cf. *Ibid.*, p. 213, and William H. Brownlee, "The Text of Isaiah VI:13 in the Light of the Dead Sea Scroll," *Vetus Testamentum* I (1951), 296-98.

It shall be consumed and shall be
As an oak, when it is thrown down,
And as the terebinth, by the sacred column of a high place,
Which, when felled, a stump remains in it."

B. THE DAY OF THE LORD

The theme of Isaiah's earliest message is the day of the Lord. It clearly reveals the influence of the prophet Amos of Tekoa, who had proclaimed at Bethel:

Woe to you who desire the day of the Lord!
    Why would you have the day of the Lord?
It is darkness, and not light. (Amos 5:18.)

The date of this first prophetic utterance of Isaiah is 742. It was Uzziah's leprosy that had brought his son Jotham to the throne as regent for him during the last eight years of his reign (750-742). From his father's death in 742 until 735 Jotham was king of Judah in his own right. In this latter period the nation of Judah experienced considerable material prosperity, but Jotham was not in the least responsive to Isaiah's solemn prophetic warnings. Isaiah took up Amos' theme but carried it further. He announced the imminent self-manifestation of the Lord in a day near at hand, when all merely human glory would experience humiliation. This earliest message, arranged in correct order, consists of Isa. 2:19, 6, 7-13; 10:33-34; and 2:14-22. At Bethel Amos, the herdsman prophet of Tekoa, had warned the Israelites against the widespread popular expectation that the day of the Lord was destined to bring salvation to Judah and destruction to its foes. Rather that day would be for Judah itself a day of "darkness, and not light."

This earliest prophetic utterance of Isaiah reveals him as already a skilled poet. The refrain of vss. 19, 10, and 21 is an opening refrain which, as Gray suggests, also originally preceded Isa. 2:6, while vss. 9 and 17 are closing refrains.

1. Flee in Dread Before the Lord's Judgment

In rhetorical, poetic vigor Isaiah calls upon his fellow countrymen to flee in dread from the imminent majestic self-manifestation of the Lord when he rises up to bring judgment upon his people. Having deserted the Lord, their real strength, the Judeans had substituted for the true worship of God pagan rites of divination and prediction, such rituals as those for which the Philistines were famous. Isaiah begins with an opening refrain (vs. 19) and then in vs. 6 accuses his people, whom he calls "the house of Jacob," of seeking divine guidance through pagan rituals which Judah had absorbed (2:19, 6).

> 2:19 Enter into caverns of rocks,
>   And into holes of earth,
>   Away from the dread [presence] of the Lord,
>   And from before his majestic splendor,
>   When he shall arise to cause the earth to tremble.
> 6 Because you have abandoned your strength,
>   O house of Jacob,
>   For they[5] are full of diviners from the east,
>   And of foretellers like the Philistines,
>   And they strike hands with descendants of foreigners.

2. The Judean Worship of Material Things

Judah had become a wealthy nation, having extravagantly furnished itself with rich material resources and treasure store. It was equipped with horses and chariots and had manufactured for itself skillfully wrought idols. Such luxury in the material realm resulted in the worship of material things, with the result that the citizens of Judah, destitute of real moral strength, were making no ethical or spiritual advance, their lives being empty of dignity and worth. Cries the prophet, describing contemporary Judah's crass materialism, militarism, and idolatry:

> 2:7 So their land is full
>   Of silver and gold,
>   And there is no end to their treasures;
>   And their land is full of horses,
>   And there is no end to their chariots.
> 8 And their land is full of idols;
>   To the work wrought by their own hands, they bow them-
>   selves down.
> 9 So human beings have become empty,
>   And mankind degraded,
>   And there is no dignity in them.

3. The Humbling of the Haughty

Again resounds the refrain with which the message had opened (vs. 19) warning haughty Israel that its own pride was laying it low (vss. 10-11):

[5] The Judeans.

> 2:10 Enter into the rocks,
>   And hide yourself in the dust
>   From before the dread presence of the Lord,
>   And from before the splendor of his majesty,
>   When he rises up to cause the earth to tremble.
>   11 The haughty eyes of man shall be humbled,
>   And the pride of men shall be brought low;
>   And the Lord alone shall be exalted
>   In that day.

4. The Lord's Antagonism to Human Pride

In 2:12-13 Isaiah conceives the day of the Lord as being antagonistic to all human pride and as depicted in nature as that which is lofty and exalted. Physical symbols of such exaltation on the part of man are the majestic cedars of Lebanon and the famed oaks of Bashan in the ancient kingdom of Oz, which may still be seen on the western slope of the mountains of Hauran, stretching from the stream of Jabbok north to Mount Hermon.

> 2:12 For the Lord of hosts has a day
>   Against everything that is elevated and lofty,
>   Against everything that is lifted up and exalted;
>   13 And against all the cedars of the Lebanon! *
>   And against all the oaks of Bashan.

Isa. 10:33-34 rightly belongs here. The prophet's antagonism to human pride continues, as he uses Lebanon's towering cedars and its forest thickets as symbols of it. Accordingly, the nation of Judah is doomed to destruction.

> 10:33 Behold, the Lord God of hosts
>   Will lop off the crown of branches with an axe,
>   And the heights of the lofty trees shall be hewn down,
>   And the haughty shall be brought low.
>   34 And the thickets of the forest shall be struck away,
>   And Lebanon, with its majestic trees, shall fall.

5. Symbols of the Pride of Man

In 2:14-19 the prophet paints other pictures which symbolize human pride, illustrations of which he saw upon every hand—mountains and hills, towers and fortresses of man's construction, the proud ships which ploughed

---

* Omitting with BH the second clause of Isa. 2:13.

the Mediterranean Sea to Tarshish, famed western commercial port—all of them pictures of the materialistic spirit that prevailed in Judah. The thing most lacking in the nation was humility, the modest recognition that the ultimate source of every mental achievement and physical glory in the nation was God. Accordingly the sole object worthy of appreciation and exaltation in the Lord's day of crisis is not man-made idols, which are utterly impotent, having no hold upon reality, but the majestic spiritual being of the unseen Lord, himself alone. From before his august majesty and splendor let sinful Judah flee in awe and dread! In Isaiah's continuing thought (vss. 14-18) he maintains that the Lord is against everything that symbolizes or gives expression to human pride and glory as a basis of national security.

> 2:14 And against all the high mountains,
>   And against all the lofty hills;
> 15 And against every high tower,
>   And against every fortified wall;
> 16 And against all the ships bound for Tarshish,
>   And against all the panelled vessels.
> 17 And the pride of man shall be humbled,
>   And the haughtiness of men shall be abased;
>   And the Lord alone shall be exalted
>   In that day.
> 18 But the idols shall entirely vanish.

Again comes the refrain:

> 19 Enter into caverns of rocks,
>   And into holes of earth,
>   Away from the dread [presence] of the Lord,
>   And from before his majestic splendor,
>   When he shall arise to cause the earth to tremble.

6. Terror Before the Lord of Judgment

In 2:20-22 the keynote is awesome terror before the mighty Lord of judgment. We feel how transient is mere man before the terrors of the trembling earth, which is viewed as a manifestation of the divine judgment. How utterly unimportant and impotent are mere human beings and the idols which they worship! In the day of the Lord's judgment mankind will realize how futile and valueless is human pride. In the trembling of the earth, John Skinner senses the deep impression made on Isaiah's youthful mind by the earthquake which occurred in King Uzziah's reign (cf. Amos 1:1; Zech.

14:5), and how it "furnished him with a presentiment of the terror of the great day of the Lord." [7]

> 20 In that day men shall fling away
>   Their silver idols and their golden idols,
>   Which they had made for themselves to worship,
>   To the moles and to the bats,
> 21 To go to the crevices of the rocks,
>   And into the clefts of the cliffs,
>   From before the dread of the Lord,
>   And from the splendor of his majesty,
>   When he rises to cause the earth to tremble!
> 22 Cease regarding man,
>   In whose nostrils is but a breath,
>   At what worth is he esteemed?

C. ISAIAH'S INDICTMENT OF JUDAH

1. Isaiah's Vineyard Song

A. THE PROPHET SINGS HIS MESSAGE

Isa. 5:1-7 is a charming vineyard song which most likely was actually sung by Isaiah at the autumnal festival of Booths. We are in the reign of Jotham. Vineyard songs with a love motif were in the air at this greatest and most popular of the Judean festivals. We know how real is the owner's love of his farm, orchard, and vineyard. We are likewise aware that when a Christian minister who is also a good soloist on occasion sings a spiritual message, it is usually to the delight and edification of the congregation. It is evident that in addition to his power as a spiritual spokesman for God Isaiah had a singing voice which, in such a moment, became a unique channel of spiritual ministry as he sang the message he would impart. Thus he introduces this innovation in an inspiring manner and shares with the congregation of Judah the Lord's "love song concerning his vineyard," as he interprets God's message to the Judean nation. The "beloved" is the Lord, and Judah is the object of his loving concern. We can imagine the eager silence of the Judean congregation as Isaiah resorts to prophetic song.

> 5:1 Pray let me sing for my beloved
>   My love song concerning his vineyard:
>   My beloved had a vineyard
>   On a very fertile hill.
> 2 And he dug it carefully round about, and freed it from stones,
>   And planted it with a choice vine;

---

[7] *The Book of the Prophet Isaiah, Cambridge Bible,* pt. I, 23. Used by permission of Cambridge University Press.

> And built a watchtower in the midst of it,
> And also hewed out in it a wine vat;
> And he looked expectantly for it to bear grapes,
> But it bore worthless, stinking things.

We can readily imagine the intense interest with which the prophet's hearers, up to this moment, had attended this quite unexpected procedure on Isaiah's part as he passed from prophetic speech to prophetic song.

B. ISAIAH'S APPEAL TO THE RESIDENTS OF JERUSALEM

In vs. 3 he resumes the technique of prophetic speech. He appeals to the residents of Jerusalem and to his fellow Judeans generally. Who is to blame for the disappointing yield of the Lord's vineyard? What could the Lord of his vineyard, Judah, still do to assure a bountiful spiritual harvest, the bearing of the good and abundant fruit of moral and spiritual living? In vss. 3-4 God speaks:

> 5:3 So now, you who dwell in Jerusalem,
> And men of Judah,
> Judge, I pray, between me
> And my vineyard.
> 4 What is there still to do to my vineyard,
> That I have not done to it?
> Why have I expected that it would bear grapes,
> When it yielded but worthless, stinking things?

C. HOW THE LORD PROPOSED TO DEAL WITH JUDAH

Isaiah paused a moment in order to give his question time to penetrate Judah's ethically dull conscience. Then through his revelation to Isaiah, in all solemnity, the Lord imparted what he proposes to do to his beloved vineyard, the Judean nation.

> 5:5 So now, pray let me tell you
> What I am about to do to my vineyard.
> I will take away its hedge,
> And it shall be burned down;
> I will break through its enclosing wall,
> And it shall be trampled down.
> 6 And I will exterminate it;
> It shall not be pruned, neither shall it be hoed,
> But thorns and thorn bushes shall spring up;
> And I will command the clouds
> Not to send rain upon it.

D. THE LORD'S DISAPPOINTED APPEAL FOR JUSTICE AND RIGHTEOUSNESS

Not until this moment does it dawn upon Isaiah's hearers that his interesting and attractive vineyard song is in fact an original and indeed brilliant prophetic appeal to the house of Israel, the Northern Kingdom, and to the house of Judah, the Southern Kingdom, for justice and righteousness of conduct in every human relationship. In the last three lines of vs. 7 Isaiah resorts to the prophetic technique of assonance, using Hebrew words that are similar in sound but have a drastic contrast in meaning. Cries the prophet:

> 5:7 For the vineyard of the Lord of hosts
>   Is the house of Israel,
>   And the men of Judah
>   Are the plantation of his delight;
>   And he waited eagerly for *mishpat* [justice]
>   But lo! *mispah* [bloodshed];
>   For çedhāqāh [righteousness]
>   But lo! çeʻāqāh [a cry of distress]!

2. *Isaiah's Sevenfold Woe Upon Judah*

Isa. 5:8-24 and 10:1-4 belong in the same context of prophetic utterance. We are in the late reign of Jotham. With an evident intention both of completeness and of solemnity, they embody the prophet's sevenfold condemnation of Judah. Each member of this series opens with the expressive and solemn interjection, "Woe!" which suggests grief, disaster, trouble, or misery. Taken as a whole these woes give concrete glimpses of the moral and spiritual conditions in contemporary Judean society which called forth the prophet's lament and condemnation.

A. WOE UPON GREEDY LANDHOLDERS

The first woe (5:8-10) falls upon greedy landholders who, equipped with the power of their material wealth, buy up large tracts of land, then through remote control force out the former dwellers from their ancestral holdings. These covetous land-grabbers have no conception whatever of property as a sacred, social trust. The Lord's judgment upon them will be expressed in the scanty yield of the soil. Cries the prophet:

> 5:8 Woe to those who join house to house,
>   Who join field to field,
>   Until there is no more room, and you will dwell
>   By yourself alone in the midst of the land.
> 9 Therefore, in my ears,
>   The Lord of hosts
>   Has sworn:
>   "Surely many houses shall become desolate,
>   Large and beautiful [ones],

> Without inhabitant.
> 10 For ten acres of vineyard
>   Shall yield but one bath[8]
>   And a homer[9] of seed
>   Shall yield but an ephah." [10]

B. WOE UPON INDULGERS IN INTOXICATING DRINK

The second woe (5:11-13) falls upon those in Judean society who are excessive indulgers in intoxicating liquor. At their banquets they start imbibing early in the morning to the music of lyre and lute and carry on late into the night until their minds are aflame with intoxication. They are blissfully unaware of what Isaiah perceives to be their certain fate—captivity to a foreign power—and that simply because of their fatal lack of knowledge.

> 5:11 Woe to those who arise early in the morning,
>   To pursue strong drink,[11]
>   Who tarry on into the twilight
>   Until wine inflames them!
> 12 And lyre and harp,
>   Timbrel and flute,
>   And wine are at their discretion.
>   But to the [providential] work of the Lord they pay no heed,
>   Nor do they perceive the work of his hands.
> 13 Therefore my people will surely go into captivity
>   From lack of knowledge;
>   And their glory will be emptied from hunger,
>   And their population parched from thirst.

The Humbling of Man and the Exaltation of God

In vss. 14-17 Sheol, the realm of the dead, is conceived of as "a country under the earth" [12] and is imaginatively pictured as an insatiable and devouring monster (vs. 14) which is at the point of swallowing down the superficially pompous, jubilant Judean capital and its gay, irresponsible city throng. Thus will the Lord bring utter humiliation and complete destruction upon the haughty Judeans.

That very judgment, so rightly deserved, will lift into sharp and condemning awareness on their part the righteousness and majesty of the Lord. In these verses there is given a glimpse of Isaiah's philosophy of history. In the anticipated destruction of the capital city he sees the working

---

[8] *Ca.* eight gallons.
[9] Ten ephahs.
[10] Nine gallons.
[11] When the evening breeze springs up.
[12] Gray, *The Book of Isaiah*, I, 92. Used by permission of Charles Scribner's Sons.

of the moral law. Regions once inhabited by human beings shall then have become but the haunt of hungry, devouring lambs.

> 5:14 Therefore Sheol has increased its appetite
>   And has opened its mouth immeasurably wide,
>   And its[13] majesty and its multitude shall descend,
>   With its noisy clamor, and jubilance along with it.
> 15 So mankind is humbled,
>   And human beings are degraded,
>   And the eyes of the haughty are humiliated.
> 16 But the Lord of hosts will be exalted in justice,
>   And the Holy God
>   Will show himself majestic in righteousness.
> 17 Then lambs shall feed as in their pasture,
>   And fatlings shall devour amid desolations.

C. WOE UPON THOSE WHO TOIL AT SIN

In 5:18-19 the prophet utters the third woe. He pronounces a threat of disaster upon those who are actually *toiling* at sin just as men must toil who have to drag along unruly cattle with strong ropes. He puts in the mouth of sinful Judeans a daring, disdainful challenge to the Lord on the part of men who have no faith whatever in his existence.

> 5:18 Woe to those who drag along the evil
>   As with calf ropes,
>   And the sin, with cordage.
> 19 Those who keep saying, "Let him hurry up!
>   Let the Lord hasten his work,
>   That it may be seen!
> And let the counsel of the Holy one of Israel
>   Come into being and draw near,
>   That we may see it!"

D. WOE UPON JUDEAN STATESMEN

In 5:20 is spoken the fourth woe, wherein the prophet condemns the Judean statesmen who do not concern themselves with moral distinctions and who attempt to justify abuses in society such as men of integrity under no circumstances could condone.

> 20 Woe to those who keep calling
>   What is evil, good,
>   And what is good, evil,

[13] Jerusalem's.

> Who keep substituting darkness for light, and light for darkness;
> Who keep putting bitterness for sweetness,
> And sweetness for bitterness.

E. WOE UPON THOSE WISE IN THEIR OWN EYES

In the fifth woe (5:21) Isaiah seems to have haughty Judean statesmen in mind. He has no respect for these leaders whose own self-admitted shrewdness has made them arrogant. Cries the prophet:

> 21 Woe to those who are wise in their own eyes,
> And, in their own view, intelligent!

F. WOE UPON VALIANT WINE-MIXERS

In the sixth woe (5:22-24) we feel the sarcastic humor of the prophet's words as he criticizes the valiant (!) wine-spicers and wine-mixers! It is the judgment of Isaiah that drunkenness is the basic cause of injustice on the bench, and next to this comes bribery. Spiritually speaking the Lord's people are no more substantial than chaff, and since the root of the nation is rotten, there can be no national advance. The Lord's law and teaching are spurned.

> 5:22 Woe to those who are valiant to drink wine,
> And men of valour to mix intoxicating drink,
> 23 Who declare the wicked righteous, in consequence of a bribe,
> And take away the righteousness of the righteous from him!
> 24 Therefore, as a tongue of fire eats up stubble,
> And as chaff sinks down in the flame,
> Their root will be as rottenness,
> And their bud will go up like the dust;
> For they have rejected the law of the Lord of hosts,
> And they have spurned the word of the Holy One of Israel.

G. WOE AGAINST JUDICIAL OFFICIALS WHO THWART JUSTICE

The seventh and final woe is uttered in 10:1-4, and, as Kittel points out, rightly belongs immediately after 5:21-24.[14] It is a climactic woe and is directed against the judicial officials who defame the dignity of their high office by writing legal decrees that thwart rather than promote justice. Consequently, those who suffer are the poor and defenseless widows and orphans. Isaiah warns the responsible but unworthy officials of the inevitable punishment which will eventually overtake such miscarriage of justice. The

---

[14] *Great Men and Movements*, p. 616.

popular foreign deities—such as the Babylonian Beltis (Bel Marduk) and the Egyptian Osiris—in whose protection many Judeans confide, Isaiah pronounces to be utterly impotent, and Judah's worship of such nonentities arouses the anger of Judah's Lord. Cries the prophet:

> 10:1 Woe to those who inscribe unjust decrees,
>   And write damaging decisions,
>   2 So as to thrust aside the afflicted from justice[16]
>   And rob, by judicial decree, the poor of my people.[16]
>   So widows become their plunder,
>   And orphans, they take as spoil!
>   3 Now what will you do in the day of punishment,
>   And of devastation that is coming from afar?
>   To whom will you flee for help,
>   And where will you bring your wealth into safety? [17]
>   4 Beltis is crouching, Osiris is shattered,[18]
>   And under the slain they fall.
>   In all this his anger is not turned away.
>   But his hand is stretched out still.

D. SOCIAL WRONGS IN JUDAH AND DOOM OF THE NORTHERN KINGDOM

In 735 Ahaz, son of Jotham, became king of Judah. Ahaz had no interest in religion. Whatever loyalty to the Lord he may have revealed was but a surface loyalty like that of his fathers, as Isaiah was quick to discern.

Beginning with the reign of Ahaz, Isaiah had to deal with pressing external problems concerning Judah's international relations. The Syrians and the Philistines threatened the destruction of Judah. In 734, in less than a year's time, Syria made an alliance with the Northern Kingdom, Israel, against Judah, the Southern Kingdom. This complicated Isaiah's task. Consequently he had to deal with threats of attack from without as well as with moral corruption from within. Grappling with these problems led him to new heights of religious insight.

1. Social Wrongs in the Reign of Ahaz

In 3:1-15 Isaiah is concerned primarily with specific social wrongs that existed unrestrained in Judean society during the reign of Ahaz (735-715) and which were driving the nation to destruction. He singles out five partic-

---

[15] Reading רין with LXX and Syriac.
[16] Reading במשפט with Targum.
[17] Reading with BH.
[18] Reading with BH בלת כרעת הת אסיר.

ular groups of Judah's citizens for specific condemnation: Men in public office, such as (1) military commanders and soldiers, (2) judges appointed by the government to administer law and order, (3) elders, the mature heads of prominent Judean families, (4) counselors, a select few of distinguished and honorable Judeans who had the ear of the king, and (5) prophets, whose sacred responsibility it was to seek out and declare to monarch and people the word of the Lord. These should have been the pillars of the Judean state.

A. ANARCHY IN JUDEAN SOCIETY

Instead of offices filled by reliable, conscientious, and social-minded men, Isaiah saw them usurped by incompetent and irresponsible young upstarts motivated by no concern whatever for the welfare of the nation, but moved merely by selfish whim. The consequence of such leadership in the Judean nation mounted to social anarchy, a situation in which able and competent men who had ability to lead selfishly refused public office, rejecting with finality such responsibility and interpreting their refusal to serve as the rejection of the rôle of national dictator. Cries the prophet:

3:1 For lo, the Lord,
    Yahweh of hosts,
        Is in process of removing from Jerusalem and Judah
    Stay and staff,[19]
  2 Valiant men and men of war,
    Judges and prophets,
        And predictors and elders,
  3 Captains in battle array
    And eminent citizens,
  And counselors and wise men,
  And those skilled in charms.
  4 And (so says the Lord) I will make *mere boys* their officials,
    And caprice shall rule them.
  5 So the people shall draw near,
    Man against man,
        And each against his neighbor.
  The young men shall act arrogantly toward the aged,
    And the lightly-esteemed toward the distinguished.
  6 When a person lays hold of his brother
    [In] his own father's house [and says]
  "Take for yourself a mantle;
  "Become dictator over us,
  And let this heap of ruins

[19] Omitting as an insertion "Every staff of bread and every support of water."

> Be under your hands!"
> 7 He will say in protest in that day,
> "I will not be a restorer of fortunes.
> No, in my house there is no bread
> And no mantle;
> You cannot make *me*
>   Dictator over the people."

B. SINS OF THE CITIZENS OF JUDAH

Judah and Jerusalem had indeed fallen upon hard times. The conversation and the conduct of the leaders in the capital city were so disapproved by the Lord that their spiritual rejection of him had manifested itself in their very facial features. In blatant boldness, comparable to the wickedness of the notorious Sodomites, the sin of Judah's citizens was manifesting itself. However nonchalant these Judeans might appear to be among their fellowmen they could not hide the inner misery of their souls, which was indeed the fruit of their own sinful conduct for theirs is a wickedness comparable to that of Sodom and Gomorrah. Cries Isaiah:

> 3:8 For Jerusalem has stumbled,
> And Judah has fallen;
>   Yes, whatever they say and whatever they do is against the Lord.
>   Thus rebelling against the eyes of his glory.
> 9 The expression on their faces witnesses against them;
> And their own sin they proclaim like Sodom.
> They cannot hide the woe of their soul
> Because they have dealt out evil to them.

C. A LATE MARGINAL COMMENT

It is likely, as Duhm and Marti maintain,[20] that Isa. 3:10-11 is a late marginal comment intended for the consolation of the reader. This passage views the Judean people as divided sharply into two classes, the God-fearing and the wicked. Most likely it was inserted after the law book of Deuteronomy had been introduced into Judah in 621 B.C. This unknown person, stressing one of the greatest principles of ethics, the moral boomerang of Judean conduct, their deeds bringing upon themselves either good or bad, writes:

> 3:10 Oh the happiness of the righteous, for it will go well with him,
> For he shall eat the fruit of his deeds.

---

[20] *Das Buch Jesaja*, p. 39.

> 11 Woe to the wicked! It will go ill with him,
>   For what his own hands deal out will come back upon him.

On the throne of Judah at the time was King Ahaz, an inexperienced and timid youth who lacked both courage and a sense of national responsibility. Isaiah had already made implicit reference to this unfortunate condition of affairs as in itself a divine judgment upon the nation when he had said, "And I will make [mere] boys their rulers
    And [the spirit of] recklessness shall govern them." (3:4.)
Furthermore it is probably the pathetic figure of this youthful, fearful Judean king which the later author of the Book of Ecclesiastes had in mind when he said: "Woe to you, O land, when your king is a child." (10:16a.)

D. THE LORD'S JUDGMENT UPON THE RULERS OF JUDAH

It is with reference to this young monarch, ruled by his harem, that Isaiah now speaks:

> 3:12 O my people, their leader is a child,
>   And women rule over him.
>   O my people, those leading you are causing you to err,
>   And they have confused the way of your paths.

E. THE LORD AS JUDGE OF HIS PEOPLE

In vss. 13-15 the Lord is portrayed as the judge of his people. There opens before our eyes a scene of judgment. The Lord here plays a threefold role. He is at the same time accuser, judge, and vindicator of his people. He comes in regal dignity to call the rulers and princes to responsibility for the welfare of Judah.

> 3:13 The Lord has taken his stand to plead,
>   Yes, he stands up to judge his people.
> 14 The Lord enters into judgment
>   With the rulers of his people and its princes:
>   "It is you who have devoured the vineyard
>   The plunder of the poor is in your houses.
> 15 What do you mean that you crush my people,
>   And grind the faces of the poor?"

2. The Daughters of Zion Are Passing By

In 3:16-4:1 the prophet's conception of the certainty of the Lord's judgment is focused upon the young women of Jerusalem, to whom Isaiah gives the beautiful designation "the daughters of Zion." How alive is his firsthand description! We can *see* the proud daughters of Zion passing by! We note their haughty bearing and their bold sensualism as they trip along with the "come-hither" look in their eyes, the decorative bangles on their feet tinkling to attract the attention of Jerusalem's young men. Incidentally this passage is instructive regarding the dress of the upper-class young women in the capital city of Judah. We see their attractively "set" hair, the necklaces, the ear and nose rings, and the decorative anklets. We note their colorful sashes. We can almost catch the aroma of the perfume which fills the air when the daughters of Jerusalem pass by, the tinkle of their decorative step chains calling attention to them. As we admire the beauty and up-to-the-minute fashion of their raiment we appreciate the vivid details in this living picture painted by the young prophet.

A. THE TRAGIC FUTURE OF THE DAUGHTERS OF ZION

However attracted by their feminine charms young men may have been, Isaiah, with imaginative power and solemn prophetic sensitivity, saw into the future of the daughters of Zion. He envisaged these same young women stripped of their ornaments, captives of the ruthless enemies of Judah, their heads bald, their expensive, fashionable garments stripped off and replaced with the sackcloth of captives. The climax of their chagrin and dismay is portrayed in what Skinner calls "a companion picture to Isa. 3:6, where efforts, frantic but unsuccessful, are made to induce some person to accept the task of maintaining order in the existing chaos." [21]

3:16 And the Lord said:
 Because the daughters of Zion
  Are haughty,
 And walk with necks outstretched,
  And ogling eyes,
 Walking and tripping along quickly as they go,
 And tinkling their bangles on their feet;
17 The Lord will smite with a scab
 The scalps of the daughters of Zion,
 And the Lord will lay bare their foreheads.[22]
18 On that day the Lord will remove the beauty of the anklets, the necklaces, the crescents, 19 the pendants, the ear-rings and the veils, 20 the turbans, the step chains, and the sashes, the perfume and the charms; 21 the seal rings and the nose rings, 22 the stately robes and the over-tunics, the cloaks and the purses, 23 the mirrors, the linen wrappers, the turbans and the mantles.
24 And it shall be that

[21] *Op. cit.*, p. 31.
[22] So render instead of "their secret parts," "for cutting off the hair as a sign of shame, cf. 7:20." *Interpreter's Bible*, V, 192.

> Instead of perfume there shall be rottenness,
> And instead of a mantle, a captive's rope,
> And instead of a rich robe, a girdle of sackcloth;
> Branding instead of beauty.
> 25 Your men shall fall by the sword,
> And your might in battle,
> 26 And her gates will lament and mourn,
> And cleaned out, she will sit on the ground.

B. THEIR ATTEMPT TO ESCAPE DISGRACE

The climax of the chaos portrays Judean young women feeling it a disgrace to be unmarried. Seven of them dare to take the initiative in romance and lay hold on one man, promising to provide for their own maintenance of food and clothing if they can but escape disgrace by being called by his name.

> 4:1 And seven women will lay hold
> Upon one man in that day,
> Saying, "We will eat our own bread
> And we will wear our own clothes,
> If only we can be called by your name;
> Remove our disgrace."

C. SELF-INDULGENT AND UNCONCERNED WOMANHOOD

Isa. 32:9-14 is parallel to Isa. 3:16-4:1. Just as in 3:16-4:1 Isaiah is concerned with the social wrongs which characterized Judean women during the reign of Ahaz (735-715). The self-indulgence and utter lack of social concern on their part are quite apparent. The prophet seeks to arouse them from their complacency. At the moment there was in the Judean nation a seeming security, but Isaiah is convinced that although next year's grape and fruit harvest may be gathered, beyond that it will fail. Isaiah has no uncertainty regarding Judah's destruction. He believes it is near at hand and is convinced that the extent of it will be so great as to leave even the Temple hill, Ophel, deserted of all human occupancy. The Judean women who outwardly seemed to be so secure were solemnly summoned to lamentation by Isaiah, whose insight penetrates the tragic future of Judah. Cries the prophet:

> 32:9 Self-indulgent women,
> Listen to my voice;
> Daughters so secure,
> Give ear to what I say.
> 10 In little more than a year

> You who are complacent will be perturbed;
>   For the vintage shall be at an end,
>   Ingathering shall not take place.
> 11 Tremble, be perturbed, careless daughters;
>   Strip, and make yourselves naked,
>   And gird sackcloth upon your loins.
> 12 There will be wailing over your fields,
>   Over [your] delightful fields,
>   Over [your] fruitful vines.
> 13 Upon the soil of my people
>   You have caused thorns and thornbushes to grow,
>   Upon all the joyous houses of the rejoicing city.
> 14 For the palaces will be abandoned,
>   The roaring city forsaken,
>   Ophel and watchtower will become dens forever.
>   The exultation of wild asses,
>   A pasturage for flocks.

E. The Doom of the Northern Kingdom of Israel

Isa. 9:8-21 dates from the early part of the sixteen-year reign of King Ahaz of Judah (*ca.* 735). These verses deal with the doom of "Jacob," the Northern Kingdom of Israel—designated here by its leading tribe, "Ephraim"—and the inhabitants of its capital, Samaria.

The time is before Ephraim, the prophet's name for the Northern Kingdom of Israel, and Syria had become allies against Judah. Israel, the Northern Kingdom, is haughty in spirit, superficially optimistic, and seemingly quite unaware of the doom which Isaiah is convinced is soon to overtake it. Cries the prophet:

> 9:8 The Lord has sent a word against Jacob,
>   And it will fall upon Israel;
> 9 And the people, all of them, will know,
>   Ephraim and those dwelling in Samaria,
>   Who speak in haughtiness,
>   And in insolence of heart, saying:
> 10 "Bricks have fallen,
>   But we will build with hewn stone.
>   Sycamores have been hewn down,
>   But we will substitute cedars."

1. The Lord's Use of Nations as Instruments of Judgment

The Lord is about to bring his judgment upon these proud and self-confident Israelites. The instruments conceived by the prophet as the mediators of that judgment are the Syrians to the east and the Philistines on the west—these are the adversaries of Zion who will destroy, yes, consume, Israel. But even then the Lord's judgment upon Israel will not have been accomplished. Still will his hand be stretched out in further discipline.

The last two lines of vss. 12, 17, and 21 form an impressive refrain which affirms in awesome solemnity the persisting judgment of the Lord. The effect of this is cumulative and fills the reader's mind with awe.

Speaks the prophet:

> 9:11 So the Lord will exalt in effective hostility[23]
> The adversaries of Mount Zion against it,
> And his adversaries will pierce you through.
> 12 The Syrians on the east,
> And the Philistines on the west;
> Shall devour Israel with open mouth.
> For all this his anger is not turned away,
> But his hand is stretched out still.

2. The Failure of Military Disaster to Turn Israel to God

In vss. 13-14 Isaiah makes it clear that the military blows dealt Israel by the Syrians and Philistines—which he views as a concrete expression of the judgment of God—did not arouse the nation, as was divinely intended that it should, to confident trust in him. Accordingly Israel, the Northern Kingdom, is doomed to swift and devastating destruction.

> 9:13 But the people have not turned unto him who smote them,
> Nor have they sought the Lord of hosts,
> 14 So the Lord will cut off from Israel head and tail,
> Branch and rush, [in] one day.

Vs. 15 is a marginal comment on vs. 14 by a later reader which has crept into the text. Whoever inserted it quite misunderstood the prophet's meaning in the above two verses.

> 9:15 The elder and eminent one, he is the head,
> And the prophet who teaches deception, he is the tail!

3. The Awful Effects of Corrupt Leadership

In vss. 16-17 Isaiah focuses solemn attention on the effects upon Judean life in general of irresponsible and corrupt leadership. Isaiah continues:

[23] So read with LXX.

9:16 And those who are leading this people on
   Are causing them to err;
   And those who are being led
   Are being engulfed in ruin.
17 Therefore the Lord does not rejoice over their young men,
   And he does not have compassion for their orphans and
   widows,
   For all of them are profane and evil doers,
   And every mouth keeps uttering disgraceful folly.
   For all this his anger has not turned away,
   But his hand is stretched out still.

4. The Wickedness of the Northern Kingdom

In vss. 18-21, in picturesque, living style, Isaiah portrays the wickedness of
the Northern Kingdom, Israel. These verses form an impressive and awful
climax to the entire chapter. First, in vs. 18 Israel's wickedness is vividly
pictured as a burning fire. Following the prophet's keen imagination we
see the dense forest thickets aflame. We hear the crackle and roar of burning timber and watch the great columns of smoke rolling up to the sky.
It is a solemnizing imaginary picture of the Lord's fury consuming in judgment the Northern Kingdom of his people, leaving Israel a desolate land.
Isaiah's picture goes beyond the realm of physical nature, however, for
among those destined for destruction are *people*, so hungry that all self-con-
trol, all decent self-restraint is gone. It is a picture of mankind reduced in
dire straits to cannibalism. Not only civil war between Manasseh, the
Israelites who lived east of the Jordan, and Ephraim, Israel's supreme tribe,
is in Isaiah's prospect, but the chief Northern tribes will combine together
against Judah, the sole Southern tribe, and destroy it. Even then the Lord's
judgment is not at an end.

Cries the prophet:

9:18 For wickedness burns like fire,
   It consumes thorns and thorn-bushes;
   And it kindles in thickets of the forest,
   And they roll up a column of smoke.
19a The land will be desolated by the fury of the Lord,
   And the people are like consuming fire.
19b A man will have no compassion toward his brother,
20c   They will eat, each the flesh of his fellow,
20a And one will slice off on the right hand, yet be hungry.
20b And one will eat on the left hand, yet not be satisfied.
19c   No man will spare his fellow man.

21 Manasseh will consume Ephraim,
    And Ephraim, Manasseh,
    Together they shall be against Judah.
    Because of all this his anger has not turned away,
    But his hand is stretched out still.

F. THE DOOM OF SYRO-EPHRAIMITE ALLIANCE

1. An Oracle Concerning Damascus

Isa. 17:1-11, the oracle of Damascus, dates from shortly after the formation of the alliance (ca. 734 B.C.) between Ephraim—which, as its leading tribe, was Isaiah's designation of the Northern Kingdom of Israel—and Syria, whose capital was Damascus. Upon the throne of Syria was Rezin, and Pekah, the son of Remaliah, was upon the throne of Israel. With profound religious and political insight, Isaiah stood against that alliance. At the present moment Damascus formed a bulwark of protection between mighty Assyria and Israel. The prophet speaks with an insight that is both religious and practical. Syria's fall is sure and imminent, and Israel's fall will then be certain. Speaks Isaiah:

17:1 An Oracle concerning Damascus:
    Lo, Damascus is about to be removed from being a city,
    And will become a heap of ruins.
   2 Its cities will be forsaken forever.
    Flocks will possess them,
        And they shall lie down, and no one shall terrify them.
   3 Thus a bulwark shall be removed from Ephraim,
    And sovereignty from Damascus,
    And the remnant of Syria will be
    Like the glory of the sons of Israel,
        Says the Lord of hosts.

2. The Doom of the Northern Kingdom, Israel

Isaiah describes vividly in anticipation the sure fate of Ephraim, the Northern Kingdom, as will be manifest when Assyria has done its work of destruction (vss. 4-6). The prophet has three figures of speech to portray that certain fate—wasting disease, the reaping of corn, and the gathering of olives (vss. 4-6). "The glory of Jacob" is the prophet's loving and unique designation of the Northern Kingdom, Israel. The valley of Rephaim (vs. 5) is a fertile grain area, "southwest of Jerusalem toward Bethlehem." [24]

[24] Bewer, *The Book of Isaiah*, V, 49. Used by permission of Harper & Row, Publishers.

17:4 And it shall be in that day
   That the glory of Jacob will be laid low,
   And instead of fat, his flesh will grow lean.
5 And it shall be as when the reaper is gathering standing grain,
   And his arm reaps [the] ears.
   And it shall be as when one harvests the ears of grain
   In the Valley of Rephaim,
6 And there will be left in it mere gleanings,
   Just as at the beating of olive trees, [Isa. 24:13]
   Two, three berries,
      On the top of a bough,
   Four, five,
      On the branches of a fruit tree,
      Says the Lord God of Israel.

3. The Utter Futility of Idol Worship

Gray rightly views vss. 7-8 as coming from "an early annotator whose notes have crept into the text." [25] However, his words effectively emphasize both the utter futility of the worship of idols and the reality and power of the living God. The annotator feels keenly the contrast between the Asherim on the one hand—sacred wooden poles representing living trees, but lifeless and shaped by merely human hands—which used to stand beside the altars of Canaan and on the other hand, the might of Israel's invisible, spiritual Creator. Says this annotator:

17:7 In that day, mankind will gaze upon his Maker and his eyes will behold the Holy One of Israel.
    8 But they will not regard [with favor] the altars, the work of their own hands, neither will they fear that which their own fingers have made, the Asherim and the sun pillars.

4. Forsaking the Lord to Worship Adonis

In 17:9-11 the prophet addresses himself to the question, What has Israel done which has laid the nation low? The answer is clear to Isaiah, and with it he confronts Judah. The Judean nation, influenced by certain popular features of the nature and fertility cults of Syrian and Babylon religion which had crept into Judah, had turned away from—indeed, had forgotten —the spiritual and ethical worship of the Lord. In vss. 10-11 Isaiah makes specific reference to an alien but exceedingly popular cult which had crept into Judaism, the plantings of Adonis. Describing this, Cheyne says, the

[25] *Op. cit.*, chaps. 1-39, I, 301.

gardens of Adonis—which were planted by women—consisted of "pots or baskets filled with herbs, which soon withered in the sun." The prophet Isaiah seems to have extracted from this custom an omen of the speedy fall of the Northern Kingdom.[26] Says the prophet:

17:9 In that day your cities shall be deserted like the forsaken ruins of the wooded heights of the Amorites, which they abandoned from before the Israelites, and [which] became a desolation.

10 For you have forgotten the God of your salvation,
And the rock of your protection you have not remembered;
Therefore, though you plant plantings of Adonis,
And though you set out the vine slips of a strange god,

11 [Though] in the day of your planting you fence it carefully about,
and in the morning when you sow it, you cause it to sprout,
Fled away will be the harvest in the day of sickness
And of incurable pain!

G. The Syro-Ephraimitic War

In 7:1-25 we have a narrative of the Syro-Ephraimitic war (734). In its present context it contrasts sharply with the vivid first person experience of Isaiah's call, as recorded in ch. 6. The narrative is in the third person and deals with events in which Isaiah takes significant part.

The combined forces of Syria and Ephraim, Isaiah's designation of the Northern Kingdom of Israel, attacked Jerusalem, capital of Judah. The narrative is in part dependent upon the summary account as given in II Kings 16:5: "Then Rezin king of Syria and Pekah the son of Remaliah, king of Israel, came up to wage war on Jerusalem, and they besieged Ahaz but could not conquer him." Vs. 1 is Isaiah's own brief summary of this Syro-Ephraimite attack upon Judah and its outcome.

Isa. 7:1 In the days of Ahaz, son of Jotham, and grandson of Uzziah, king of Judah, Rezin, king of Syria, and Pekah, son of Remaliah, king of Israel, went up to Jerusalem to fight against it, but they could not conquer it.

In 7:2 the effect which the news of the threatened combined campaign against the Judean capital had upon King Ahaz—here designated as "the house of David"—and upon the Judeans generally is vividly described:

7:2 When it was reported to the house of David, "Syria is in league with Ephraim," his heart trembled, and the heart of his people, as trees of the forest tremble before the wind.

[26] *The Prophecies of Isaiah*, I, 108.

1. Isaiah's Call to Calm Faith in the Lord

In this crisis hour when Judah was in grave peril an impulse came to Isaiah from the Lord to go and confront King Ahaz in Jerusalem at the hour and place where the king was inspecting the adequacy of his water supply in the event of siege. At this time the tunnel for bringing the water within the city walls had not as yet been constructed.

The prophet took with him his son—whose very name, Shear-Jashub, bore the ominous message that "[only] a remnant will return." Thus his presence was intended as a message of solemn warning to Judah. He was to confront King Ahaz in the crisis and counsel calm faith on his part. Ahaz was to have no fear or anxiety before the threat of attack now being plotted by the allies, Rezin, king of Syria, whose capital is Damascus, and Pekah, king of Israel, whose capital is at Samaria. Their plot—to attack Judah, to bring it under domination, and to set up over it a puppet king whom Syria and Ephraim, the Northern Kingdom, could control—will fail.

Thus runs the narrative:

> 7:3 Then the Lord said to me, "Pray go forth to meet Ahaz, you and Shear-Jashub, your son, at the end of the aqueduct of the upper pool on the highway to the Fuller's Field, 4 And say to him: 'Take care to be quiet. Do not be afraid and do not let your heart grow faint before these two fag ends of firebrands, because of the burning anger of Rezin and Syria, and the son of Remaliah. 5 Because Syria has advised evil against you, saying 6 "Let us go up against Judah and bring her into straits, and let us lay her open to us and let us set up a king in her midst, the son of Tabeel."' "

2. Faith Alone Leads to Staith

In 7:7-9 in the Lord's name Isaiah maintains that this Syro-Ephraimite plot against the Davidic monarch of Judah will fail because at its heart there is no concern as to whether it is in accord with the will of God. Rezin, the Syrian king, and the son of Remaliah—whose name, Pekah, the disdainful prophet does not even mention—are national, political monarchs who have no concern whatever for the accomplishment of the Lord's will. With a brilliant word-play in the climactic sentence of vs. 9b upon two Hebrew words of similar sound but of different yet related meaning (tha'ᵃmīnū and thē'ᵃmēnū), Isaiah gives classic utterance to the necessity of Judah's basing its security upon faith in God and in a national policy which will give expression to that faith in *staith,* that is, steadiness, through confidence in God's presence and power. The order of verses as Scott suggests should be 7, 8a, 9a, 8b, 9b.[27] Says Isaiah:

[27] So *Interpreter's Bible,* V, 216.

7:7   Thus says the Lord God:
      It shall not stand,
          And it shall not be realized.
8a For the head of Syria is Damascus,
          And the head of Damascus is Rezin.
9a And the head of Ephraim is Samaria,
          And the head of Samaria is the son of Remaliah.
8b Yet six, nay five years more and Syria
          Shall be shattered, Ephraim diminished! [28]
9b If you will not have faith,
          Surely you shall not have staith.

3. With Us Is God

At a slightly later time, but probably in the same year, Isaiah received another impulse from the Lord which led him to speak again to King Ahaz. The king, seeking aid against the alliance of Syria and the Northern Kingdom of Israel which had been formed against him, made overtures to Assyria. The prophet, sure of the truth he is proclaiming and with a deep desire to influence the youthful king to put his trust for protection in God and not to resort to help from Assyria, speaks again to King Ahaz. With profound conviction, Isaiah offers him and his counselors a sign—that is, an event soon to take place—which would confirm and prove that what he is counseling is truly the Lord's word. Isaiah gives the young king the privilege of naming a sign such as would give assurance of the validity of his counsel—whether the sign be from the realm of the dead or from the height of the heavens. Ahaz, in mock piety, covers up his real lack of faith by refusing to put God to such a test. Whereupon (vs. 13) Isaiah takes the initiative and speaks the Lord's message to Ahaz. The sign—a young woman with child—as Scott rightly maintains, has nothing to do with the virgin birth, but simply "refers to a young woman well known to both king and prophet . . . (perhaps a new wife of Ahaz.) " [29] "The king of Assyria" in vs. 17 is a marginal note which was inserted by a later reader. Scott, in rejecting the messianic interpretation, says that a prediction of the marvelous birth of a Messiah more than seven centuries later could hardly have served as a sign to Ahaz.

7:10 Again Isaiah spoke to Ahaz saying, 11 "Ask for yourself a sign from the Lord your God. Ask the depth of Sheol or the height of heaven. 12 But Ahaz said, "I will not ask, and I will not put the Lord to the test." 13 Then he said, "Hear,

[28] Kissane, *The Book of Isaiah*, I, 78-79, 82.
[29] *Interpreter's Bible*, V, 219.

I pray, house of David, is it too little a thing for you to weary men that you weary my God also? 14 Therefore the Lord himself will give you a sign. Behold a young woman has conceived and is about to bear a son, and you shall call his name Immanuel [With us is God]. 15 Leben and honey he shall eat until he knows to reject the evil and to choose the good. 16 For before the boy knows to reject the evil and to choose the good, the land before whose two kings you are in dread will be forsaken. 17 The Lord will bring upon you and upon your land, and upon your father's house, days such as have not come since the day when Ephraim departed from Judah.[30]

4. The Tragic Results of Foreign Invasion

In 7:18-25 threats are uttered against Judah. The first two verses look forward in predictive fashion to the invasion of Judah and the ruin which the invading forces will bring about. To portray such an invasion Isaiah uses the fly to represent Egypt and the bee to represent Assyria. These swarms of flies and bees are agents of the Lord's judgment upon Judah (vss. 18-19). Vss. 20-22 embody Ahaz's appeal to Assyria, his hiring the Assyrian forces from beyond the Euphrates who will come in sweeping destruction but will utterly humiliate the Lord's people, shaving the nation as with a razor—head, feet and beard—reducing the desolated population to poor peasant survivors living in utter simplicity like nomads. Vss. 23-25 look ahead to the result of such foreign intrusion viewing it as the reduction of the land to briars and thorns so it will be fit only for the grazing of stray cattle and sheep. Thus Isaiah speaks:

> 7:18 And it shall be in that day,
>   The Lord will hiss for the fly
>   Which is in the extremity of the Nile canals of Egypt,
>   And for the bee which is in the land of Assyria.
>   19 And they will come and settle down, all of them,
>   In the ravines of the precipices,
>   And in the clefts of the cliffs,
>   And on all the thorn bushes,
>   And on all the pastures.
>   20 In that day the Lord will shave with a razor that is hired in the region beyond the Euphrates,[31] the head and hair of the private parts and he will also sweep away the beard.
>   21 And it shall be in that day,
>   That a man will keep alive a heifer cow and two sheep.
>   22 And because of abundant
>   Yield of milk,

[30] Omitting "The king of Assyria" as an unnecessary marginal note.
[31] Omitting with BH "with the king of Assyria."

Every one who is left in the midst of the land
   Shall eat leben and honey.
23 And in that day
   Every place
      Where there used to be
   A thousand vines
      At a thousand shekels of silver,
         Will be but briars and thorns.
24 With bows and arrows
   Men will go there,
For all the land will be
   Briars and thorns.
25 And as for all the hills
   Which used to be hoed with hoes,
You shall not enter there.
   For fear of briars and thorns;
But it will have become [merely] a place for letting cattle loose,
   And a trampling place for sheep.

5. The Coming Desolation of the Land

Isa. 8:21-22 rightly belong after 7:18-25. It is a fragmentary passage which portrays a few survivors, hungry and distressed, passing through a desolate land. In desperation they look upward toward God who has thrust them into the darkness of anguish and distress and downward to their king who has failed them.

8:21 And they will pass through the land,
   Hard-pressed and hungry.
      And because they are hungry they will put themselves into a rage,
  And they will curse their king and their God.
      And they will turn their faces upward,
22   And they will look to the earth.
  But behold distress and darkness,
   Gloom of distress
      And darkness so one cannot see.

6. Only a Remnant Shall Return

When the youthful King Ahaz of Judah received the news that Syria was in league with Ephraim, Isaiah's name for the Northern Kingdom of Israel, and that the two nations were about to come against Jerusalem he was desperately frightened. At an impulse from the Lord Isaiah and his son, whose name, Shear-Jashub, bore the frightening message that "only a remnant shall return," confronted the timid young monarch. This name accordingly embodied an oracle of doom which is given expression by his son's presence. "Only a remnant shall return." We are here in harmony with the meaning to which the prophet's solemn thought gives utterance, for that seeming annihilation overflows with such righteousness as is the essence of the divine nature. Isaiah's words are intended to save Ahaz from mastery by fear.

> 10:22 For although
> Thy people Israel be
> As the sand of the sea,
> Only a remnant of them shall return.
> An annihilation is strictly determined,
> Overflowing with righteousness.
> 23 For an end, and that decisive, the Lord of hosts is making, in the midst of the land.

7. The Advance of an Invading Army

In 10:27d-32 Isaiah imaginatively pictures the advance of an invading army. We follow with breathless interest and concern the steady approach of enemy forces against Judah. It is a fragment of poetry which reports, as it were, from moment to moment the march of the united forces of Syria and Israel in the Syro-Ephraimitic war from the vicinity of Samaria, capital of the Northern Kingdom, Israel, against Jerusalem. The date is 734. Although the poetry is imaginative the author knows his geography. Aiath lay near Bethel to the southeast. Migron lay north of Mikhmash, a city in the tribal area of Benjamin, north of Geba and Jerusalem. Geba lay south of the pass of Mikhmash. Ramah is Er-Râm, less than two miles due west of Geba. Gibeah of Saul lay about half way between Geba and Jerusalem. Anathoth is modern Anata. Madmenah was in the tribal area of Benjamin which lay about three miles north-northeast from Jerusalem. Gebhim, meaning "trenches," also lay north of Jerusalem. Nob probably lay on the height of Scopus, overlooking the city from the north.[32]

> 10:27d He has gone up from the vicinity of Samaria,[33]
> 28   He has come to Aiath;
> He has crossed into Migron,
> At Mikhmash he will deposit his baggage;
> 29 They have crossed the pass,
> Geba is a lodging place for the night;

[32] So Skinner, op. cit., p. 102.
[33] Scott, Interpreter's Bible, V, 246.

Ramah is terrified,
Gibeah of Saul has taken flight.
30 Cry shrilly with thy voice, daughter of Gallim!
Give attention, Laishah!
Answer her, Anathoth!
31 Madmenah has fled,
Bring into safety the inhabitants of Gebim!
32 Yet today he will take his stand in Nob,
Brandishing his hand in defiance toward the mount of the
daughter of Zion,
The hill of Jerusalem.[34]

8. The Certain Doom of the Northern Kingdom, Israel, Prophetic Autobiography

In 8:1-15 we have a good illustration of prophetic autobiography wherein Isaiah anticipates the sure and imminent conquest of Damascus, capital of Syria, and of Samaria, capital of the Northern Kingdom, Israel. We are still in the reign of Ahaz. Moved by an impulse from the Lord, Isaiah took a great tablet and in large letters in Hebrew script clearly legible to all onlookers wrote upon it, "LeMaher Shalal HashBaz," which means "Concerning Spoil Speeds, Prey Hastens." Isaiah considered what he was doing to be so important that he took with him two prominent Judeans as witnesses. These were Uriah, the priest who had just built in Jerusalem an altar after a Syrian pattern before King Ahaz had arrived home from Damascus, and Zechariah, who, as Bewer says, was apparently well known at the time and an unimpeachable witness.[35]

9. The Birth and Naming of Isaiah's Second Child

8:1 Now the Lord said to me, "Take for yourself a large tablet and write on it with an ordinary stylus: "CONCERNING MAHER SHALAL HASHBAZ!" 2 So I took for myself as reliable witnesses Uriah, the priest, and Zechariah, son of Jeberechiah. 3 And I approached the prophetess [Isaiah's wife], and she conceived and bore a son; and the Lord said to me, "Call his name Maher Shalal HashBaz; 4 For before the child will know to cry 'my father' and 'my mother,' the wealth of Damascus and the booty of Samaria will be carried off before the king of Assyria."

10. The Rejection of Faith and the Resulting Destruction of Judah

In 8:5-8, in vivid word pictures and using symbolic language, the prophet charges the inhabitants of Judah with having rejected as the basis of Judean

---

[34] Reading with BH בת instead of בית.
[35] Op. cit., p. 30.

security the quietly flowing waters of the Pool of Siloam, which waters are to the prophet a symbol of calm and effective faith and confidence in the Lord. In place of them the Judeans sought security through reliance upon the protection of powerful war-skilled Assyria, here symbolized by the mighty, abundant, and destructive waters of the Euphrates River. These are pictured as sweeping on into Judah, and while not wholly submerging that nation, they are bringing it into extreme danger. The prophet urges that the awful threat of Assyrian domination and the destruction of Judah be met by faith in God, such as the import of the name Immanuel implies (with us, i.e., Judah, is God).

8:5 Now the Lord spoke yet again to me saying: 6 "Because this people have rejected the waters of the Pool of Siloam, which flow along softly, and despond before Rezin and the son of Remaliah; 7 therefore, behold, the Lord is bringing up against them waters of the River, the mighty and the many; and it shall overflow all its channels, 8 and it shall sweep on into Judah, and shall overflow and pass on, and reach unto the neck; and the outspreading of its wings will fill the breadth of your land, O Immanuel."

11. A Summons to Calm Faith in the Face of International Intrigue

In vss. 9-10 in the very midst of destruction-bringing international intrigue we are given a deep inner glimpse into the prophet's calm faith. However severe the threat of the coalition between Syria and the Northern Kingdom, Israel, or any other plot of nations against Judah may be, these peoples have not taken into account the potent and steadying presence in Judah of the living God. Cried the prophet in dramatic utterance to all the nations, even to far-away peoples of the earth:

8:9 Take knowledge, peoples, and be broken in pieces;
    And give ear, all distant places of earth;
  Gird yourselves, but be shattered;
  Gird yourselves, but be shattered;
10 Plot together, but you shall be frustrated;
    Speak a word, but it shall not come to be,
    For God is with us!

12. Fear and Revere the Lord Only

In the crisis Isaiah receives a stirring revelation from the Lord that he is not to be influenced in his judgment by the people generally nor is he to share their fears. With all his soul he is to reverence the Lord and be inspired and led solely by him. Thus the prophet reports this revelation:

8:11 For thus the Lord admonished me, with urgency of his hand, not to walk in the way of this people, saying: 12 "Do not call holy everything which this people calls holy, and you are not to fear what it fears; and you are not to regard it as striking terror. 13 With the Lord of hosts, with him you shall make a league; and he shall be your awe-inspirer. 14 But he shall be as a snare, and like a stone against which one strikes one's foot, and like a rock over which one stumbles, to both the houses of Israel and, as an agent of calamity to those dwelling in Jerusalem. 15 And they shall fall and be maimed, and they shall be ensnared and captured."

CHAPTER II

The Period of Withdrawal From Public Ministry (734-715)

THE SECOND PERIOD OF ISAIAH'S PROPHETIC MINISTRY WAS A TIME OF WITH-DRAWAL FROM PUBLIC TEACHING. THE ATTITUDE OF KING AHAZ OF JUDAH during his entire reign of twenty years (735-715) was that of rejection of the prophetic counsel or utter ignoring of it. Frightened by the alliance of Syria and Ephraim, the Northern Kingdom of Israel, against Judah, Ahaz rejected Isaiah's counsel and ignored the prophetic words. Against the warning of Isaiah he appealed to Assyria for support. Although Ahaz of Judah rejected the prophet's counsel there were in Judah true disciples of Isaiah who would listen to and heed his words.

A. The Lord's Woe Upon the Drunkards of Ephraim

The only prophetic oracle which we can be sure came from this period of Isaiah's ministry is 28:1-4. Bewer says, "This prophecy was originally given to the northern kingdom of Israel at the time after Hoshea's defection from Assyria, ca. 726 or 725." According to II Kings 17:4, Hoshea, King of Israel, had withheld the annual tribute from Assyria which he had regularly sent, and as a consequence the Assyrian king had imprisoned him. As Bewer says, "The protecting walls of Samaria's hills are as powerless as a wreath of fading flowers worn on the heads of Ephraim's [i.e. Israel's] leaders" [1]—"drunkards," Isaiah sarcastically dubs them—men who were in no condition to give national leadership, who were dissolute, licentious, and under the influence of strong drink. In vivid figures of speech Isaiah portrays the fading away of Israel's strength before the might of Assyria, here viewed as the agent of the Lord's discipline. It is uttered against the "drunkards of Ephraim," the dissipated leaders of Ephraim, the Northern Kingdom.

> 28:1 Woe to the proud crown,
> Of the drunkards of Ephraim,
> Who are overcome with wine.
> Its glorious beauty at the top of the fertile valley,

[1] Bewer, The Book of Isaiah, I, 71.

> Shall be a fading flower.[2]
> 2 Behold, the Lord has a mighty and strong one,
>   With which, like a tempest of hail and a destructive storm,
>   Like a downpour of water,
>   He will thrust down with violence to the earth.
> 3 The crown of pride of
>   The drunkards of Ephraim,
>   Shall be trampled under foot;
> 4 And the languishing flower
>   Of its glorious beauty,
> Which is upon the head
>   Of the fertile valley,
> Shall be as a first ripe fig
>   Before harvest,
>   Which he that sees it picks, and eats it up,
>   As soon as it is in his hand.[3]

B. ISAIAH'S RESORT TO PRIVATE TEACHING OF HIS DISCIPLES

In 8:16-17 Isaiah reports a clear summons from the Lord to use this period as a time for concentrated private teaching of his disciples. They are to wait in faith, in quiet trust in the Lord, whose purposes at the moment seem beyond ferreting out. They are to become aware that as the prophet teaches and his disciples humbly receive, they will tend to arouse Judah to knowledge of and to faith in the purposes and power of God. When the desperate need of the times drives men to summon up, through necromancy, the spirits of the dead, in search for information from them as to what should be done to ward off catastrophe, Isaiah, in deep earnestness, directs his disciples to seek to learn the divine will for them by direct contact with the living God. As one seals up a valuable document, so the prophet is divinely counseled to seal up in the hearts and minds of his disciples—that intimate inner circle of responsive minds—the Lord's words of revelation and direction.

8:16 I will bind up the testimony. I will seal the teaching among my disciples. 17 And I will wait for the Lord, who is hiding his face from the house of Jacob, and I will look eagerly for him.

1. The Prophet and His Disciples as Living Epistles

Isaiah feels toward his disciples as a father toward his children. He senses most keenly the tremendous responsibility which rests upon himself and them—those, as Mowinckel puts it, "who had said 'Yes' to the will and call of God and were willing to submit to his plan for Israel, even through

---

[2] Following Bewer's translation of this verse, *The Book of Isaiah*, I, 71.
[3] *Ibid.*, p. 72.

affliction." [4] They, as well as he, have prophetic significance. Isaiah lovingly calls them "the sons whom the Lord has given me." They serve as portents of a future. They look ahead to the new society, and they help to build it. They have a mission from the Lord whose dwelling is the Temple. When the popular trend is to seek guidance by consulting the "familiar spirits"— those supposedly acquainted with the secrets of the unseen world—Isaiah summons his disciples to the basic insights given by the true prophets, which insights he designates by the two great words "teaching" and "testimony," —that is, prophetic exhortations. What folly it is to consult the dead on behalf of the living! Says the prophet:

8:18 Lo, I and the sons whom the Lord has given me, are for signs and for portents in Israel, from the Lord of hosts who dwells on Mount Zion.

19 And when they say to you, "Resort to the necromancers and to the familiar spirits that chirp and mutter," should not a people seek unto its God? On behalf of the living [should they seek unto] the dead? 20 To the teaching and to the testimony! If they do not speak in accordance with this word, then there can be no dawn for them.

2. Philistia, Now Superficially Rejoicing, Will Be Destroyed

Isa. 14:28-32 presents a prophetic oracle definitely dating from the year of the death of King Ahaz of Judah (715 B.C.). Ahaz of Judah had united with the king of Hamath against Assyria. Isaiah warns Philistia that its joy over the death of King Ahaz is premature, for while the Assyrians will utterly destroy the Philistine nation, Zion, Judah's beloved capital, stands secure, and the needy young nations as well, under the protection of God.

14:28 In the year that King Ahaz died came this oracle:
29 Do not rejoice, Philistia, all of you,
　　Because the rod smiting you has been broken,
　　For from the root of the serpent will come a hissing serpent,
　　And its offspring will be a flying serpent,
30 And the poorest of the poor shall feed,
　　And needy ones shall lie down in confidence.
　　But I will kill your root with famine,
　　And your remnant I will slay.
31 Howl, O gate of the elders of the city.
　　Melt away, Philistia, all of you,
　　For smoke is coming from the north,
　　And there is not a straggler in his ranks.
32 So what shall my people answer messengers of nations?
　　That the Lord has founded Zion,
　　And in her shall the poor of his people seek refuge.

[4] The Book of Isaiah, p. 134.

CHAPTER III

The Third Period of Isaiah's Ministry —His Middle Ministry (715-705)

THE THIRD PERIOD OF ISAIAH'S MINISTRY EXTENDED FROM 715, THE YEAR OF THE DEATH OF KING AHAZ OF JUDAH, TO 705. THIS IS A PERIOD OF ONLY TEN years, but the events that took place during it were momentous. The period opens with two dynastic oracles which are of great importance. Ahaz has died, and Hezekiah is to become king of Judah. It is in this period that we meet with intrigues of political leaders in Judah, Egypt, and Assyria. It is also in this period that we sense the purpose of the Lord as it manifests itself in political events. This period may rightly be designated Isaiah's Middle Ministry.[1]

A. The Messianic Teaching of Isaiah

In 9:2-7 and 11:1-9 we have two dynastic oracles. The first is a liturgy of enthronement which has been linked with King Hezekiah by persistent Jewish tradition. The second is one of the royal accession ceremonies, wherein the monarch of the Davidic dynasty is viewed "as a sacred, even semi-divine, person." It is the reasoned judgment of Scott that this also "may well have been composed by Isaiah for the occasion of the anointing of Hezekiah." [2]

These two passages relate to a succession of kings of the same line or family. They present what has ever since been an ideal in the Judean nation, never fully achieved by any monarch yet tremendously influential, not only in Judean history, but in that of other nations as well.

Martin Buber in *The Prophetic Faith*, as Will Herberg interprets his view, sees messianism in its connection with the kingship and prophecy.[3] He says: "The way of the kingship is the way from failure to failure in the dialogue between the people and God." "As the failure of the Judge leads to the King, and the failure of the King to the Prophet, so the failure of

---

[1] See Scott, *Interpreter's Bible*, V, 161.
[2] *Ibid.*, p. 247.
[3] Herberg, *Profeten Jesaja en Bibelstudiebok*, p. 252.

the Prophet in his opposition to the King leads to new types of leader who
will set the dialogue aright—the Messiah of Yahweh, as interpreted by
Isaiah, and the suffering servant of the Lord as interpreted by the Second
Isaiah." The Messiah, "the anointed one," is seen as the king of the remnant
from which the people will renew itself.[4]

In these two references (9:2-7; 11:1-9) we also have prophetic passages
which look ahead in passionately eager expectancy to the mounting of the
throne of David by an anointed, and indeed, ideal monarch. Among the
most beloved of Old Testament passages on the part of Christians are these
two sections of Isaiah. They inspire the souls of those who believe that in
Jesus of Nazareth the messianic hope of Judaism is fulfilled. The term
"messiah" simply means "anointed one." The term Christ means the same,
the anointed one. For the rank and file of Christians the coming of Jesus
as the messiah is foretold in the above two passages. Both of them deal with
the messianic king. The sacred and joyous religious rite of anointing made
a man king (II Sam. 2:4) over the house of Judah. In the presence of the
newly anointed monarch, just as in the crowning proclamation and anointing of Joash (II Kings 11:12), his subjects clapped their hands and cried,
"Long live the king!" We must keep clearly in mind that the ceremony of
anointing was not merely royal and political. It was deeply spiritual as
well. It is a true instinct that in ancient Israel led the subjects to view their
newly anointed monarch as a sacred person.

In the light of such thoughts Margaret B. Crook in her article "A Suggested Occasion for Isa. 9:2-7 and 11:1-9" is probably right in viewing these
two sections as being, respectively, a liturgy of enthronement and a coro-
nation liturgy. The monarch, as Scott says, "is no longer, in the thought of
the poet, an ordinary man but is the chosen and anointed son of Yahweh." [5]
Isa. 9:1 is a transition verse. It simply explains that in the former time
(733-732) the Assyrian monarch Tiglath-pileser had taken over into Assyrian
domination the caravan route which ran from Damascus to the Mediterranean Sea at Acre.[6] The historian says that the tribal areas of Zebulun and
Naphtali, which had been ruthlessly overrun, in the latter time were to be
restored to honor. Isaiah utters words of hope and promise to Judah. The
verses numbered in the Hebrew text Isa. 8:23-9:6 are numbered in the
Revised Standard Version as Isa. 9:1-7, which numbering is here followed.

9:1 But gloom shall not continue
To her who was in distress.
In the former time he treated with dishonor the land of Zebulum and the land of Naphtali, but in the latter time he will bring to honor the way of the sea, from the land beyond the Jordan to Galilee of the nations.[7]

1. Glorious Light and Gladness Under a Messianic King

Isa. 9:2-7 which follows, as Scott maintains, is a dynastic oracle which was most probably composed by Isaiah "to celebrate the accession of an actual Judean king" [8] and was uttered on that occasion. That the king was Hezekiah is the more probable as well as the more general supposition. This would date the oracle at 715. A study of Isaiah's career reveals his intimate association with both the royal court and the Temple.

In 9:2-3 the prophet represents the darkness of the period of which he speaks—darkness of uncertainty and even of despair—but the darkness is now to be succeeded by such light as will bring rejoicing and happiness comparable to that when, as victors in war, the winners fall upon the plunder of the enemy and divide it among themselves. Vs. 3 is addressed directly to the Lord. Thus the prophet speaks:

> 9:2 The people who are walking in the darkness
> Have seen a great light;
> Those who have been dwelling in the land of deep darkness,
> Upon them light has shone.
> 3 Thou hast increased the rejoicing,
> Thou hast magnified the gladness;
> They rejoice before thee like gaity in the harvest time,
> Just as they rejoice
> When they divide spoil.

In 9:4-5 the prophet exults in what the Lord has done in breaking the burdensome yoke of the Assyrian oppression of Judah. This is similar to that which had been accomplished in the long ago by Gideon when he broke the yoke of the Midianite oppression of the Israelites, as is vividly described in Judg. 6-7. Then the spirit of the Lord took possession of Gideon (Judg. 6:34). The Israelite forces, reduced to but three hundred courageous and dependable troops (Judg. 7:6-8), at the call of the trumpet and the battle cry, "For the Lord and for Gideon" (Judg. 7:18), had defeated and routed the Midianites and won a decisive triumph over those foreign forces

[7] Procksch, *Isaiah*, p. 144.
[8] *Interpreter's Bible*, V, 232.

invading the nation. Similarly has the Lord now done on behalf of his people.

> 9:4 For his burdensome yoke
> And that which bows down his shoulder,
> The rod of his oppressor,
> Thou hast shattered as in the day of Midian.
>
> 5 For every boot of him who shakes the earth by tramping.
> And every garment stained with blood
> Will be but for burning,
> Fuel for fire.

In 9:6-7 the prophet looks ahead with joy to what the Lord is about to bring to pass. The verbs are simple perfects. In vs. 6*f* Isaiah anticipates days of glorious light for Judah under a God-given king. In the third sentence, "The government shall be upon his shoulder," as E. R. Goodenough suggests, the word refers to "some symbol of majesty such as a rosette embroidered on the royal robe." [9] Thus Isaiah speaks:

> 9:6 For to us a child is born,
> To us a son is given;
> And the government will be upon his shoulder,
> And his name will be called
> Wonderful Counselor,
> Divine in might,
> A father forever
> Prince of peace.
> 7 Great shall be his dominion, and to peace there will be no end,
> Upon the throne of David and over his kingdom,
> To establish it,
> And to sustain it,
> With justice and with righteousness,
> From now on, even forever.
> The zeal of the Lord of hosts
> Will do this.

2. A Second Presentation of the Messianic Hope

In 11:1-9 we have another passage similar to 9:2-7, which presents the messianic hope as portrayed in the book of Isaiah. We must keep in mind that, as Scott has said, "every monarch of the Davidic dynasty was an anointed representative of Yahweh." [10] We are not to think here of a messianic age remote in the future. The superlatives are an attempt "to describe

[9] "Kingship in Early Israel," JBL, 48 (1929), 190.
[10] *Interpreter's Bible*, V, 247.

the kingship of one who on his accession was adopted as Yahweh's son." [11] It is likely, as is the case with ch. 9, that this passage also was composed by Isaiah for the anointing of King Hezekiah.

In 11:1-5 the anointed ruler has his roots in the Davidic dynasty. Jesse was the father of David. To David the ruler will trace his ancestry, and he will be imbued with the Lord's spirit which will manifest itself in eight designated qualities—wisdom, understanding, counsel, valor, knowledge, reverence, righteousness, and faithfulness.

11:1 And there shall come forth a branch from the stem of Jesse,
And a sprout from his stock shall send out shoots.
2 And the spirit of the Lord shall rest upon him,
The spirit of wisdom and understanding,
The spirit of counsel and valor,
The spirit of knowledge and the fear of the Lord.
3 And he shall cause reverence for the Lord to rest on him.
He shall not judge by what his eyes see,
Nor shall he decide by what his ears hear;
4 But he shall judge the poor with righteousness,
And shall decide with uprightness for the weak of the earth;
And he shall smite the ruthless with the rod of his mouth,
And with the breath of his lips he shall slay the wicked.
5 And righteousness shall be the girdle of his waist,
And faithfulness the waistcloth of his loins.

A. A CHARACTERISTIC FEATURE OF THE MESSIANIC HOPE

In 11:6-9 there is lifted up a characteristic feature of the messianic hope which includes peace between animals and human beings and between men themselves. The climactic feature of this hope is that just as waters cover the deep, so knowledge of the Lord will fill the whole earth.

11:6 And wolves shall dwell with lambs,
And leopards shall lie down with young goats,
And calves and young lions shall feed together,
With a little child leading them.
7 And the cow and bear shall be each others' companions;
Their offspring will stretch themselves out together;
And a lion shall eat straw like an ox.
8 And a babe shall play upon the hole of a cobra,
And upon a viper's den
A weaned child shall stretch out its hand.

[11] *Ibid.*

9 They shall do no injury and shall not destroy
  In all my holy mountain;
  For the earth shall be full
  Of the knowledge of the Lord,
  As the waters covering the sea.

B. THE COUNSEL TO JUDAH TO REJECT ALLIANCE WITH EGYPT AND ETHIOPIA

In 20:1-6 is reported an activity on the part of Isaiah, which from the inscription of Sargon II can be definitely dated as continuing three years (714-711 B.C.). We have here an illustration of symbolic prophecy, the aim of which in this instance, as Gray says, was "keeping Hezekiah and Judah out of an anti-Assyrian alliance with the neighbouring states." [12]

It was at the beginning of this period (714 B.C.) that Isaiah received a prophetic impulse from the Lord—in the very year when the Tartan, the officer of the Assyrian army who ranked next to the king, captured the city of Ashdod, one of the five principalities of the Philistines. A prophetic impulse from the Lord (20:2a) led Isaiah to remove his rough mantle of haircloth and the leather girdle which, as Gray says, represents "a distinctive but regular dress of the prophet" and to go about half clad, "wearing the inner garment only." [13] Thus for a three-year period (714-711) he exposed himself to the jeers and popular contempt of Jerusalem generally. Then in vss. 3-6 follows the message which it was the Lord's will that he proclaim in this startling way.

20:1 In the year that the field marshal went to Ashdod, when Sargon, king of Assyria, sent him, and he engaged in battle against Ashdod and captured it, 2 At that time the Lord spoke to Isaiah, son of Amoz, saying, "Go, loosen and remove the sackcloth from your loins, and loose your sandals from your feet." Accordingly he did so, going half clad and barefoot, and he continued thus clad for three years.

3 Then the Lord said: "Just as my servant Isaiah has gone half clad and barefoot for three years, as a sign and a portent concerning Egypt and Ethiopia, 4 So shall the king of Assyria drive off captives of Egypt and exiles of Ethiopia, young and old, naked and barefoot and buttocks bare. 5 And they shall be dismayed and ashamed because of Cush their [basis of] expectation, and because of Egypt their object of boasting. 6 And those who live on this[14] coast in that day shall say: 'Lo! such is our basis of hope to which we have fled for help to be delivered from the king of Assyria, but how can we escape?'"

[12] Gray, op. cit., I, 342.
[13] Ibid., p. 345-46.
[14] I.e., the Palestinians.

1. Judah and Alliance with Ethiopia

The occasion which called forth Isaiah's message in 18:1-6 was the sudden appearance at the Judean court in Jerusalem of ambassadors from Ethiopia. I have seen citizens from Ethiopia on the streets of Jerusalem and can well appreciate Herodotus' reference to them as "the tallest and handsomest of all men." They came from Cush, the governmental district which extended from Elephantine at the first cataract of the Nile far down to the fourth cataract, just above Napata. Isaiah's hailing of this region as the "land of the winged ship," as G. R. Driver suggests, refers "to sails used by the Egpytian craft on the Nile, as a supplement to oars." [15]

A new Egyptian dynasty, the twenty-fifth, began *ca.* 714, and it was not long after this date that the intrigues of Egypt stimulated a revolt against Assyria on the part of the smaller subject peoples of Philistia, Moab, Edom, and Judah.

2. Ethiopian Statesmen in Jerusalem

These Ethiopian statesmen from Napata, pursuing this aim, suddenly showed up at the Judean court in Jerusalem (vs. 2) about 712. They had come in vessels made of papyrus. Isaiah's keen political insight discerned the purpose of this mission. Under the Nubian prince Shabaka and from then onward under the victorious careers of the native Ethiopian kings Piankhi, Shabaka, and Taharqah Egypt had achieved a place among the leading powers of the Middle East. It now seemed evident that Egypt's purpose was, by the negotiation of an alliance with Judah, to halt effectively the ruthless domination of the whole Middle East by the powerful military machine of Assyria, their common foe. The phrase "by the sea" (vs. 2) refers to the Nile River (*el bahr*). Isaiah's curiosity and spiritual concern are sharply aroused by the appearance of this distinguished delegation of handsome Ethiopians at the court of Judah. Isaiah speaks:

> 18:1 Ah! land of the winged ships[16]
> Which lies on the other side of the rivers of Ethiopia;
> 2a Which is sending envoys by the Nile,
> And vessels of papyrus on the face of the waters.[17]

3. Judah Must Not Ally Itself with Ethiopia

To these envoys from the mysterious land of Ethiopia Isaiah now speaks,

---

[15] "Difficult Words in the Hebrew Prophets," H. H. Rowley, ed., *Studies in Old Testament Prophecy*, p. 59.
[16] See *Interpreter's Bible*, V, 276.
[17] *Ibid.*

bidding them to depart and to return to their own land. Judah must not accept alliance with them.

> 18:2*b* Go, swift messengers,
>   To a nation, tall and of shining skin,
>   To a people dreaded
>   From near and far,
>   To a nation of might and all-subduing,
>   Whose land rivers cut through.

4. The Calm and Potency of Judah's God

Suddenly the prophet turns from his specific words to these Ethiopian embassadors and speaks the Lord's message to all mankind. Judah needs no material or military alliance, whether with Ethiopia or with any other human power, however strategic the hour may seem. God has spoken to Isaiah counseling him that the crucial situation calls not for international intrigue and alliance, but for vital, positive faith in God who, although unseen, is actually at work. Moreover, supreme over the trouble which this hour seems to be shaping in Judah, and immeasurably potent over it, is the calm, untroubled, but watchful and caring God. Thus speaks Isaiah:

> 18:3 All inhabitants of the world,
>   And you who dwell upon the earth,
>   At the lifting up of a signal you shall see,
>   And like a blast of a trumpet you shall hear!

> 4 For thus the Lord spoke to me:
>   "I will be quiet and will look forth from my abode,
>   Like glowing heat in sunshine,
>   Like a night mist in the time of harvest."

5. The Lord's Message for Ethiopia and the Nations

Now Judah trembles before the military might of the world power of Ethiopia, but Judah has not adequately reckoned with what God is about to do. Isaiah grows more specific. He uses two figures of speech. First, in vs. 5 the Ethiopians are as a grapevine which before the grapes ripen is cut down. The second figure of speech which Isaiah uses for the Ethiopians (vs. 6) is that of an army utterly destroyed and left on the battlefield as putrid, decaying flesh to be consumed as carrion by wild beasts and birds of prey.

18:5 For before the vintage which he causes to sprout is as a complete bud,
And unripe grapes become ripe,
There will be a berry-cluster.
But he will cut off the quivering tendrils with the pruning knives,
And the spreading twigs he will strike away.
6 They will be left, all alike,
To the birds [of prey] of the mountains,
And to the beasts of the earth.
And the birds of prey will feel a sickening dread toward them,
And all of the beasts of the earth
Will taunt them.

6. The Lord Is Coming in Judgment Upon Egypt

Isa. 19:1-4 imaginatively picture the Lord as coming against Egypt in judgment, riding upon a rapidly moving cloud. Before the power of his august presence the heart of the nation trembles in terror and the whole land is reduced to anarchy—Egyptian principality fighting against principality and city against city until, driven by the extremity of need, they resort to idolatry and to the consultation of the spirits of the dead. The "formidable king" (vs. 4), as Scott suggests, refers either to the Ethiopian invader Piankhi or to Shabaka (*ca.* 711-699), who succeeded Piankhi to found the twenty-fifth, or Ethiopian, dynasty.[18]

19:1 Oracle of Egypt,
Lo, the Lord is riding upon a swift cloud
And is coming to Egypt:
And the idols of Egypt
Will tremble at his presence,
And the heart of the Egyptians
Will melt within them.
2 And I will pierce Egypt in Egypt
And they will fight, each his brother,
One will fight his neighbor,
City against city,
Kingdom against kingdom;
3 And the spirit of Egypt will be laid waste within them,
And their sagacity I will confuse;
And they will resort to the idols and the ventriloquists,
And to the necromancers, and to the familiar spirits.
4 And I will deliver Egypt
Into the hands of a rough lord;

[18] *Ibid.*, p. 279.

> And a formidable king will rule over them,
> Says Yahweh of hosts.[19]

7. The Failure of the Waters of the Nile

In vss. 5-10 we sense the life-giving importance of the Nile River, for here is pictured what happens when the waters of the Nile fail. The branches of the river stink; the reeds shrivel. Fishermen return from their fishing with their nets empty, and those whose livelihood is dependent upon the sea are left humiliated and insecure.

> 19:5 And water of the Nile will be dried up,
> And the river will be parched and become dry;
> 6 And the branches of the Nile will stink;
> The canals of Egypt will become low and dry up;
> Branches and rushes will decay,
> 7 And all reeds will shrivel up,
> And all sea land of the Nile,
> Will be dried up, will wither away until there is nought of it.
> 8 So the fishermen will mourn and lament:
> All who cast hooks in the Nile will mourn,
> And those who spread out fishing nets
> Upon the face of the waters will languish.
> 9 And weavers of combed flax will be ashamed,
> And those wearing white stuff will be humbled,
> 10 And their foundations will be shattered,
> All who work for hire, the lowly of soul.

8. There Is Not in Egypt a Man of Action

In vss. 11-15 the prophet has in mind the worldwide repute in which at that time the Egyptian wise men of Tanis (Zoan), in the northwest part of the Delta, were held, and their consequent pride. They had, however, no spiritual discernment whatever regarding the Lord's will, and no motive of human justice governed their conduct. Consequently their judgments were distorted. Among the most searching of prophetic utterances of the Lord's judgment upon those who, although in positions of authoritative leadership, fail utterly to lead is expressed in these verses. In all Egyptian society, high or low, says Isaiah, there is not a man of action.

> 19:11 Surely the chieftains of Tanis are foolish;
> Its wise men have counseled Pharaoh

[19] Omitting "The Lord."

With stupid counsel,
How can you say to Pharaoh,
"A son of learned men am I,
I am a member of the Ancient Royal Council!"
12 Where now, are your wise men?
Pray let them declare and make known to you,
What the Lord of hosts counsels
Against Egypt.
13 The princes of Zoan (Tanis) have become fools,
The princes of Memphis (Noph) have been deluded;
The rulers of its tribes
Have misled Egypt.
14 The Lord has poured out in their midst
The spirit of distorted judgment;
And they have caused Egypt to err
In all its undertaking,
Like a drunkard and staggering in his vomit.
15 And there is not for Egypt a man of action
Who does things be it
Head or tail [i.e., high or low]
Branch or rush.

C. REVELRY ON THE BRINK OF DISASTER

The date of 22:1-14 is usually set by scholars as 701, when Jerusalem experienced a remarkable deliverance from Sennacherib. R. B. Y. Scott, however, has called attention to the fact that "this date is not compatible with an expected attack by forces from Elam and Kir [22:6], nor with Isaiah's attitude to that deliverance (cf. 37:33-35) ." He says: "It seems that a similarly unexpected if less spectacular escape from the horrors of siege took place in 711, when Sargon struck down Ashdod (cf. ch. 20) but left Jerusalem unmolested, although she had taken part in the conspiracy." [20]

The news of the unexpected retirement of the Assyrian forces naturally was greeted by the citizens with great joy. Isaiah, however, sees far beyond the shallow and noisy revelry of the people of Jerusalem and weeps bitter tears (vs. 4). As Scott says, the reference to "the valley of vision" is probably to divination at an altar in the Valley of Hinnom at Jerusalem, to which the later prophet Jeremiah refers (Jer. 7:31-34) .[21]

22:1 Oracle of the Valley of Hinnom,
What is the matter with you, pray, that you have gone up,
Everyone of you, to the roofs,

[20] Interpreter's Bible, V, 289.
[21] Ibid., p. 290.

2   Full of shoutings,
         A city in commotion,
         A jubilant town?
    Your slain are not slain by the sword,
    And not dead from battle.
3b All your mighty men have been taken prisoner together,
    Without use of bow.
3a All your chieftains have fled together,
    To a distance, they have fled.

1. Isaiah's Lament Over Judah

In sharp contrast to this superficial jubilation of the people of Jerusalem comes the lament of the prophet who is sensitively aware of just how shallow and premature that jubilation is. Disappointed with his people, he cries:

4   Therefore I say: "Turn away your gaze from me,
    I will weep bitterly;
    Do not hasten to comfort me,
    Because of the ruin of the daughter of my people."

In vss. 5-8a in poetic words carefully chosen for their sound effect (vs. 5, mᵉhumah, mᵉbhusah, mᵉbukah, and mᵉqarqarqir) Isaiah dscribs what has been revealed to him in prophetic vision that Judah will experience in the valley. Elam, a well-known country and people northeast of the Lower Tigris, and Syria and Kir, a tribe in South Babylonia east of the Tigris, furnished troops to the Assyrian army. Says the prophet:

22:5 For it is a day of distraction, and desecration, and disturbance
         Of the Lord God of hosts
         In the valley of Hinnom;
             A breaking down of walls
             And a cry to the mountains for help.
6   And Elam bore the quiver,
         Syria mounted horses,
         And Kir lay bare the shield.
7   And the choicest of your valleys
         Were full of chariots,
             And horsemen set their faces toward the gates.
8a   And thy terror, O Judah, was revealed.

2. Judah's Concern for Its Physical Security

In vss. 8b-11 Isaiah describes in some detail the careful attention Judah had paid to its physical security through armed protection such as "the

House of the Forest" so called, as Scott points out, "because of the many pillars supporting the roof." 22 We learn later that it was used as an armory, for here were kept "three hundred shields of beaten gold" (I Kings 10:17). They took careful account of Jerusalem's houses and broke down those that could be spared, and with timber thus secured they fortified the wall. They also took care to make sure of adequate water supply in case of siege. Judah acted in these matters without seeking any guidance whatever from the Lord of all history. Says Isaiah:

22:8b In that day you paid attention to the weapons of the House of the Forest, 9 and as for the breaches of the city of David, you saw that there were many, and you collected the waters of the pool, the lower one, 10 and you counted the houses of Jerusalem, and broke down the houses to fortify the wall. 11 And you made a reservoir between the two walls for the waters of the old pool. But you did not pay attention to him who did it, even to him who had determined it long ago.

3. The Serious Prophet and the Reckless Leaders

In 22:12-14 Isaiah brings this prophecy to a solemn end. In his mind are those Judeans who are committed to a plot of revolt against Assyria. What God intends, however—by the solemnizing events that are taking place in Judah—is to bring the nation to divine judgment. We sense the sharp contrast between the serious prophet and the utterly reckless leaders, who have no sense of the reality of that divine judgment, but are solely intent upon their enjoyment of the present moment. Isaiah is absolutely certain that those responsible Judean leaders who stand for such a policy, or lack any considered policy, are committing an unpardonable sin. Their iniquity can never be forgiven. Cries the prophet:

22:12 And the Lord called,
    Yahweh of hosts,
      On that day,
   To weeping and to wailing,
    And to baldness and to girding on sackcloth.
  13 But look, exultation and mirth,
    Slaying oxen and slaughtering sheep,
   Eating flesh and drinking wine!
    "Let us eat and drink,
      For tomorrow we shall die!"

22 Ibid., p. 291.

14 But the Lord of hosts has himself revealed in my ears:
"Surely this iniquity cannot be atoned for by you
Until you die."

D. ISAIAH'S CONDEMNATION OF SHEBNA

In 22:15-19 Isaiah utters in the Lord's name a sharp condemnation of
Shebna, the steward of the Judean court, a high royal official. The prophet
speaks of him as "this steward" with a tinge of contempt. He was over the
household of the king in charge of the royal palace. Although Shebna had
no family pedigree or hereditary claim he asserted his right to a royal tomb,
which he carved out for himself on a prominent height in the rock. Moved
by an intuition from the Lord Isaiah confronted him at what was for Shebna
an embarrassing moment, when he was at work upon the project. Respond-
ing to a specific prophetic intuition from the Lord Isaiah uttered a straight-
forward, stinging rebuke. Using direct and penetrating questions the
prophet criticizes this presumptuous official for his unworthy reach after enduring prestige at the very moment when he was egotistically attempting
"to feather his own nest."

22:15 Thus says the Lord God of hosts, "Go in to this steward, to Shebna, who
is over the palace, 16b who is hewing out a place for his sepulchre, cutting out in
the rock a tomb for himself, and say to him: 16a 'What [right] have you here and
whom have you here, that you have here hewn out a tomb for yourself? 17 Lo, the
Lord will hurl you, violently, O man, grasping you forcibly, 18 and rolling you
up tightly in a bundle, he will throw you like a ball into a wide-stretching
country; there shall you die and there shall be your splendid tomb, you shame
of your Lord's house! 19 And I will depose you from your station, and I will
cast you down from your office.' "

1. Eliakim Will Succeed Shebna as Steward

Isa. 22:20-23 states that the office in the Judean state now held by Shebna
will be placed firmly in the hands of Eliakim, the son of Hilkiah, into
whose absolute control will be given the right to admit or deny access to
the king's presence. Eliakim will bring glory to Judah, but if by any
chance he should resort to the policy of putting his own relatives in places
of national responsibility he will be removed along with his hangers-on.

22:20 And it shall be in that day I will call to my servant, Eliakim, son of
Hilkiah, 21 And I will clothe him with your[23] tunic, and your sash[24] I will bind

[23] Linen.
[24] I.e., of office.

firmly about him, and your staff I will put in his hand. And he shall be as a father to those who dwell in Jerusalem and to the house of Judah. 22 And I will lay the keys of the house of David upon his shoulder, and he shall open with no one closing, and shall shut, with no one opening. 23 And I will drive him, like a tent peg, in a firm place, and he will be as a throne of glory to his father's house.

2. *The Nepotism of Shebna*

In 22:24-25 we have a vivid picture of Shebna, who is here denounced, although not by name, because of his nepotism—his showing favoritism to his relatives in dealing out patronage.

22:24 And they will hang on him the entire weight of his father's house, the offspring and the issue. 25 In that day, says the Lord of hosts, the peg that has been driven in a sure place shall be removed and shall be hewn off and shall fall: and the weight which was on it shall be cut off, for the Lord has spoken.

CHAPTER IV

The Fourth and Final Period of Isaiah's Ministry (705-701)

THIS PERIOD BEGINS AT 705 AND EXTENDS UNTIL THE END OF ISAIAH'S PROPHETIC CAREER IN 701, OR POSSIBLY, AS SOME SCHOLARS BELIEVE, UNTIL 700.

It was the death of Sargon, king of Assyria, in 705 that awakened Judean interest in revolt against Assyrian domination and accordingly led them to seek alliance with Egypt, the other contemporary world power of the Middle East. This forms the political background of Isa. 30.

A. A COVENANT WITH DEATH

With keen political insight, as we have seen, Isaiah viewed the Judean alliance with Egypt against Assyria in 705 as a "covenant with death" (28:15). He had made it clear that the only secure foundation for Zion— that is, for Jerusalem, capital of Judah—is that which the Lord God himself is laying, the cornerstone of which is calm belief, unalarmed trust in God, and a constructive national policy based on that confidence (28:16). Isaiah had frankly said, when he saw what Judah was doing in seeking security through alliance with Egypt, that the Judeans were making lies their refuge and falsehood their shelter (28:15).

In 30:1-3 Isaiah definitely denounces the secretive Judean policy to secure protection from Assyria by alliance with Egypt. He sees Judean envoys headed south. The Judean political leaders already know all too well Isaiah's opposition to this trend of dependence upon Egypt. Accordingly they have not sought his counsel. The prophet is perfectly clear that such dependence is at best a shadow security which will eventually bring upon Judah utter disgrace. He represents God speaking.

1. Judah's Refuge in the Shadow of Egypt

>   30:1 "Ah! stubborn sons,"
>   Says the Lord,

"Who take counsel,
But not from me;
And weave a web,[1]
But not of my spirit,
So that they add
Sin to sin;[2]
2 Who are setting out to go down to Egypt,
But have not asked at my mouth,
To take refuge in the protection of Pharaoh,
And to seek shelter in the shadow of Egypt!
3 But the protection of Pharaoh will be to you a shame,
And the refuge in the shadow of Egypt, a disgrace."

In vss. 4-5 we learn of the power and reach of the Ethiopian empire in Egypt. Ethiopian princes have an official residence at Zoan, which is identical with Tanis at the extreme north of Egypt very close to the Palestinian border. The Ethiopian envoys sent on a special mission by their government have already come north as far as Hanes, today called Ahnas, which is situated in Middle Egypt on an island in the Nile south of Memphis. These facts "had given the Judeans hope that Egypt was strong enough to face Assyria." [3] but Isaiah clearly saw that it was futile hope and an unreliable dependence.

30:4 "For although his[4] princes are in Zoan,
And his messengers have reached Hanes,
5 All of them[5] bring a gift as homage
To a people[6] who cannot confer benefit."

2. The Futility of Expecting Help from Egypt

Vss. 6-7 continue the thought of vss. 4-5 and repeat the refrain of vs. 5b. Isaiah pictures the Judeans carrying tribute to Egypt, whose help they are seeking against Assyria, but he knows it is futile for Judah to expect assistance from that quarter. In vs. 7 there is an implicit reference to a myth which portrays the Lord's overthrow of a dragon, as Barton says.[7] This was "a mythical sea monster, one of its names being Rahab, which becomes an emblematic name of Egypt." [8] Just so the monster will be destroyed.

[1] I.e., negotiations with Egypt.
[2] So Scott, Interpreter's Bible, V, 329.
[3] Ibid., 330.
[4] Judah's.
[5] I.e., Judeans.
[6] I.e., Egypt.
[7] Barton, Archeology and the Bible, pp. 298-302.
[8] BDB, p. 923.

30:6 They carry, through the heat of the southland,
Through a land of drought and anguish,
From whence come lions and lionesses,
Vipers and flying fiery serpents;
They carry their wealth on the shoulders of asses,
And their treasures upon the humps of camels,
To a people who cannot confer benefit.
7   Vainly and emptily does Egypt help:
Therefore I call her
"Rahab [monster], the destroyed."

3. Write Down the True Message of God

Just as before (30:16-18) Isaiah had recorded his message in the calm
conviction that the future would demonstrate its truthfulness, so again
(30:8) he obeys the Lord's summons to *write it down* for a later day to read
that men may know what God had taught at that earlier time regardless of
the present spiritual dullness of Judah. Isaiah was keenly sensitive to the
fact that the Judeans to whom he spoke were not receptive toward God's
will. Rather were they rebellious, unwilling to listen to the Lord's teaching
as it came through his words because it was contrary to what they wanted
to hear and do. What they wanted to hear (vs. 10) was something smooth,
agreeable flattery.

Accordingly, now again there comes to Isaiah an impulse from the Lord
to write down the true message God had given him so that, although ignored
by Judah in the present, it would be an abiding witness as to what God had
then willed and taught.

God speaks to Isaiah:

30:8 So now, go in, write it
Upon a tablet, in their presence,
And inscribe it in a book,
That it may be for a later day,
A witness forever.
9 For it is a rebellious people,
Deceptive sons,
Sons who are not willing
To hear the teaching of the Lord.
10 Who say to the seers, "Do not see";
And to the prophets, "Do not prophesy to us true things,
Speak to us agreeable things,
Prophesy deceitful things.
11 Get out of our way,
Turn aside from the path;

> Stop talking in our presence,
> Of 'the Holy One of Israel.' "

4. The Iniquity of Rejecting the Prophetic Word

To such impatient words on the part of Isaiah's hearers who have thus rejected the Lord's message and would indeed silence the Lord's true messenger the Holy One of Israel has a solemn answer to give through his prophet (vss. 12-14). The Judeans have summarily ignored the words of Isaiah and have trusted in their own willful interpretation of events. Their iniquity of thus rejecting God's word is comparable in Isaiah's conception to a breach in a high wall that suddenly brings the wall shattering and crashing down, broken into fragments so small that not even one potsherd could be found in the debris that was big enough with which to snatch fire from a hearth or to draw water from a cistern.

> 30:12 Therefore thus says the Holy One of Israel,
> "Because of your rejection
> Of this word,
> And [because] you have trusted in perversion and cunning,
> And have leaned upon it,
> 13 Therefore this iniquity
> Will be to you
> Like a falling breach
> In a high wall,
> Which, suddenly, at an instant,
> Comes crashing down.
> 14 Like the breaking of a jar of pottery,
> He will not spare [it],
> Until there cannot be found
> In its crushed fragments, even a potsherd,
> For snatching up fire from a hearth,
> Or for drawing water from a cistern."

5. The Essence of Isaiah's Teaching

In 30:15 the prophet contrasts the headstrong, willful attitude of the Judeans with his own teaching regarding the Lord's fourfold call to Judah: (1) A call to return to God, (2) to rest in calm surrender to his will, (3) to practice quietness of mind, free from inner turmoil, and (4) to trust in God with perfect confidence in him. Here is the essence of Isaiah's teaching and its greatest compact summary.

> 30:15 For thus says
> The Lord God,
> The Holy One of Israel,
> "In returning and rest shall you be saved;
> In quietness and in trusting
> Shall be your strength."

6. Judah's Trust in a Military Basis of Security

The nation was unwilling to follow such counsel, however. Rather they sought a military basis for Judean security—speed upon war horses, "swift steeds." Accordingly Isaiah deals with the utter disobedience of Judah to his clear call (30:16) and the consequent pursuit by the enemy of those very Judeans as reduced to a powerless few, they will flee in terror and in panic before him.

> 30:16 But you said, "No! but
> Upon horses we shall fly," [9]
> Therefore you shall *surely flee!*
> "And upon swift [horses] we shall ride":
> Therefore shall those who will be pursuing you be swift.
> 17 A thousand shall be terrified
> At the threat of one;
> From before the threat
> Of five, you shall flee
> Until you are left alone,
> Like a [solitary] flagstaff upon the top of a mountain,
> Or like a [lone] signal on a hill.

7. The Intervention of the Lord in Judgment Upon Assyria

In 30:27-28, 30, which rightly connects with 30:17, the prophet uses the imagery of a thunderstorm as the vehicle of the Lord's judgment on Assyria. Scott rightly maintains that the threat of judgment on the Assyrians is Isaiah's, but the picture of the Temple celebration (vss. 29, 31-33) owes its origin to a later hand.[10]

In terms of a theophany, the manifestation of the presence of the Lord **is** pictured as coming like a thunderstorm, the progress of which as it approaches from a distance is imaginatively portrayed.

> 30:27 Behold, the manifestation of the presence of the Lord is coming from afar,

[9] I.e., Attacking the enemy.
[10] *Interpreter's Bible*, V, 336.

His anger burning and with weight of uplifted clouds;[11]
His lips are full of indignation,
And his tongue is like consuming fire.
28 And his breath, like an overflowing torrent,
Shall reach to the neck.[12]
To sift nations in a sieve of destruction,
And with a halter on the jaws of the people, causing them to wander about.
30 And the Lord will cause
His glorious voice to be heard,
And he will cause them to see the descent of his arm
In raging of anger,
And flame of devouring fire,
And bursting of clouds and hail stones.

8. The Egyptians Are Men and Not God

In 31:1-3 Isaiah sharply condemns the spirit of Judah which bases its security upon the military strength of Egypt, with whom it is seeking alliance against Assyria. The date is 705. Judah's policy utterly ignores Isaiah's insistent call to trust in the protection of the Lord and in the action that will result from such trust as the basis for national security. There is a touch of irony and sarcasm in the prophet's words in vs. 2. It is the clear conviction of Isaiah that stronger than the horses and chariots of Egypt, to which Judah is now turning for national security, is quiet confidence in the protection of the spirit of the living God. "This conception of history," as Bewer says, "is one of the profoundest insights of religion." [13] Thus Isaiah counsels Judah in the crisis:

31:1 Woe to those who are going down to Egypt for help,
And who lean upon horses,
And trust in chariots, because they are many,
And in horsemen, because they are very strong,
But do not regard with trust the Holy One of Israel,
And do not resort to the Lord!
2 Yet he also is wise, and will bring calamity.
And does not retract His words,
But will arise against the house of evildoers,
And against the help of workers of iniquity.
3 Yes, the Egyptians are men, and not God;
And their horses are flesh, and not spirit.

[11] BDB, p. 673.
[12] Shall reach to the neck and so divide.
[13] The Book of Isaiah, I, 82.

> And the Lord will stretch out His hand,
> And he who helps will stumble,
> And he who is helped will fall,
> And all at once all of them shall be destroyed together.

9. God's Use of Assyria as an Instrument of Judgment.

In vss. 4-5 Isaiah emphasizes the certainty that God will continue to use the Assyrian army to discipline his people Judah. He will destroy the Egyptians—here pictured as shepherds—when they come on a mission to relieve Jerusalem from the peril of destruction at Assyrian hands. Cries the prophet:

> 31:4 For thus has the Lord said to me:
> Just as a lion that growls,
> And a young lion, over its prey—
> When there is called out against him
> A multitude of shepherds—
> Is not dismayed at their cries,
> And is not thwarted at their number,
> So will the Lord of hosts descend
> To fight upon Mount Zion and upon its hill.
> 5 Like hovering birds, so will
> The Lord of hosts defend Jerusalem;
> Defending and snatching away,
> Sparing and delivering [it].

In vss. 6-7 Isaiah calls his fellow Judeans to turn away from their apostasy to other gods, rejecting the images which they themselves fashioned.

31:6 Turn back to him from whom the sons of Israel have made deep their apostasy. 7 For in that day men will reject their silver idols and their golden idols which your own hands have made for yourselves.

10. The Fall of Assyria at the Lord's Volition

Then, not by military defeat, but at the volition of the Lord in Zion Assyria shall fall. The officers of that army, the elite core of the greatest fighting machine of the ancient Middle East, reduced to panic—probably, as Bewer suggests, by a storm of thunder and lightning [14]—will desert and flee (vss. 8-9).

> 31:8 "Then Assyria shall fall,
> By a sword, not of man,
> And a sword, not of man, shall devour him.

[14] *Ibid.*

And he shall flee from before the sword,
And his chieftains shall become labor gangs.
9 And his rock [elite of his army] shall pass away in terror,
And his officers shall desert the standard in panic."
Says the Lord,
Whose flame is in Zion,
And whose fire pot is in Jerusalem.

11. A Secret Plot of the Political Leaders of Judah

In 29:15-16 Isaiah clearly demonstrates that he knows what is taking place in the political machinations of the hour. It is the secret plot of the political leaders of Judah to form an alliance with Egypt in order to revolt against Assyria. In this phase of national policy Isaiah is all too aware that the Judeans are seeking no counsel from the Lord. Indeed their plotting leaders are ignoring the counsel given by Isaiah and, in fact, are concealing from him their real designs. The date is 703. Cries the prophet:

29:15 Woe to those who deeply hide from the Lord,
To conceal their designs;
And whose plots are in secrecy,
And who say, "Who sees us?" and "Who knows us?"
16 O your perversity! Just as though the potter
Is esteemed as clay!
For does the pottery say
Concerning its maker, "He did not make me"?
Or does the pottery say
As regards him who fashions it, "He does not understand"?

12. The Chaldean Envoys Pay a Visit to King Hezekiah

In 39:1-8 we have an episode which dates *ca.* 703. The Chaldean prince of Bit-Yakin, whose name is Merodach Baladan, having heard that King Hezekiah of Judah had been ill but had recovered, sent envoys officially equipped with letters and a gift for Hezekiah to congratulate him. Flattered by such recognition, Hezekiah showed the envoys every courtesy and displayed all his resources including the armory (vss. 1-2).

39:1 At that time Merodach Baladan, son of Baladan, king of Babylon, sent scribes and a gift to Hezekiah, for he had heard that he had been sick, but had recovered. 2 And Hezekiah took pleasure in their visit and showed them his treasure house, the silver and the gold and the spices and the good oil, and his treasury and all which was found in his storehouses. There was not a thing in his house which Hezekiah did not show them.

13. Isaiah's Penetrating Questions to Hezekiah

Upon hearing of this, Isaiah came to King Hezekiah and asked him three penetrating questions, which the king frankly answered (vss. 3-4). Reports the prophet:

39:3 Then Isaiah the prophet came to king Hezekiah and said to him, "What did these men say, and from where did they come to you?" And Hezekiah said, "They came from a far distant land, from Babylon." 4 Then he said, "What did they see in your house?" And Hezekiah said, "They saw all that was in my house. There was not a thing which I did not show them in my storehouses."

14. Solemn Prediction of the Babylonian Captivity

In vss. 5-8 Isaiah proclaims to King Hezekiah a solemn message from the Lord. The time is coming when all Judean possessions will be taken to Babylon and some of Judah's own sons will be made eunuchs at the Babylonian court. Hezekiah respectfully answers the prophet, but with a quite unjustified confidence in Judean security, so far as his own lifetime is concerned (vs. 8b).

39:5 Then said Isaiah to Hezekiah, "Hear the word of the Lord of hosts. 6 Lo, days are coming when everything that is in your house, and which your fathers have stored up, unto this day shall be taken to Babylon. Nothing shall be left, says the Lord. 7 And some of your sons which will be born to you, which you will beget, will be taken, and they will be eunuchs in the palace of the king of Babylon."

In 39:8a Hezekiah respectfully receives the prophet's words.

39:8a Then said Hezekiah to Isaiah, "The word of the Lord which you have spoken is acceptable."

The last sentence (vs. 8b), as Scott points out is an editorial addition to the text which wrongly portrays Hezekiah as feeling relieved that the punishment will not come within his lifetime.[15] The comment reads:

39:8b For he said, "There will be peace and security in my days."

B. THE CORRUPT LEADERSHIP OF JUDAH

In 28:7-29 we are presented with a vivid and realistic picture of the corrupt and dissipated spiritual leadership of Judah, such a condition as

[15] Interpreter's Bible, V, 381.

cuts Isaiah to the quick. These verses date from before and during Sennacherib's invasion of Judah (701). The "tables" of vs. 8, judging from an early description of such an occasion, which were presided over by Samuel (I Sam. 9:12-13) are those of a sacrificial feast where drunkenness and filthy vomit utterly destroy all its spiritual symbolism as well as the beauty and dignity of true worship. This corrupt materialism extended even to the priests and prophets who were attached to the sanctuary in Samaria, where the earlier prophet Amos had once preached. The spiritual leaders themselves stagger and reel in drunkenness, and thus unfit themselves for their holy office.[16] It is a realistic and revolting picture which the prophet paints:

> 28:7 And these also
> Reel with wine,
> And stagger with strong drink;
> Priests and prophets
> Reel from intoxicating liquor;
> They are swallowed up by wine!
> They stagger from strong drink,
> They err in vision,
> They reel in the giving of decisions.
> 8 For all tables
> Are full of filthy vomit;
> There is no place clean.

1. The Scoffing and Corrupt Leaders of Judah

Such on-the-spot, frank criticism by Isaiah aroused the ire of these corrupt Judean spiritual leaders. "Who is this upstart that would teach us? Does he think he is teaching mere babes?" Such is their reaction, and Procksch suggests as likely that vs. 13d in sarcasm represents the words of the teacher calling on "the little one here," "the little one there," to repeat the lesson.[17] Thus Isaiah's scoffing hearers speak (vss. 9-10) :

> 9 "Whom would he teach knowledge?
> And whom would he make to understand the message?
> Those just weaned from milk?
> Those just removed from the breasts?
> 10 For it is line upon line, line upon line,
> Rule upon rule, rule upon rule,
> 'The little one here' and 'the little one there.' "

---

[16] Bewer, *The Book of Isaiah*, I, 72.
[17] *Isaiah*, p. 316.

2. A Message of the Lord's Doom Upon Judah

With a grave solemnity made all the more serious because of the Judeans'
superficiality and their mocking reception of his words, Isaiah counters
their sarcasm by solemnly warning his hearers of their sure defeat and
capture at foreign hands. As Scott says: "The strange and apparently stam-
mering speech of barbarians [vs. 13] will speak a word of doom to those
who would not find rest and "repose" in Yahweh." [18]

> 28:11 Surely in stammering speech
> And in an alien tongue
> Will I speak to this people.
> 12 To whom I said,
> "This is the resting place;
> Give rest to the weary;
> And this is the repose."
> But they were not willing to listen.
> 13 So the word of the Lord will be to them:
> Precept upon precept, precept upon precept,
> Line upon line, line upon line.
> The little one here,
> And the little one there;
> In order that they may go and stagger backwards,
> And be broken and ensnared and captured.

3. The Cornerstone of Sure Foundation

In 28:14-17a Isaiah speaks directly to the utterly irreligious political leaders of Jerusalem who have come into control in the Judean state. Evidently
in the case of making important decisions such as that of forming a political
and military alliance with Egypt, as Bewer tentatively suggests, they have
resorted to the art of divination by summoning the spirits of the dead to
obtain information from them.[19] Such grounds for guidance and protection
as those which these Judean leaders are seeking are deceitful and utterly
futile. In contrast to these deceptive bases of national security, the Lord
speaks through his prophet one of the profoundest religious utterances of
his entire ministry. Reliance upon God is the sole dependable basis of
Judean security. A political policy based upon belief in God, with confidence alone in his presence and protection, will save Judah from humiliation and shame. This, not political alliance, is the cornerstone of Judean
security. Isaiah calls the leaders of Judah to such faith. He who acts upon

---

[18] *Interpreter's Bible*, V, 316-17.
[19] *The Book of Isaiah*, p. 73.

faith such as this will never experience humiliation. Isaiah puts into the mouth of his people as purposive (vs. 15) what he emphasizes as a moral result.

>28:14 Therefore hear the word of the Lord,
>   Scoffing men,
>   Rulers of this people,
>   Who are in Jerusalem.
>15 Because you have said, "We have made
>   A covenant with death
>   And with Sheol
>   We have made a pact;
>   The overflowing scourge, when it passes through,
>   Will not come to us;
>   For we have made deceit our refuge,
>   And in deception have we hidden ourselves."
>16 Therefore thus says
>   The Lord God,
>   "Behold I am laying in Zion a stone,
>   A tested stone,
>   A precious cornerstone, of sure foundation,
>   'A people that keeps faith has no cause for panic.'
>17a And I will make justice the line
>   And righteousness as a level."

4. The Foundations of National Security

As regards 28:17b-20, Isaiah implies that if Judah bases its course of action upon anything other than justice and righteousness its foundation as a nation will surely prove false. As Skinner has said: "The purpose of God, as embodied in his revelation in the life of Israel, is the one element in human history which is indestructible." [20] National conduct must be based upon justice and righteousness if the nation is to persist. Otherwise the judgment of the Lord upon Judah will be, as he states it, "a protracted visitation and will continue till every one of the conspirators has been carried away." [21] To escape the divine judgment is impossible. The prophet uses a vivid and very human illustration of one who attempts to do it. It is like sleeping on a bed that is too short, with covers that are entirely too narrow and too short the whole night.

>28:17b "And a hailstorm will sweep away the refuge of lies,
>   And a flood will overflow the shelter."

[20] Skinner, *The Book of the Prophet Isaiah*, p. 226.
[21] *Ibid.*, p. 227.

18 Then your covenant with death will be broken,
    And your agreement with Sheol will not stand;
    When the overflowing scourge passes through,
    You will be trampled down by it.
19 As often as it passes
    It will take you;
    For morning by morning it will pass through.
    By day and by night;
    And it will be sheer terror
    To understand the message.
20 For the bed is too short to stretch oneself upon it,
    And the covering is too narrow to wrap one's self in it.

5. The Lord's Strange Work and Judgment

In 28:21-22 Isaiah represents the Lord as acting as the punisher of his people and the Assyrians as being used by him as the instrument of the divine judgment. He harks back to the time of David when, having defeated the Philistines, he gave the place of his victory the memorial name Baal-perazim, meaning "Lord of breaking through" (II Sam. 5:20). It is the conviction of Isaiah that similarly in his day the God of majesty will arise in his mighty power and break through in his "strange" but essential work of judgment and of discipline upon Judah.

28:21 For as at Mount Perazim, the Lord will rise up,
       As in the lowland in Gibeon, he will be provoked to wrath;
       To do his work—
       Strange is his work!
       And to do his task—
       Strange is his task!
    22 So now, do not act as scorner,
       Lest your chastisement prevail over you;
       For a decree of complete and decisive destruction,
       I have heard from the Lord of hosts,
       Upon the whole land.

6. A Prophetic Parable

In 28:23-26 Isaiah resorts to prophetic parable as an instrument of teaching and focuses upon the carefully instructed skill of the Judean farmer. He makes no application of his parable, but his words must have searched the hearts of his fellow Judeans to take home to their own consideration the example of the capable, experienced farmer whose use of his farm implements is both informed and efficient. The prophet leaves us with a new sense of the skill of God the creator and with a challenge to wisdom and common sense in the acceptance and use of all humanity's God-provided skills for the performance of life's routine tasks, which to him are as sacred as worship.

> 28:23 Give ear, and hear my voice;
> Give attention, and hear what I say.
> 24 Does the ploughman plough every day?
> Does he continually harrow his land?
> 25 Does he not, when he has leveled its surface,
> Scatter black cummin abundantly,
> And plant wheat in rows,
> And barley with spelt as its border?
> 26 For the Lord trains him properly;
> His God teaches him.

7. Glimpses of Agricultural Procedure

In 28:27-29 the prophet deals with ordinary skills of the farmer which are to a great extent taken for granted by him. He gives us instructive glimpses of ordinary agricultural procedure which are both informing and interesting. We learn that dill, an annual, sweet-smelling plant, was not threshed. We are informed as to how cummin and black cummin and dill, both of the nature of herbs, were beaten out and used for seasoning. We also learn how the noisily moving cart wheel crushed for effective use the grain from which bread was made. The prophet is keenly interested in agricultural procedures as well as in the results of the farmers' toil. And the God whose counsel and presence are writ large in the growth of black cummin and cummin and of corn for human consumption is Israel's God, the Lord of hosts, wonderful in counsel to his sons and daughters and sound and efficient in his guidance of their lives.

> 28:27 For black cummin is not threshed with a threshing sledge,
> Nor is a cart wheel rolled over cummin;
> But black cummin is beaten out with a staff,
> And cummin with a rod.
> 28 Does one grind bread grain?
> Surely not forever.
> Will one continue to thresh it?
> When he drives his wagon wheels over it,
> And spreads it out, he will not crush it.
> 29 This also goes forth
> From the Lord of hosts.

He makes counsel wondrous;
He makes wisdom great.

C. The Invasion of Judah by Sennacherib

In 36:1-37:9a and 37:9b-36 we have two accounts, respectively, of the attempt on the part of Sennacherib, king of Assyria, to accomplish the surrender of Jerusalem. The type of writing which we have in these two accounts is prophetic biography. As Bewer says, "They are probably parallel stories of the same event." [22]

The historical kernel of both of these accounts is II Kings 18:13-19:37. There are, however, three verses which are of prime importance in the passage from II Kings that do not appear in either of the above designated accounts in Isaiah. These are II Kings 18:14-16, which tell of Hezekiah's willingness to pay whatever Sennacherib imposes if the Assyrian monarch will withdraw (vs. 14). Sennacherib required three hundred talents of silver and thirty talents of gold. Hezekiah gave Sennacherib all the silver in the royal treasury and stripped the gold from the temple doors and door posts. No indication of any such abject surrender by Hezekiah appears in either version of the event as described by Isaiah.

1. The First Account of the Invasion of Sennacherib

The first account of Sennacherib's attempt to secure the surrender of Jerusalem is introduced in 36:1. The year is 701 B.C., the fourteenth year of the reign of King Hezekiah of Judah.

36:1 Now it came to pass in the fourteenth year of King Hezekiah, the king of Assyria came up against all the fortified cities of Judah and seized them.

A. THE SUDDEN APPEARANCE OF THE CHIEF ENVOY

In vss. 2-3 Isaiah narrates the sudden appearance of the Rab-Shakeh, the chief Assyrian envoy, who came to Jerusalem from Lachish, which was the Palestinian headquarters of the Assyrian forces. The designation Rab-Shakeh is not a proper name but an official title meaning "principal envoy." [23] He came, not to besiege Jerusalem, but merely to display Assyria's military strength.

The principal envoy stood at the very place where, in the days of King Ahaz of Judah, Isaiah and his son Shear-Jashub had confronted that young monarch, exhorting him to courage and faith in the Lord.

[22] *The Book of Isaiah,* I, 91.
[23] *Interpreter's Bible, op. cit.,* p. 362.

36:2 And the king of Assyria sent the principal envoy from Lachish to Jerusalem, to King Hezekiah, with a great army, and he went and stood by the water course of the upper pool on the highway of the fuller's field. 3 Then Eliakim, son of Hilkiah, who was over the palace, and Shebna, the secretary, and Joah, son of Asaph, the chancellor, went out to him.

B. JUDAH'S TRUST IN EGYPT

In vss. 4-6 the chief of the Assyrian forces asks Hezekiah what his basis of confidence is that he has rebelled against Assyria and has put his trust in the Pharaoh of Egypt. Such dependence, as the chief envoy maintains, is really self-destructive.

36:4 And the chief envoy said to them, "Please say to Hezekiah, Thus says the great king, king of Assyria, 'What is the confidence in which you trust? 5 Do you think that merely empty words are strategy and power for war? Now in whom do you trust that you have rebelled against me? 6 Behold now, you trust in this crushed staff of reed, in Egypt, which, if one supports oneself on it, will go into his hand and pierce it; so is Pharaoh, king of Egypt to all who trust in him.' "

C. JUDAH'S TRUST IN THE LORD

In vs. 7 the chief envoy says that if Hezekiah maintains that the Judeans should trust in the Lord for protection let them remember that it was the Lord's own high places, the altars of which had been removed by Hezekiah, insisting that Judean worship is to be carried on solely in the Temple of Jerusalem.

36:7 And if you say to me, "We trust in the Lord our God," is it not he whose altars Hezekiah removed and said to Judah and Jerusalem, "Before this altar shall you worship"?

D. LET JUDAH TRUST IN ASSYRIA

In 36:8-10 the chief Assyrian envoy calls the Judeans to be faithful to Assyria, who will provide horses for all the horsemen they can muster. Why then should Judah turn to Egypt for support? The Assyrian principal envoy even infers that Israel's own Lord had counseled the destruction of Judah.

36:8 So now, pray make a wager with my lord, the king of Assyria, that I shall give you two thousand horses if, on your part, you can put riders upon them. 9 How then can you decline the offer of the one of the least of my master's servants and trust in Egypt for chariots and horsemen? 10 And have I now come up against this place, without the Lord, to destroy it? The Lord said to me,[24] "Go up against this land and destroy it."

[24] So Bewer, The Prophets, p. 91, adding "attah."

E. LET THE ASSYRIAN ENVOY SPEAK IN ARAMAIC

In vss. 11-12 the Judean delegation, aware that their own people are listening in, urges the Assyrian envoy to speak to them, not in Hebrew but in Aramaic, the official language of diplomacy, so that the rank and file Judeans who are eagerly listening will not understand what the envoy says. The principal envoy continues in Hebrew, however, because he wants to reach the ear of the rank and file Judeans. He even has the nerve to say that it was Judah's own God who had sent him to speak in such words as the Judeans generally would understand!

36:11 Then Eliakim and Shebna and Joah said to the chief envoy, "Please speak to your servants in Aramaic for we understand it, but do not speak to us in Hebrew in the hearing of the people who are on the wall." 12 But the chief envoy said: "Has your Lord and God sent me to your master and to you to speak these words, but not to the men who are sitting on the wall, that they may eat their own dung and drink their own urine with you?"

F. THE ASSYRIAN APPEAL TO JUDAH TO SURRENDER

In 36:13-15 the Assyrian official persists in his appeal now directly to the Judeans, to surrender. If they do they will be permitted to live normally. They are not to pay heed to Hezekiah. They are to make their peace with Assyria, which is now the lord of the Middle East. The Assyrian spokesman is careful not to call Hezekiah king.

36:13 Then the Assyrian official stood and cried with a loud voice in Hebrew, saying, "Hear the words of the great king, king of Assyria. 14 Thus says the king: 'Do not let Hezekiah deceive you, for he is not able to deliver you. 15 And do not trust Hezekiah when he says, "the Lord will surely deliver you. This city shall not be given into the hand of the king of Assyria."' "

G. LET JUDAH SURRENDER TO ASSYRIA

In 36:16-21 the Assyrian official urges the Judeans not to heed King Hezekiah but to surrender. Then they will be permitted to live normally until the Assyrians, having triumphed over Egypt and being ready to return home, will deport the Judeans to Assyria.

36:16 Do not listen to Hezekiah; for thus says the king of Assyria: "Make a treaty of peace with me and come out to me and eat, each of his own vine and fig tree, and drink each from his own cistern, 17 until I come and take you to a land like your own land, a land of grain and new wine, a land of bread and vineyards. 18 Beware lest Hezekiah persuade you, saying, 'The Lord will surely deliver us.' Have the gods of the nations delivered—each his own land—out of the hand of the king of Assyria. 19 Where are the gods of Hamath and Arpad? Where are the gods of Sibraim? [25] And when have they delivered Samaria out of my hand? 20 Who are there among all gods of the nations who have delivered their land out of my hand, that the Lord would deliver Jerusalem out of my hand?" 21 But they were silent and did not answer him a word, for the command of the king was, "you are not to answer."

H. THE LAMENTING REPORT TO HEZEKIAH

Isa. 36:22 records how the Judean officials, in the mood of solemn lamentation, reported the words of the chief Assyrian envoy to King Hezekiah.

36:22 Then Eliakim, son of Hilkiah who was over the palace, and Shebna, the Scribe, and Joah, the recorder, went to the king with torn garments and reported to him the words of the chief Assyrian envoy.

I. HEZEKIAH SENDS A DELEGATION TO ISAIAH REQUESTING PRAYER

In 37:1-9a we learn how King Hezekiah reacted to the attempt of Sennacherib to secure Jerusalem's surrender. In the mood and attire of lamentation he went to the Temple. He sent Eliakim, Shebna the scribe, and the experienced priests, covered with sackcloth, to Isaiah the prophet. They are to describe the situation interpreting it as a threefold calamity. They are asked by the king to seek out Isaiah, report to him the crisis, and beseech him to pray that the Lord will rebuke Assyria and save the remnant of Judah.

37:1 And it came to pass when King Hezekiah heard he tore his garments, covered himself with sackcloth and went to the house of the Lord. 2 And he sent Eliakim, who was over the palace, and Shebna, the scribe, and the elders of the priests, covered with sackcloth, to Isaiah, son of Amoz, the prophet 3 And they said to him, "Thus says Hezekiah. 'This day is a day of distress and reproof and humiliation, for children have come to the mouth of the womb but there is no strength to give birth. 4 Perhaps the Lord thy God will hear the words of the chief envoy which the king of Assyria, his lord, sent to reproach the living God, and reprove the words which the Lord your God has heard; wherefore lift up a prayer on behalf of the remnant that is left!' "

J. THE LORD WILL BRING ABOUT THE RETURN OF SENNACHERIB TO NINEVEH

In 37:5-7 to the servants of Hezekiah who came to Isaiah for counsel from the Lord, he counseled them to have no fear before the irreverent servants of the Assyrian king who had blasphemed the Lord. The Lord will put a

---

[25] Located on the border between Hamath and Damascus and destroyed by Shalmaneser in 727; so read with Bewer, *The Book of Isaiah*, I, 92.

spirit in him that will impel him to return to Assyria, to his capital at Nineveh, where he will be overthrown.

37:5 So the servants of King Hezekiah came to Isaiah 6 and Isaiah said to them, "Thus shall you say unto your master: Thus says the Lord: 'Be not afraid of the words that you have heard, wherewith the servants of the king of Assyria have blashphemed me. 7 Behold I will put a spirit in him and he shall hear a rumor and return to his own land and I will cause him to fall by the sword in his own land.' "

K. THE RETURN OF THE CHIEF ASSYRIAN ENVOY

In 37:8-9a we are informed of the return of the chief Assyrian envoy to find Sennacherib warring against Libnah, which is "a fortified city in the foothills of Judah, near modern Beit Jibrin," [26] and we learn also of the approach of Tirhakah, nephew of king Shabaka, who was destined to be the last king of the twenty-fifth, or Ethiopian, Dynasty in Egypt. At the moment he was not yet king but the nephew of king Shabaka.[27]

37:8 So the chief envoy returned and found the king of Assyria fighting against Libnah, for he had heard that the king had departed from Lachish. 9a And he heard say concerning Tirhakah, king of Ethiopia, "he has gone forth to fight against you."

2. *The Second Account of Sennacherib's Attempt to Secure the Surrender of Jerusalem*

In 37:9b-36 we have the second account of Sennacherib's attempt to se-cure the surrender of Jerusalem. This passage is simply a later version of 36:1-37:9a. The editor who connects the parallel accounts, as Bewer says, repeats the beginning of 20:9 "and he heard," where II Kings 19:9 reads, "and he again sent." [28] The Rab-Shakeh, the chief envoy, is the subject of Isa. 37:9b, who sent messengers to Hezekiah urging him not to be deceived by those who were maintaining the inviolability of Jerusalem. The destruc-tive power that Assyria had already shown should make Jerusalem doubly anxious as to its own fate. Gozen of vs. 12 is the Assyrian Guzana in Meso-potamia, on the river Chabor. Haran is in northern Mesopotamia. Reseph is the modern Rusafe, situated between Palmyra and the Euphrates River. Eden is the Assyrian Bit-Adini, on both sides of the Euphrates. Telassar is the Assyrian Til-ashuri near Edissa. Hamath is modern Hama on the Orontes River, north of Damascus.

[26] *Ibid.*
[27] *Ibid.*
[28] *Ibid.*, p. 93.

37:9*b* And he again[29] sent messengers to Hezekiah, saying 10 "Let not your God in whom you are trusting, say: 'Jerusalem shall not be given into the hand of the king of Assyria.' 11 Behold you have heard what the kings of Assyria have done to all the lands, to exterminate them, and will you be delivered? 12 Have the gods of the nation delivered them whom my fathers destroyed, Gozan and Haran and Reseph, and the sons of Eden, and those who were in Telassar? 13 Where is the king of Hamath and the king of Arpad and the king of the city of Sepharvaim, of Hena and Ivah and Samaria?" [30]

A. THE ASSYRIAN GODS ARE NO GODS

In 37:14-20 Hezekiah received and read the letter,[31] then went to the Temple and spread it before the Lord. He prayed to the Lord beseeching him to see what is taking place and to hear Sennacherib's words which defy the Lord. The Assyrian gods are in reality no gods, but mere lifeless images which human hands have made and can destroy. He calls upon God to save the Judeans from Sennacherib's hands so that the kingdoms of earth may know that the Lord whom Israel worships, and he alone, is God.

37:14 And Hezekiah received the letter from the hand of the messengers and read it, and went up to the house of the Lord, and Hezekiah spread it out before the Lord. 15 And Hezekiah prayed to the Lord, saying: 16 "O Lord of hosts, God of Israel, that art enthroned above the cherubim, Thou alone art the God of all the kingdoms of the earth. Thou hast made the heavens and the earth 17 Incline thine ear, O Lord and hear; open thine eyes, O Lord and see, and hear[32] the words of Sennacherib which he has sent to defy the living God. 18 Truly, O Lord, the kings of Assyria have laid waste all the nations and their lands, 19 and have cast their gods into the fire, for they are not gods but the work of men's hands, wood and stone, and they could destroy them. 20 So now, O Lord our God, deliver us from his hand that all kingdoms of the earth may know that Thou, alone art the Lord."

B. A TAUNT SONG AGAINST SENNACHERIB

In 37:21-29 we have a taunt song uttered against Sennacherib. Isaiah introduces it as an answer to Hezekiah because he had prayed to the Lord against the Assyrian monarch. As Scott says concerning the prophet's oracle of defiance, it "sets forth the impending doom of the overweening pride of the Assyrian king." [33]

---

[29] So read with II Kings 19:2. This is, as Bewer says, "the editor's connecting link between the parallel accounts." *Ibid.*
[30] Adding Samaria, with the Dead Sea Scroll, as in Isa. 36:19.
[31] So read as single following the LXX.
[32] Omit all with LXX and II Kings.
[33] *Interpreter's Bible,* V, 368.

37:21 Then Isaiah, son of Amoz, sent to Hezekiah, saying, "Thus says the Lord
God of Israel to whom thou hast prayed, against[34] Sennacherib king of Assyria,
and I have heard. 22 This is the word which the Lord has spoken concerning him:

"The Virgin daughter of Zion,
    Hath despised thee, hath derided thee;
The daughter of Jerusalem
    Hath shaken her head at thee.

23 Whom hast thou defied and blasphemed?
    And against whom hast thou lifted up thy voice,
And lifted up thine eyes on high?
    Against the Holy One of Israel!

24 By your servants you have reproached the Lord,
    And you have said, 'By the multitude of my chariots
Have I come up to the height of mountains,
    To the recesses[35] of Lebanon.

And I have cut down its tall cedars
    And its choice fir trees.
And I have entered its farthest height,
    Its densest forest.

25 I have dug and drunk water,
    And with the sole of my feet I have dried up
    All the canals of Egypt.'

26 Have you not heard long ago
    How I did it,
And of ancient times that I fashioned it?
    Now have I brought it to pass,
That thou shouldst lay waste
    Defenced cities into ruin-heaps.

27 Therefore their inhabitants, shorn of strength,
    Were dismayed and ashamed;
They have become as the grass of the field,
    And as the green herb,
As grass on the housetops, and as corn
    Blasted before it is grown up.

28 I know your sitting down,
    And your going out and coming in,
    And your raging against me.

[34] Reading with II Kings עַל instead of אֶל.
[35] So Bewer, The Book of Isaiah, I, 94.

> 29 Because you have raged against me,
> And your arrogance has come up to my ears,
> I will put my hook in your nose,
> And my bit in your mouth,
> And I will turn you back by the way
> In which you came."

C. THE DEPARTURE OF SENNACHERIB

In 37:33-35 we have a continuation of the second account of Sennacherib's attempt to gain the surrender of Jerusalem. The prophet gives the Judeans confidence that Sennacherib of Assyria will not come into Jerusalem, nor will he cast up a mound there such as is used in attacking a walled city. He will return as he came, for Jerusalem, in the divine intention, is inviolable. Thus Isaiah interprets the Lord's intention.

> 37:33 Therefore, thus says the Lord concerning the king of Assyria:

> "He shall not come into this city,
> Nor shoot an arrow there;
> And he shall not confront it with shields,
> Nor cast up a mound against it.

> 34 By the way he came,
> By it he shall return,
> And shall not come into this city,
> Says the Lord.

> 35 For I will defend this city to save it
> For my own sake and for the sake of David, my servant."

D. THE ESCAPED REMNANT AS THE NUCLEUS OF A NEW JUDAH

Isa. 37:30-32 belongs, as Scott says, between vss. 35 and 36. These verses give great encouragement. The escaped remnant of Judeans are a vital nucleus of a new day for Judah. It is not merely human power and skill that will bring this about, however. Rather it is the divine initiative, the zeal of the Lord, his ardent interest in his people, that will accomplish it.

> 37:30 And this shall be a sign to you: Eat this year what shall grow from spilled kernels, and in the second year grain that shoots up of itself. And in the third year sow and reap, and plant vineyards and eat their fruit. 31 And the remnant that is escaped, of the house of Judah, will again take root downward and bear fruit upwards. 32 For out of Jerusalem there shall go forth a remnant, and they that escape out of Mount Zion. The zeal of the Lord of hosts will accomplish this.

E. THE LEGEND OF THE DESTRUCTION OF THE ASSYRIAN FORCES

Herodotus preserves an Egyptian tradition which narrates a disaster of the army of Sennacherib at the border of Egypt when field mice invaded the camp and gnawed the bows and the shields. Mice were carriers of the plague. In the present account it is an angel of the Lord who destroys the army by pestilence.[36]

37:36 And it came about, in that night, that the angel of the Lord went forth and smote in the camp of Assyria, a hundred and eighty-five thousand; and when men arose early in the morning, behold all these were dead bodies.

F. SENNACHERIB'S RETURN TO NINEVEH AND HOW HE MET HIS DEATH

In 37:37-38 we have the narrative of the departure of Sennacherib to the Assyrian capital city of Nineveh, and we are informed as to how he met his death and the secession to his throne.

37:37 Then Sennacherib, king of Assyria, departed and went home and dwelt in Nineveh. 38 And as he was worshiping in the house of Nisroch his god, Adrammelech and Sharezer, his sons, smote him with the sword, and he escaped to the land of Ararat, and, Esarhaddon, his son, ruled in his stead.

The basic source (II Kings 18:14-16) makes it perfectly clear that King Hezekiah submitted to Assyria and agreed to pay whatever the king of Assyria demanded. Sennacherib demanded of him three hundred talents of silver and thirty talents of gold. To pay it Hezekiah took all the silver from the treasures of palace and Temple. Such submission on the part of Hezekiah ignored Isaiah's oracle of 37:22-29, which was an oracle of defiance. How deeply disappointed Isaiah must have been, when, because of the likelihood of a long siege, Hezekiah submitted to Sennacherib! Sidney Smith says that "the prospect of a long siege caused Hezekiah to submit. . . . The campaign had been absolutely successful, and Palestine remained at peace and faithful to Assyria for the remainder of Sennacherib's reign!" [37]

D. HEZEKIAH'S ILLNESS AND RECOVERY

Isa. 38:1-22, which gives an account of King Hezekiah's illness and his recovery which took place during the siege, is quoted from II Kings 20:1-11, but it includes qualities which, as Sheldon Blank says, "along with the element of prediction give a strong impression of the legendary." As he suggests, these words "have much in common with the miracle tales of the 'early prophets' to be found in the books of Samuel and Kings." [38]

[36] Henry Cary, *The History of Herodotus*, Book II, 141, 79.
[37] Cf. J. B. Bury, S. A. Cook, and F. E. Adcock, *Cambridge Ancient History*, III, 74.
[38] *The Prophetic Faith in Isaiah*, p. 13.

To Hezekiah, dangerously ill, Isaiah comes and summons the king to prepare for imminent death. Hezekiah, weeping bitter tears, utters a prayer to the Lord, urging upon him his faithfulness, whereupon the Lord sends Isaiah to the king to impart to him the comforting assurance of an extension of his days and deliverance from Assyrian dominion. The prophet also gives the king counsel regarding the treatment of his illness (38:1-6, 21, 7).

38:1 In those days King Hezekiah became deathly sick. And Isaiah, son of Amoz, the prophet, came to him and said to him, "Thus says the Lord: 'Give charge to your household, for you are about to die and not live.'" 2 Then Hezekiah turned his face to the wall, and weeping bitter tears, prayed to the Lord. 3 And said: "Ah now, Lord, remember, I pray, that I have walked before thee in faithfulness and with a heart at peace, and have done what is good in thy sight." And Hezekiah wept profusely. 4 Then the word of the Lord came to Isaiah, saying, 5 "Return and say to Hezekiah, 'Thus says the Lord, God of David, your father: I have heard your prayer, I have seen your tears; behold, I will add fifteen years to your life. 6 I will deliver you from the hand of the king of Assyria, and I will defend this city.'"

1. Isaiah in the Rôle of Physician

Vss. 21-22 rightly belong between vs. 6 and vs. 7, as we see from II Kings 20:6-9. As Scott has noted they give "one of several slight indications that he [Isaiah] may have known and practiced the arts of the physician." [39]

38:21 Now Isaiah had said, "Let them take a hot poultice of figs and rub it upon the boil that he may live." 22 Hezekiah had also said, "this[40] is the sign that I shall go up to the house of the Lord."

2. The Covered Way for the Sabbath

In vss. 7-8 is imaginatively pictured the shadow of the declining sun miraculously turning backward ten steps on a private stairway which Ahaz had erected. Probably this is "the covered way for the Sabbath" which had been built inside the palace, to which reference is made in II Kings 16:18.

38:7 And this is the sign to you from the Lord that the Lord will do this thing which he has said. 8 Lo, I am about to turn backward the sun's shadow on the steps which the sun has gone down on, the steps of Ahaz, ten steps. So the sun turned back on the dial the ten steps which it had gone down.

3. A Liturgy for a Sacrifice of Thanksgiving

For 38:9-20 there is no parallel in the books of Kings, and it is generally recognized that we here have legendary material. As Scott says, "The so-

[39] *Interpreter's Bible,* V, 378.
[40] So LXX, reading וְעָלִיתִי with II Kings.

called 'psalm of Hezekiah' . . . like the 'song of Hannah' (I Sam. 2:1-10) and the 'prayer of Jonah' (Jonah 2:2-9), is a liturgical composition for use in the temple service at the private presentation of a sacrifice of thanksgiving for some personal deliverance!" The title (vs. 9) rightly interprets it as a "mikhtam," which is "an appeal for divine help ending on a note of confidence." [41] It is not part of the poem, but was added by the compiler of the psalm book from which it was derived. The setting of the liturgy is given in vs. 9.

38:9 A writing of Hezekiah, king of Judah, when he had been sick and had recovered from his illness.

A. ANGUISH AT THE EXPECTATION OF DEATH

In 38:10-14, the first part of the poem, is described the anguish of soul that our psalmist had experienced when he had despaired of his life and felt himself to be at the very gates of Sheol, the realm of the dead, soon to be cut off prematurely from the life which, with such joy, he had shared with mankind. In deep distress he cried out unto the Lord:

> 38:10 I said in the even tenor
> Of my days, I must go
> To the gates of Sheol. I have been deprived
> Of the residue of my years.
> 11 I said, "I shall not see the Lord
> In the land of the living;
> I shall not look upon mankind anymore,
> Along with the inhabitants of the world.
> 12 My dwelling has been plucked up and removed from me
> Like a shepherd's tent;
> He has rolled up, as a weaver, my life;
> He will dissever me from the thrum;[42]
> Between day and night, thou wilt make an end of me;
> 13 I have cried out for help until morning;
> Like a lion, so he breaks
> All my bones;
> 14 Like a twittering swallow, so I chirp;
> I moan like a dove.
> My eyes look languishingly on high.
> My Lord has oppressed me;
> Let him go surety for me."

[41] *Interpreter's Bible*, V, 374.
[42] Fringe of such threads remaining on the loom when the web has been cut off.

B. HEZEKIAH'S PRAYER FOR RESTORATION TO HEALTH

In 38:15-17 Hezekiah speaks meditatively and in the mood of wonder. He could not sleep because of his bitterness of soul, but in the inner darkness of his spirit he is somehow led to look up to the heights where God dwells, and he experiences the wonderful realization that from on high the Lord heard his lamenting petition and acted. This changes his bitterness of spirit into calm and hope such as lead him to wait in quiet certainty of soul for restoration to life and health.

> 38:15 What shall I say? I spoke to him
> And he acted.
> All my sleep had fled
> Because of the bitterness of my soul.
> 16 O Lord, with thee are the days of my life.
> Thine alone is the life of my spirit.[43]
> O restore me to health and let me live.
> 17 And my bitterness shall become peace.[44]
> Yea, thou hast held back my soul
> From the pit of destruction.
> For thou hast cast behind thy back
> All my sins.

C. PRAISE CAN COME ONLY FROM THE LIVING

In vss. 18-20 Isaiah asserts that praise songs will never arise to the Lord from Sheol, "the land of no return," nor can those who are no longer in the land of the living praise God as his character deserves. Praise can come only from the living, whose responsibility it is to pass on to the next generation the psalms, hymns, and spiritual songs of the Temple, the grateful recognition of God's faithfulness.

> 38:18 For Sheol cannot praise thee,
> The dead cannot celebrate thee;
> Those who go down to the grave cannot praise thee
> For thy lovingkindness.
> 19 The living, the living, he shall praise thee,
> As I do this day;
> A father to sons
> Will declare thy faithfulness.
> 20 The Lord will make haste[45] to save me,

---

[43] So read with Targum.
[44] Reading with BH וחיה instead of הנה.
[45] Insert with BH הושה.

And to my stringed instruments we shall sing
All the days of our life,
In the house of the Lord.

E. THE ALTAR HEARTH AN EMBLEM OF JERUSALEM'S FATE

In 29:1-4 worshipers in the Temple at Jerusalem are addressed as *"ariel,*
which means 'altar hearth of God.' " [46] As Bewer says: "It may be a varia-
tion of the ancient name of Jerusalem, Uri-Salimu, with El (God) taking
the place of the god Salem." [47] The Septuagint designates Jerusalem as
"the city against which David encamped," the reference being to II Sam.
5:9, which verse, informing us of his success, says, "David dwelt in the
stronghold and called it the city of David."

This famous capital of Judah is soon to be reduced to an ariel, an altar
hearth, as Skinner says, "either a place where the flames of war rage fiercely
or a place reeking with the blood of countless human beings." [48] We may
suppose that Isaiah addressed these words to worshipers in the Temple and
that the great altar with its bleeding victims stood out before his mind as
an emblem of Jerusalem's fate. The Lord himself is in ultimate command
of forces surrounding Jerusalem in a siege to master that city, which he is
about to bring to the ground. And low from the ground, like a ghost chirp-
ing from the dust, Jerusalem shall humbly speak. Cries the prophet:

29:1 Ah! altar-hearth, altar-hearth
       City in which David encamped!
    Add year to year;
       Let feasts run the year's round.
2 And I will bring the altar-hearth into straits,
       And there shall be mourning and lamentation,
       And you shall be to me like a [true] altar-hearth.
3 And I will besiege you with siege works,
       And I will command an intrenchment against you.
4 And you shall speak low out of the ground,
       Aye your speech shall proceed humbly from the dust,
    And your voice shall be from the ground like a ghost,
       And your speech shall chirp from the dust.

1. Isaiah's Faith in the Intervention of the Lord

In vss. 5-8 there is reflected the tension which, in one period of his career,
existed in Isaiah's mind. It grew out of a conflict which he experienced

[46] Ezek. 43:15, *Cambridge Bible.*
[47] *The Book of Isaiah,* I, 75.
[48] *The Book of the Prophet Isaiah,* p. 231.

between his anticipation of the Lord's judgment upon his people and the assurance which he had that what was good in the nation of Judah would not be destroyed. Isaiah pictures Israel's multitudinous foes like dust and chaff whirled over that nation by a mighty wind. All seems lost.

The enemies of Judah have not reckoned with the Lord, however. "At an instant" the nation will be visited, not in destruction, but in salvation. We hear the thunder of God's voice. The ground is shaken as by an earthquake. The prophet thus portrays his sure faith in the intervention of the Lord on behalf of his people. That roar of nations against Zion, which is laden with the intention to destroy and extinguish Judah, is impotent before the divine initiative. Isaiah has received from the Lord the assurance of "ultimate salvation of what is good in Israel." [49]

> 29:5 And your foes shall be like dust of a multitude,
>   And like chaff passing over a crowd.
>   And it shall be, at an instant, with a roar,
>   Suddenly you shall be visited by the Lord of hosts
>   6 With thunder and earthquake and a loud noise,
>   Stormwind and tempest,
>   And consuming flame of fire.
>   7 And it shall be like a dream,
>   A night vision,
>   A multitude of all the nations
>   Fighting against Ariel,
>   And all that besiege her, and press hard upon her,
>   Shall be like a dream:
>   8 It shall be as when a hungry person
>   Dreams and behold he is eating,
>   But he awakes and his body is faint;
>   Just so shall be the multitude of all the nations
>   That wage war against Mount Zion.

2. The Spiritual Blindness of Judah's Leaders

In 29:9-12 Isaiah criticizes Judah because of the spiritual blindness and seeming stupor of its leaders. We remember that in the prophet's call there was revealed to him the needed warning that those to whom he would speak would not grasp the meaning of his message. Yet he was to keep preaching. The Judeans seem unable to discern what is happening to Judah right before their eyes. They move with uncertain steps. They stagger, not in drunkenness, but in spiritual insensibility. Those in the nation who should be able to discern, have to admit their ignorance. The leaders

---

[49] *Ibid.,* p. 232.

wash their hands of all responsibility to make God's will known to Judah. As Jesus put it centuries later, "They have eyes but see not; they have ears but hear not." Consequently the available revelation of God's will in the crisis is withheld by leaders who wash their hands of responsibility to guide the conduct of their fellowmen.

> 29:9 Astonish yourselves and be dumfounded,
>   Blind yourselves and be sightless,
>   Get drunk, but not with wine;
>   Stagger, but not with strong drink!
> 10 For the Lord has poured out on you the spirit of deep sleep,
>   And he has tightly shut your eyes;
>   And your heads he has covered.

11 And the vision of the whole has become to you like words of a book that is sealed, such as they give to one who knows how to read, saying, "Please read this," but he will say, "I cannot for it is sealed." 12 So he will give the book to one who does not know books saying, "Please read this," and he will say, "I do not know how to read."

3. The Religion of Judah Is Words, Not Deeds

In 29:13-14 Isaiah sharply criticizes the religion of Judah because it is a religion of words but not of deeds. Their words appear to honor God, but their minds and hearts, which to Isaiah are the very center of religion and are here conceived of as the seat of the intellect and the will, neither think of God nor will to do what God desires. Consequently religion has become divorced from conduct. It is lip service and does not spring from the heart, the inner spirit of the people. It is words not deeds, talk not behavior. The "wonders" which the Lord will do to his people are to be the expression of his condemnation of their spiritual superficiality which issues in a religion that is utterly impotent. Accordingly the Lord's "marvelous things" that he will do are to be conceived in terms, not of blessing, but of discipline and judgment. We are very close here to New Testament thought.

> 13 And the Lord said:
>   "Because this people draw near with their mouth,
>   And honor me with their lips,
>   But their hearts are far distant from me,
>   And their fear of me has become
>   A commandment of learned men;
> 14 Therefore, lo I will again do wonderfully,
>   A wonder extraordinary.
>   And the wisdom of their wise men shall perish
>   And the understanding of their intelligentsia shall hide itself."

F. THE GOOD RESULTS OF A RIGHTEOUS RULE

In 32:1-8 the prophet's theme is the good results that accrue from a righteous rule. Scott is right in rejecting any messianic interpretation of this passage.[50] There is no adequate justification, however, for his viewing it as the product of later wisdom writers. Isaiah saw the vast need in Judah for righteous manhood with the capacity to lead. As Skinner says, "It is perhaps most naturally assigned to the close of Isaiah's ministry, ca. 701 when his mind was occupied with the hope of the ideal future." [51] "The main ideas can be paralleled from Isaiah." Here he takes pains to paint a picture which has had a great influence across the centuries in the development of disinterested leadership. First, in vs. 1 he singles out king and princes for special attention; then in vs. 2 he paints a picture of Judean manhood in general as it should be, wherein any representative man will feel the responsibility to protect his fellow men in stormy and tempestuous times and to be to them a source of inspiration and of security. Those now spiritually and morally blind will then be awakened to insight (vs. 3). Those now seemingly deaf to prophetic teaching will listen receptively. Those now precipitant in judgment will learn calm discernment, and those whose utterance is now inarticulate or entirely lacking will speak with clarity and courage (vs. 4). No rascal will be reputed to be noble. Fools will continue on in their evil motivation with reckless speech and blasphemous conduct and with no concern whatever for the elemental physical needs of the hungry and thirsty in Judah (vs. 5). Judean society will continue to have its fraudulent rascals who ignore every attempt on the part of the needy person with justice on his side to secure a fair deal (vss. 6-7). But over against such persisting corruption—and here the prophet reveals an ultimate optimism—there is a righteous core in the Judean society; there are those who are noble in character, in conduct, and in counsel (vs. 8).

> 32:1 Lo, a king shall reign in righteousness,
>   And princes shall govern in justice.
> 2 And a man shall be like a hiding place from wind,
>   And a shelter from a rain storm,
>   Like canals of water in parched ground,
>   Like the shade of a massive rock
>   In a weary land.
> 3 And the eyes of those who see will not be blinded,
>   And the ears of those who hear will give attention.

---

[50] *Interpreter's Bible*, V, 342.
[51] *Op. cit.*, 239.

4 And the heart of the hasty shall discern knowledge,
   And the tongue of the inarticulate shall hasten to speak
      clearly.
5 The fool shall no more be called honorable,
   And the rascal shall not be called noble.
6 For the fool will keep on speaking folly,
   And his heart will continue to plan what is iniquitous,
   Doing what profanes the Most High,
   And speaking error concerning the Lord,
   So as to keep empty the bodies of the hungry,
   And causing the drink of the thirsty to fail.
7 And, as for the knave, his instruments are evil;
   He counsels evil practices
   To ruin the poor with fraudulent words,
   Even when the needy person speaks justly.
8 But the noble person counsels noble things,
   And upon noble things he takes his stand.

G. Isaiah's Philosophy of History

There are eight passages which, when brought together, give what may rightly be called a philosophy of history that became an abiding feature of Isaiah's message. These are (1) Isa. 10:5-19, (2) Isa. 14:24-27, (3) Isa. 10:20-21, (4) Isa. 30:25de; 30:29; 30:32c, (5) Isa. 30:31-32ab; 30:33, (6) Isa. 5:25-30, (7) Isa. 17:12-14, and (8) Isa. 10:24-27abc.

These passages date from 701 and reveal to us the breadth of his teaching and the deep conviction that the purpose of God was being expressed in the experiences through which his people were passing.

1. Assyria as Conceived in the Divine Purpose

In 10:5-19 Isaiah gives expression in its most complete form and clearest meaning to his philosophy of history. The question to which he here addresses himself is, What is Assyria as conceived in the purpose of God? Here was a great and ruthless national power. Indeed Isaiah lived in the period of Assyria's greatest strength. The date of this section is from 701 b.c., the fourteenth year of the reign of King Hezekiah of Judah, when, as we are informed by the Judean historian of the books of Kings, "Sennacherib, king of Assyria, came up against all the fortified cities of Judah and took them" (II Kings 18:13).

In the prophet's words the Lord himself is represented as speaking, not directly to Assyria, but to Judah concerning Assyria. The key thought of Isaiah comes in his opening words (10:5-6), where Judah is designated as a profane nation against which the Lord of all history is sending Assyria as a "rod" to express the divine anger and a "staff" to give vent to the divine fury. The Lord speaks:

> 10:5 Ah! Assyria! rod of my anger!
>   And staff of my fury!
>   6 Against a profane nation, I will send him,
>   And against a people who are the object of my rage, I command him,
>   To take as spoil and to plunder booty,
>   And to make it a trampling place like mire of the streets.

A. ASSYRIA IS UNAWARE OF BEING THE LORD'S AGENT

Judah is quite unaware that Assyria, its most powerful enemy, is an agent that God is using to punish his own profane people, and on the other hand Assyria has no inkling of being an agent in God's hand for such a purpose. Annihilation of the smaller peoples of the Middle East is Assyria's sole aim, as its military record clearly shows. So the prophet represents the Assyrian monarch as boasting over his conquests as he moves from Carchemish on the Euphrates River to Calneh, most likely Kullani, near Aleppo, which Tiglath-pileser of Assyria conquered in 738 B.C. Hamath (vs. 9) which name means "fortress," is the modern Hama on the Orontes River *ca.* 115 miles north of Damascus. Arpad is in northern Syria, fifteen miles north of Aleppo, modern Tel Erfad.[52] Thus the campaign of the Assyrian monarch is presented as the prophet envisions it:

> 10:7 But not so does he intend,
>   And not so does his mind think;
>   But it is in his mind to annihilate,
>   And to cut off nations, not a few;
>   8 For he says,
>   "Are not my captains all alike, kings?
>   Is not Calno like Carchemish?
>   Or is not Hamath like Arpad?
>   Is not Samaria like Damascus?
>   10 As my hand has reached
>   To the kingdoms of the idols,
>   Whose graven images
>   Were greater than those of Jerusalem and Samaria,
>   11 Shall I not, just as I did
>   To Samaria and its idols,
>   So do to Jerusalem and its idols?"

[52] So BDB, 75.

B. THE LORD WILL AT LENGTH DEAL WITH ASSYRIA

The Lord is not sitting back and looking at what is happening in the violent movement of nations in this area. When his will for Jerusalem shall have been accomplished he will deal with haughty Assyria. That ruthless nation is quite unaware that God is using it to accomplish his will, as an agent of discipline upon his people, but feels itself to be its own lord.

12 And it shall be that when the Lord shall have finished all his work on Mount Zion and in Jerusalem, he shall pay attention to the fruit of insolence in the heart of the king of Assyria and to the glorying of his haughty eyes.
13   For he says,
      "By the strength of my hand I have done it,
      And by my wisdom, for I have understanding;
      And I have removed the boundaries of peoples,
      And their stores I have plundered;
         And I have brought down, like a bull, those [sitting on thrones].
14 And my hands have found, like a nest,
      The wealth of the nations;
      And like the gathering of eggs that have been forsaken,
      I have gathered all the earth;
      And there was none that fluttered a wing,
      Or opened the mouth or chirped."

C. ISAIAH CHALLENGES THE BOASTS OF ASSYRIA

In 10:15-16 proud Assyria's haughty boasts are challenged by Isaiah, the Lord's prophet. Assyria, glorying in its own military ruthlessness and hitherto unchallenged pagan power of harsh domination, has not taken into consideration him who is the Lord of all history and who is using Assyria to discipline his people Israel.

      10:15 Shall the ax glorify itself
            Over him who swings it,
                Or shall the saw magnify itself over him who wields it?
            As if a rod should wield him who lifts it,
                Or a staff should lift up one who is not wood.
      16 Therefore the Lord of hosts
            Shall send among his vigorous ones leanness,
            And underneath his glory
            Will be kindled a burning,
            Like a burning fire.

D. THE FIRE OF THE LORD

In 10:17-19 the Lord, the light of Israel is the fire. The land of Israel it is which is to be burned over by him. In vs. 16 the Lord sends the fire. In vs. 17 the Lord, "the light of Israel" is himself the fire.

> 17 And the light of Israel shall become a fire
>   And his holy one a flame.
>   And it shall burn and consume his thornbushes,
>   And his thorns in one day.
> 18 And the glory of his forest and his garden land,
>   Both soul and body he will bring to an end,
>   And it shall be like the wasting away of a sick man.
> 19 And the remnant of the trees of his forest
>   Will be so few
>   That a child can write them down.

2. The Purpose of the Lord Regarding Assyria

In 14:24-27, which rightly belongs before 10:20-21, the prophet maintains that it is the Lord's purpose to destroy the Assyrians on the mountains of Palestine, so that the hated Assyrian yoke will be at an end.

> 14:24 The Lord of hosts has sworn:
>   "As I have intended
>   So has it been,
>   And as I counseled
>   So will it come to be,
> 25 That I will break Assyria in my land,
>   And upon my mountains I will trample him down;
>   And his yoke shall depart from upon them,
>   And his burden shall be removed from their shoulder."
> 26 This is the counsel of wisdom that has been counseled;
>   And this is the hand that is stretched out
>   Over all the nations.
> 27 For the Lord of hosts
>   Has counseled and who can frustrate [it]?
>   And his hand is stretched out,
>   And who can turn it back?

3. A Creative Spiritual Nucleus in Judah

In 10:20-21 the prophet gives expression to a later and more positive phase of his thought. He envisions in the nation of Judah a creative spiritual nucleus, those Judeans who will have come through disaster. In the spirit of true repentance and positive trust they will have learned to lean for support, direction, and protection, not upon alliance with any foreign power, with its armaments and military prowess which would at

length smite them, but upon the Lord, in confident trust. It is God alone
who is ultimately Judah's sole basis of security. Such Judeans are the puri-
fied and disciplined remnant. The date is *ca.* 701. Thus Isaiah speaks:

> 10:20 And in that day,
>   The remnant of Israel,
>   And the escaped of the house of Jacob,
>   Shall not any more
>   Lean upon the one smiting them,
>   But shall lean upon the Lord,
>   The holy one of Israel, in faithfulness.
>   21 Only a remnant shall return,
>   The remnant of Jacob,
>   To the mighty God.

4. Assyria as the Lord's Instrument of Discipline to Judah

In 30:25*de*, 29, 32*c* the theme is the destruction of the armed forces of
Assyria, Judah's greatest and most powerful enemy, which took place in
701. Isaiah harks back to the never to be forgotten night of watching by
the Lord to bring them out of the land of Egypt (Exod. 12:41-43).

Centuries have passed since then. Now Judah's enemy is not Egypt but
Assyria, the most ruthless military machine of the ancient Middle East.
The Lord is still watchful over his people, however. He is using Assyria as
a rod of discipline to them. Let Judah accept it, however severe the rod
may be, even with music and dancing, for the Lord will bring about a new
deliverance for his people.

> 30:25*de* In the day of great slaughter, when towers fall,
>   29   You shall have a song, as in the night
>   When a holy feast is observed,
>   And gladness of heart as when one sets out with a flute,
>   To go to the mountain of the Lord, to the rock of Israel.
>   32*c* With tambourines and lyres
>   And with dancing
>   He shall engage them in battle.

5. The Lord's Judgment Upon Assyria

In 30:31-32*ab*, 33 we have a climactic passage which vividly and with imaginative skill portrays, in anticipation, the Lord's final and complete destruction of the ruthless world power, Assyria. The setting is the hallowing of
the beloved festival of Tabernacles. There will be manifest great festal
joy, with singing participants, accompanied by the flash of lightning, and

the majestic descending blow of the Lord's arm in judgment and in punishment. This judgment is not that of man but of God, who alone is powerful enough to destroy Assyria, the greatest military machine of the then-
known world. Thus Isaiah portrays it:

> 30:31 For at the voice of the Lord
>   The Assyrians will be dismayed,
>   When they are smitten[53] with the rod.
> 32a And every blow
>   By the rod of his chastisement,[54]
>   Which the Lord will lay upon them,
> 32b Shall be to the sound of tambourines and harps:
>   They shall swing to and fro in dances.
> 33 For already long laid in order as a place of burning,
>   It has been prepared,
>   Aye, for the king [i.e., of Assyria] it is ready.
>   Has he not made its pyre deep and wide with coals of fire?
>   And he has multiplied wood.
> The breath of the Lord,
>   Like a stream of brimstone
>   Is kindling it.

6. The Manifestation of the Lord's Anger Against His People

In 5:25-30 we have the manifestation of the Lord's judgment upon his
people because of their sins, as cited in the sevenfold woe. The progress of
the military forces of Assyria against Judah in 701 is here vividly portrayed.
With sensitive picturesqueness, but in great solemnity, Isaiah portrays
the anger of the Lord manifesting itself against his people. In imagination
we see the streets filled with slain corpses. But his anger has not yet sub-
sided. A hissing signal from the Lord of nations brings Assyria, that mighty,
merciless, and fully equipped nation. We see that ruthless world power
coming, armed to the hilt, skilled in war technique. We see him leap upon
the prey. It is a solemn portrayal of the divine judgment, for Assyria is but
an agent in the Lord's hands.

> 5:25 Therefore the anger of the Lord
>   Was kindled against his people,
>   And he stretched out his hand against them,
>   And smote them;
>   And the mountains quaked;

---

[53] Reading with BH יכה instead of מסריחיכה for סוסרה.
[54] Procksch, Isaiah, p. 399.

And their corpses were
  As refuse in the midst of the streets.
For all this his anger is not turned away,
  But his hand is stretched out still.
26 And he will raise a signal for a nation from afar,
  And will hiss for it from the end of the earth;
  And lo, speedily, swiftly it comes!
27 Not one is faint or stumbling among them,
  They shall not be drowsy and are not asleep;
And the girdle of their loins shall not be loosened,
  And their sandal thongs will not be snapped.
28 Whose arrows are sharpened,
  And all their bows bent,
The hoofs of their horses are esteemed as flint
  And their cartwheels are like the storm-wind.
29 Their roaring is like a lion,
  And the roar like a young lion when it growls.
And they will take hold of prey and bring it into security,
  With no one snatching it away.
30 And they will growl over it,
  In that day,
    Like the roaring of the sea.
And if one look to the land,
  Lo, darkness of distress;
    And light is darkened by the clouds.

7. The Assyrian Invasion of Judah and the Divine Rebuke

Isa. 17:12-14 dates from the time of the invasion of Judah by Sennacherib (701 B.C.). It is the army of Assyria, the greatest, most powerful and
most ruthless military machine of the ancient Middle East. That army
included many soldiers from nations other than Assyria, subject peoples
under Assyria's dominance and control. In imagination we can hear the
roar of that vigorous military machine on the march, the sound which
for decades made the whole Middle East tremble in terror. We sense the
crash and roar of vast ruthlessness and skilled, merciless dominance.

17:12 Ah, the roar of many nations,
  Like the roaring of seas, they roar!
And the crash of peoples, like the crash
  Of mighty waters, they are in uproar.

That seemingly invincible nation has met its master, however—the Lord
of nations and men. We see indicated in Isaiah's word pictures, chaff and

dust whirled away by the storm wind, the sure destruction of that ruthless world power.

> 13 But he will rebuke them,
>   And they will flee far away,
>   And they will be chased like chaff before wind,
>   And like a whirl of dust before a storm wind.
> 14 At evening time—lo, calamity!
>   And ere morning they are no more.
>   This is the award of him who is plundering us
>   And the lot of him who would take us as spoil.

8. Let Israel Now Be Fearless

In 10:24-27abc we have an oracle of encouragement to the Judeans who are residents of Zion. They are not to fear the Assyrians when they deal ruthlessly with them just as the Egyptians dealt with the nation's ancestors. Now the Assyrians are strong, but soon the Lord will scourge them just as he did the Midianites, as we learn from Judg. 7:25, when their princes Oreb and Zeeb were seized and executed. The date is 701.

10:24 Therefore thus says the Lord of hosts: "My people who are dwelling in Zion, do not fear the Assyrians when they smite with the rod and lift up their staff against you in the manner of the Egyptians. 25 For yet a little while and my indignation will be at an end, and my anger against them will be complete. 26 And the Lord will wield against them a scourge like the scourge of Midian at the rock of Oreb, and his rod will be over the sea and he will lift it up as he did in Egypt. 27 And in that day his burden will be removed from your shoulder and his yoke will be broken from your neck."

H. THE GREAT ARRAIGNMENT

Immediately following the title of the authentic message of Isaiah, son of Amoz, as given in Isa. 1:1, comes 1:2-31, which dates from 701 B.C. and was delivered by Isaiah, as Bewer says, after the Assyrian army had apparently been decimated by a pestilence which caused Sennacherib and his forces to march away from Jerusalem.[55] It was a tremendous deliverance for Judah, and it became one of the most memorable events in Judean history.

Yet the Lord's people were not moved to repentance by it, as Isaiah felt should have been the case. The final editor of the book of Isaiah, son of Amoz, accordingly summarizes Isaiah's denunciation and indictment of

---

[55] *The Literature of the Old Testament,* p. 114.

Judah in the name of the Lord. It is evidently the aim of the final editor
of chs. 1-39, within which is contained the totality of the message of Isaiah,
son of Amoz, to gather together in that crisis hour characteristic utterances
of the prophet from different periods of his career. It is rightly designated
"the great arraignment"—that is, Isaiah's summary denunciation and indictment of Judah.

1. A Summons to Heaven and Earth

Vss. 2-3 summon heaven and earth to listen attentively as the prophet
utters the Lord's condemnation of Judah. The attitude of ox and ass in
their responsiveness to their owner has much to teach the people of Israel,
who are both inattentive and rebellious to the Lord's will.

> 1:2 Hear, O heavens,
> And give ear, O earth;
> For the Lord has spoken:
> "Sons I have begotten and reared,
> But they have rebelled against me.
> 3 The ox knows its owner,
> And the ass its master's crib;
> But Israel does not know,
> My people does not show itself attentive."

2. The Destruction Wrought by Sennacherib

Judah, this sinful nation, the progeny of evildoers, is addressed in vss.
4-6 and 7-9, which uncover before our eyes what aftereffects the invasion
of Judah (701) by Sennacherib of Assyria has had upon the nation, for,
comparable to the overthrow of Sodom, when fire and brimstone from
heaven wrought destruction (Gen. 19:24-28), it had left Judah a ruins.

> 1:4 Ah, sinning nation,
> A people heavy with iniquity,
> Offspring of evildoers,
> Children who are acting corruptly!
> They have forsaken the Lord,
> They have spurned the Holy One of Israel,
> They have turned themselves backward.
> 5 How long will you still be injured,
> That you increase your apostasy?
> The whole head is sick,
> And the whole heart is faint.

6 From the sole of the foot even to the head,
   There is no soundness in it.
   [But] bruises and blows,
   And raw wounds;
   They have not been pressed out, or bound up,
   Nor have they been softened with oil.
7 Your land is a desolation,
   And your cities are burned with fire;
      As for your land, in your very presence,
   Foreigners are devouring it;
   And it is a devastation, like the overthrow of Sodom.
8 And the daughter of Zion is left
   Like a booth in a vineyard,
   Like a watchman's hut in a field of cucumbers,
   Like a blockaded city.
9 Except the Lord of hosts
   Had left to us a few survivors,
   We should have been like Sodom,
   We should have resembled Gomorrah.

3. The Prophetic Attitude Toward Sacrifice

In vss. 10-17, as Gray says, we have "one of the most notable statements of the common standpoint of the prophets" regarding sacrifices [56]—cf. Amos 5:21-25; Hos. 6:4-6; Micah 6:8. Here Isaiah, in sarcasm, addresses the officials of Judah and Jerusalem as "rulers of Sodom" and "people of Gomorrah," Sodom being "a figure of destruction," and Gomorrah, "a figure of wickedness," [57] thus implying their exceeding sinfulness and the divine judgment upon them that is inevitable (Gen. 19:24). There is no more adequate statement of the standpoint of the prophets of the eighth century on this issue than we have here.

1:10 Hear the word of the Lord,
      Rulers of Sodom!
   Give ear to the teaching of our God,
      People of Gomorrah!
11 "What, to me, is the multitude of your sacrifices?"
      Says the Lord;
   "I am sated with whole burnt-offerings of rams,
      And the fat of fattened beasts;
   And in the blood of young bulls and he-goats
      I take no delight.

[56] See The Book of Isaiah, I, 16 ff.
[57] Scott, Interpreter's Bible, V, 171.

12 When you come to see my face,
    What are you doing here?
    Who has sought this from you,
    To trample my courts?
13 Do not bring any more futile offerings;
    Incense is an abomination to me.
    New moons and sabbaths, calling of convocations—
    I cannot endure fastings and assemblies.
14 Your feasts and your sacred seasons
    My soul hates;
    They have become a burden to me,
    I make myself weary in bearing them.
15 And when you spread out your hands,
    I will hide my eyes from you;
    Moreover, even though you make many prayers,
    I am not hearing them;
    Your hands are full of blood.
16 Wash yourselves; make yourselves clean;
    Remove the evil of your practices
    From before my eyes;
    Cease to do evil,
17 Learn to do well;
    Seek justice,
    Set right the ruthlessly dealt with;
    Act as law-giver for the orphan,
    Plead for the widow.

4. Isaiah Solemnly Reasons with Judah

In vss. 18-20 the prophet summons his hearers in order to reason with them earnestly regarding sin and how it may be uprooted, eradicated, and utterly destroyed from their lives. They are to argue the matter out, correcting one another. Isaiah is in deep earnestness as he senses the shallow concepts of sin and forgiveness that the Judeans have as they stand before God. He challenges his hearers to earnest, sincere thought. The Lord is the judge; before him stands Judah, the accused. The Lord speaks to the people:

1:18 "Come now, and let us confront one another,"
        Says the Lord:
    "Though your sins are like scarlet,
        Can they be white like the snow?
    And though they emit redness like scarlet stuff,
        Shall they be like wool?

> 19 If you consent and hearken,
>   You shall eat the good of the land;
> 20 But if you refuse and rebel,
>   You shall be devoured by the sword;
>   For the mouth of the Lord has spoken."

5. Israel's Disloyalty to Her God

In vss. 21-23 to emphasize the disloyalty of Israel to her Lord, here conceived of as Judah's husband, Isaiah uses the figure of speech of a harlot. As a harlot is unfaithful to her true husband so Judah has become unfaithful to her Lord. The silver of loyalty has become the dross of infidelity, unfaithfulness. Judah's rulers are not servants of the Lord's people, but are schemers in theft, susceptible to bribery. They are men who use their high offices for selfish ends. For the cause of the widow and orphan, unprotected persons in Judean society, these rulers have no concern and take no responsibility.

> 1:21 How the faithful city
>   Has become a harlot!
>   Zion, full of justice—
>   Righteousness lodged in her,
>   But now assassins.
> 22 Your silver has become dross,
>   Your choice wine weakened [as with water].
> 23 Your rulers are rebellious
>   And companions of thieves.
>   Every one of them loves bribes
>   And aims to secure rewards.
>   Orphans they will not vindicate,
>   And the dispute of a widow does not come before them.

6. The Lord's Severe but Redemptive Judgment

In vss. 24-26 the prophet views his unfaithful people as coming under the judgment of the Lord. It is a severe judgment, but at the same time it is not primarily punitive but redemptive. The dross in Israel the Lord will smelt away. Israel's suffering will issue, as it were, in the removal of the baser metal. Again judges and counselors worthy of the name will bring about the transformation of corrupt Jerusalem to a city of righteousness, "a town of faithfulness."

> 1:24 Therefore says the Lord,
>   The Lord of hosts,
>   Mighty one of Israel:

25 "I will turn back my hand against you,
   And I will smelt away your dross in the furnace,
   And I will take away all your baser metal.
26 And I will restore your judges as at the beginning,
   And your counselors as at first;
   And afterward, thus shall you be called, 'the city of righteousness,
   A faithful town.' "

7. The Survival of the Good and the Shattering of the Evil in Zion

In vss. 27-28 the prophet reopens the thought expressed in vs. 26, the survival of what is good in Zion, and likewise that expressed in vss. 25*bc*, which is the destruction of what is bad. Deliverance is to be the lot of the true Zion, as Scott says, "the pious Jews in contrast to sinners and apostates." [58] The lot of shattering destruction awaits those who forsake the Lord.

1:27 Zion shall be ransomed in justice,
     And those dwelling in it, by righteousness.
  28 But there shall be a shattering of transgressors and sinners together,
     And those who forsake the Lord shall be destroyed.

8. Isaiah's Indictment of Nature Worshipers

In vss. 29-31 those who are indicted are nature worshipers who believe that divine beings dwell in sacred trees and gardens. The judgment of the Lord will awaken in these nature worshipers a sense of shame and a frustrated and disappointed expectancy, for to Isaiah the origin of all the creative life in nature is the Lord.

1:29 For you shall be ashamed of oaks
     In which you took pleasure;
     And you shall be abashed at the gardens
     Which you have chosen.
  30 For you shall be like an oak
     With its leaves falling,
     And like a garden in which there is no water,
  31 And the strong one shall be as a thread of hemp fibers,
     And the thing he has made as a spark,
     And they shall burn, the two of them together,
     With no one quenching them.

I. The Prophet's Hope for Universal Peace

Isa. 2:1-5, as Bewer says, "may have formed a little book by itself." [59] The same identical passage occurs in Micah 4:1-3, but the introduction as given

[58] *Ibid.*, p. 179.
[59] *The Book of Isaiah*, I, 18.

in Isa. 2:1 is there lacking, and Micah's concluding picture (4:4) of an idyllic era for Judah, of universal independence, and of peace and freedom from fear is not in Isaiah's version. It is likely that the passage dates from Isaiah's latest period of ministry, when the Assyrian siege of Jerusalem had been lifted (701). Then the prophet, with a positive and optimistic faith in Judah's final future, envisions an epoch of universal peace. The creative center of that peace will be the Temple mount at Jerusalem, in the prophet's thought, spiritually speaking, the most exalted region in the world. To that focal point the prophet pictures the nations of mankind flowing upward, as it were, in spiritual gravitation.

> 2:1 The word which Isaiah, son of Amoz, saw concerning Judah and Jerusalem.
> 2:2 It shall come to pass in the latter days,
> > That the mountain of the house of the Lord,
> > > Shall be established,
> > And the house of our God,
> > > As the highest of the mountains
> > > Shall be elevated above the hills;
> > And all the nations shall stream unto it.

1. The Nations Shall Invite One Another to Worship Israel's God

The prophet pictures the nations as inviting one another to go as pilgrims to worship the Lord at Jerusalem where they will be taught the word of the Lord, his directions as regards their conduct.

> 2:3 And many nations shall come and say:
> > "Come, and let us go up
> > > To the mountain of the Lord.
> > > To the house of the God of Jacob;
> > That he may teach us concerning his ways,
> > > And that we may walk in his paths."
> > For it is from Zion that teaching proceeds,
> > > And the word of the Lord, from Jerusalem.

2. The Nations Shall Not Learn War Anymore

There at the Judean Temple, the nations of mankind will learn how to live together, for their disputes will be decisively settled by the Lord, the righteous Judge of all mankind. Materials out of which weapons had been fashioned will then be shaped into constructive instruments for agricultural operations; the nations of mankind will cease all strife; and all instruction in military techniques will be utterly and finally eliminated.

> 2:4 And he will judge between the nations,
>   And he will decide for many peoples;
> And they shall hammer their swords into ploughshares,
>   And their spears into pruning knives;
> And nation shall not lift up the sword against nation,
>   And they shall not learn war any more.

Gray is probably right in viewing vs. 5 "as a brief homiletic reflection which unites the poem that precedes with that which follows." [60] Scott views it as "simply a textual variant of part of vs. 3." [61]

> 2:5 House of Jacob,
>   Come and let us walk
>   In the light of the Lord.

[60] *The Book of Isaiah*, I, 48.
[61] *Interpreter's Bible*, V, 182.

CHAPTER V

Seven Anonymous Prophecies (550-540)

IMMEDIATELY PRECEDING THE SECOND ISAIAH ARE SEVEN ANONYMOUS PROPHE-
CIES THAT HAVE TO DO, RESPECTIVELY, WITH BABYLON, EDOM, ARABIA,
Egypt, and Assyria.

A. THE COMING DESTRUCTION OF BABYLON

Isa. 13:1–14:1-23 is a prophetic oracle of doom in which an anonymous prophet predicts the coming destruction of Babylon by the Medes. Although it is assigned to Isaiah by the later editor (13:1), the oracle dates, as Bewer maintains, "about, or a little before 550," after the fall of Nineveh in 612 and not long before 538, when Cyrus the Persian monarch achieved the conquest of Babylon. Although this section is primarily poetry, the intro-ductory portions (13:1, 14:1-2, 3-4a) and the epilogue (14:22-23) are in prose. After the title (13:1), "Doom Oracle concerning Babylon which Isaiah, the son of Amoz, saw," the prophet, in anticipation, paints a picture of the mustering of the Median aristocrats for their attack upon that famous city.

1. The Mustering of Median Aristocrats

13:2 Upon a wind-swept mountain raise a signal,
Lift up the battle cry;

119

> Wave the hand for them[1] to enter
> The gates of the nobles.

It is the prophet's conviction that the Median military forces are on the move at the command of the Lord himself to give expression to the divine wrath. God speaks:

> 13:3 I have commanded
> My consecrated ones,
> Yes, I have called my warriors to execute my anger,
> My proudly exulting ones.

2. The Advance of the Medes Against Babylon

Vss. 4-5 portray imaginatively the assembling and advancing of the distant Medes and their allies against Babylon. This is viewed as being accomplished in obedience to the Lord's orders and as expressing his indignation. We hear the march of the assembling and the moving of these military troops, which hail from afar.

3. The Lord Is Mustering an Army

> 13:4 A cry of a multitude in the mountains,
> As of a great people;
> A cry of uproar of kingdoms
> Of nations assembling:
> The Lord is mustering
> A fighting army.
> 5 They are coming from a distant land,
> From the end of the heavens,
> The Lord and the weapons of his indignation,
> To destroy the whole earth.

4. The Lord's Judgment upon Babylon

Vss. 6-13, as Bewer says, "describe the judgment of Babylon as part of the universal judgment." [2] It comes from God upon the whole earth. Vss. 6-8 portray the terror of the people against whom these military forces march.

> 13:6 Howl ye, for near is the day of the Lord;
> As devastation from the Almighty it comes!
> 7 Therefore, every pair of hands will lose energy,
> And every man's heart will grow faint,

---

[1] I.e., the Medes.
[2] *The Book of Isaiah*, p. 40.

8 And they will be dismayed.
Pangs [of terror] and travail will take hold;
As a woman in travail, they will writhe.
Each will be astounded at his fellow,
Their faces will be as faces of flame.

5. Its Effect Upon Heaven and Earth

Vss. 9-13 portray the effect of the Lord's judgment upon heaven and earth
in the oncoming day of the Lord.

13:9 Lo, the day of the Lord is coming,
Cruel and with fury and fierce anger,
To put the earth to destruction.
And to exterminate its sinners from it.
10 For the stars of the heavens and Orion
Will not flash forth their light;
The sun will grow dark when it rises,
And the moon will not let its light shine.
11 "I will punish the world for its evil,
And the wicked for their iniquity;
And I will cause the pride of the presumptuous to cease,
And the haughtiness of the terrifiers I will lay low.
12 I will make men more rare than gold,
Even a man, than the gold of Ophir."
13 Therefore he will make the heavens quake,
And the earth will be shaken from its place,
By the fury of the Lord of hosts,
In the day when his anger burns.

6. The Flight of Foreign Residents to Their Own Lands

Vss. 14-16 describe how the foreign people in the threatened cities flee to
their own lands. Those who do not thus escape will be slaughtered, and their
wives and children violently dealt with.

13:14 And like a hunted gazelle it shall be,
And like a flock with no one to gather it.
And they shall turn, each to his nation, and each
To his own land shall flee.
15 Every one lighted upon shall be pierced through,
And every one who flees
Shall fall by the sword.
16 And their children shall be dashed in pieces
Before their eyes;

> Their houses shall be plundered,
> And their wives ravished.

7. The Medes as Agents of the Lord's Judgment

In 13:17-18 for the first time it is definitely stated that those who are the Lord's warriors as the agents of his judgment are the Medes. In 549 B.C. Media was conquered by Cyrus, the Persian, and became a part of his kingdom, the kingdom of the Medes and Persians.

> 13:17 Behold I am about to stir up against them
> The Medes,
> Who reckon not with silver, and [as for] gold,
> They take no pleasure in it.
> 18 And all young men they shall dash to pieces;
> And their maidens shall be cast away.
> Upon the fruit of the womb [babes] they shall show no compassion,
> And upon all children their eyes shall not look with pity.

8. The Desolation of Babylon

In vss. 19-22 it is definitely affirmed that the threatened city is Babylon, and the very site of Babylon will experience complete and eternal desolation as the judgment of the Lord. The Chaldeans, a people of southern Babylonia, had ruled Babylon since 625 B.C., when Nabopolassar, Nebuchadrezzar's father, had seized the throne.

> 13:19 And Babylon, the most beautiful of kingdoms,
> The glorious pride of the Chaldeans,
> Will be like God's overthrow of Sodom and Gomorrah,
> 20 It will never be inhabited, nor dwelt in,
> Unto generation after generation.
> And no Arab will pitch his tent there, and shepherds
> Will not let their sheep lie down there.
> 21 But desert yelpers will stretch themselves there,
> And jackals will fill their houses.
> And ostriches will dwell there,
> And hairy beings will leap about there.
> 22 And hyenas will howl in its citadels,
> And jackals in temples of exquisite delight.
> Aye its time[a] is nearly come,
> And its days will not be prolonged.

[a] Babylon's.

9. Israel Shall Rule Over Its Captors

To the post-exilic editor who wrote 14:1-4a probably, as Gray suggests, Babylon was "a symbolic name for all those that oppress Israel." [4] He is sure of the Lord's gracious purpose to restore Israel to its own soil in Palestine and views as certain that they who are now Israel's captors will themselves be ruled over by "the house of Jacob" and will be appropriated as male and female slaves. Writes this editor:

14:1 For the Lord will have compassion upon Jacob and will still choose Israel, and will set the Israelites down upon their own land; and the resident aliens will attach themselves to the house of Jacob. 2 And they[5] will take them along with them and bring them to their place, and Israel, the house of Jacob, will appropriate them to themselves as a possession in the land of the Lord, as male and female slaves. So they shall be captors of those who had captured them, and shall rule over their oppressors. 3 And it shall be in that day, when the Lord shall have given rest to you from your pain[6] and from your turmoil, and from your hard service, such as was performed by you, 4a you shall utter this taunt song concerning the king of Babylon.

10. The Taunt Song of Israel Over Babylon

In 14:4b-21 this "taunt song" appears. Israel is represented as rejoicing, in anticipation, over the fall of the tyrant Babylon. The song opens (vss. 4b-6) in the atmosphere of profound relief at the certainty of Babylon's ultimate fall, an event which did not actually take place until 538.

> 14:4b How hath the oppressor desisted!
> Insolent raging has ceased!
> 5 The rod of the wicked has been broken in pieces,
> The scepter of rulers,
> 6 That smote peoples in fury,
> Conquest without withdrawal,[7]
> Pursuing nations in anger,
> In intense pursuit, nothing sparing.

11. With the Destruction of Babylon the Earth Will Be at Rest

With Babylon in anticipation destroyed the whole earth is pictured as rejoicing and as at rest. Even the cypress trees and Lebanon's famous cedars glory in the certainty and finality of that destruction.

[4] *The Book of Isaiah*, I, 233.
[5] I.e., the Israelites.
[6] I.e., of exile.
[7] Of defeated troops.

14:7 At rest, in quiet, is all the earth;
    They have broken forth [with] a ringing cry.
8 Even cypress trees rejoice before thee,
    The cedars of Lebanon, [saying]
    "Since you have been laid low, there shall not arise
    The maker of a covenant against us."

12. The Ecstatic Joy of the Deceased Kings in Sheol

In vss. 9-11 the poet, in imaginative anticipation, depicts the reception on the part of the deceased kings of the nations who are already in Sheol, the land of the dead, as the once mighty and seemingly indestructible Babylon now becomes as one of them. We sense the almost ecstatic joy, mingled with scorn and hate, which our poet puts into the mouth of these kings. The prophet addresses Babylon:

14:9 Sheol from below is excited at you,
    To meet your coming.
    Inciting the shades to arise before you,
    All the chief men of the earth;
    Causing to arise from their thrones
    All the kings of the nations.
10 All of them shall answer
    And say to you:
    "Even *you* have been made weak as have we!
    You are similar to us.
11 Your majesty has been brought down to Sheol,
    The music of your lutes;
    Under you a worm has been spread,
    And your covering is worms.

13. Tyrant Babylon Will Be Brought Down to Destruction

In vss. 12-15, Babylon, the tyrant, shining star of the morning, lies hewn down upon the dead of the earth. Instead of achieving its proud boast that it would mount up to the abode of deity in the remote northland above the glorious stars in the mythical mount where the gods assemble, Babylon will be brought down to the remotest depths of Sheol. The poet writes in prophetic certainty and conceives this as though it has already happened.

14:12 "How thou hast fallen from the heavens,
    Shining One, son of Dawn!
    How thou hast been hewn down to the earth,
    Prostrate upon corpses!

13 But you said in your heart,
   "I will mount up to the heavens;
  From above the stars of God,
  I will set up my throne,
  And I will dwell in the Mount of Assembly[8]
  In the remote parts of the North;
14 I will mount up upon the high places of clouds,
  I will make myself like the Most High."
15 Nevertheless to Sheol you shall be brought down,
  To the remote parts of the pit.

14. The Awesome Destruction of the Terror-Arousing Tyrant

In 14:16-21 the prophet predicts that the once all-conquering, terror-arousing tyrant (Babylon) will at length lie prone on the battlefield where it will have fallen, a rotting, unburied corpse. "Can it possibly be," people will call as they gaze upon fallen Babylon, "that this mere corpse was once a living nation so powerful that it made mighty world kingdoms quake, ruthlessly turned the world's great cities into a wilderness, and set no prisoners free?" Those rulers, though conquered, received honorable burial. As for Babylon, however—and directly to that city the prophet now speaks— that capital will not receive, as it were, honorable interment in a magnificent tomb. Rather Babylon will be cast out tombless, abhorred by civilized men, and clothed only with those who have been slain by its cruel sword. The prophet ends this section with the passionate prayer that there be no descendant of that tyrant to repeat his ruthless career. Cries the prophet:

14:16 They who see you will gaze at you
   To you they will show themselves attentive:
   "Is this the one who kept causing the earth to tremble,
   Making kingdoms shake?
17 Who made the world like a wilderness,
   And overthrew its cities.
    Who to his prisoners did not throw open the prison-
    house?
18 All the kings of the nations,
   All of them, lie in glory,
   Each in his own tomb[9]
19a But as for you,[10] you shall be cast out tombless,
   Like an abhorred abortion,
    Clothed with the slain, pierced by the sword,

[8] I.e., the gods.
[9] Literally, house.
[10] I.e., Babylon.

19b [You] who go down to the foundations of the grave,
    Like a trodden-down corpse.
20a With them you shall not be united in burial,
20b   For your land you have destroyed,
        Your people you have slaughtered,
            Descendants of evildoers shall not ever arise.
21 Set up for his sons a slaughtering place,
    Because of the iniquity of their fathers,
    They shall not ever arise, or possess the earth,
        But they shall fill the face of the productive earth
        with heaps of ruins.

15. Babylon Swept with the Broom of Extermination

In 14:22, 23 the prophet gives expression to what he conceives to be the Lord's promise for Babylon as a nation and as a people. Babylon is to be reduced to a haunting desolation, a possession of porcupines, inhabited by no human beings, and swept with the broom of extermination.

14:22 "And I will arise against them," says the Lord of hosts, "and I will cut off from Babylon name and flesh, and offspring and progeny," says the Lord. 23 "And I will make it a possession for porcupines, and muddy pools of water and I will sweep it with the broom of extermination," says the Lord.

B. Babylon Has Fallen

Isa. 21:1-10 is an anonymous oracle concerning Babylon. It is imaginative and has to do with those who attacked and destroyed Babylon 538 B.C. The participants in this epochal event are the Elamites and the Medes under Cyrus. Cyrus was king of Anshan in Elam, which lay west of the Tigris River and north of the Persian Gulf. In 549 he also became king of Media. It was Cyrus who put an end to the Babylonian empire, attacking Babylon in 539 and capturing it in 538, thus inaugurating the Persian period of Old Testament history. In poetic words and vivid pictures this attack and capture are portrayed.

1. The Vision of the Assault Upon Babylon Causes Anguish in the Prophet's Soul

In vss. 1-2 the unknown but brilliant and imaginative poet-prophet who is responsible for the poem places its setting in the famed Negeb, the wilderness region in southern Judah that stretches some sixty miles northward from Kadesh.[11] From the Negeb the imaginative author hears a sound like

11 Gray, op. cit., I, 352.

a storm wind sweeping across the wilderness. It represents a vision of the attackers of Babylon, the Elamites and the Medes, gathering for the assault. The tables have turned, and treachery such as Babylon has dealt to other nations is at the point of being experienced by that famous world capital itself.

> 21:1 Oracle of the Negeb.
> A sound like storm winds from the Negeb sweeps on,
> From the wilderness it comes,
> From a dreadful land.
> 2 A stern vision
> Has been declared to me;
> The treacherous has been dealt with treacherously,
> And the violent has been violently destroyed.
> Go up, O Elam,
> Besiege, O Media;
> To all her haughtiness she has caused I have put an end.

Accordingly the poet is in anguish of soul at what is to take place. He is terror stricken and is keenly sensitive to the perturbation on the part of the Babylonians. Cries the prophet (vss. 3-4) :

> 3 Therefore my loins
> Are full of anguish;
> Pangs have seized me,
> Like the pangs of a woman in childbirth;
> I am bowed down at what I hear,
> I am terrified at what I see.
> 4 My mind is perplexed,
> Shuddering [fear] has overwhelmed me;
> The twilight of my longings
> Puts me to trembling.

2. The Superficial Security of Babylon

In vss. 5-7 we are suddenly transferred to a greatly contrasting scene, the Babylonian princes at a banquet. We are made vividly aware of the superficial security which these high-up Babylonians feel (vs. 5). Then suddenly there is an "alert" (vs. 6) from the Lord through his prophet:

> 21:5 [They are] preparing the table,
> [They are] laying out the carpet,
> [They are] eating, they are drinking.
> Rise up, O princes,
> And anoint the shields!

6 For thus says
  My Lord to me:
"Go, station the watchman,
  What he sees let him declare.
7 When he sees riders,
  Pairs of horsemen,
  Riders on asses,
  Riders on camels,
  Then let him give close attention,
  Very close attention."

3. Babylon's Idols Are Shattered to the Ground

From that watchtower where the seer has been stationed, he now speaks, calling in a loud, clear voice the tremendous news[12] that Babylon has fallen (vss. 8-9).

21:8 So the seer called:
"Upon the watchtower of my Lord
  I am standing,
    Continually, daily.
  And upon my watch
    I have taken my stand
    Every night.
9 And see, there comes
  A riding troop of men,
  Horsemen in pairs!"
And one said, "It has fallen,
  Babylon has fallen;
And all the idols of her gods,
  One [i.e., Cyrus] has shattered to the ground."

4. The Prophet Is Declaring to Judah God's Message

The prophet makes it clear that he is declaring to Judah, which feels now as though "threshed on the threshing floor," not the product of his own thinking, but what in prayerful brooding God has revealed to him that he might declare it (vs. 10).

21:10 O my threshed one! [18]
    And son crushed on my threshing floor,
  What I have heard
    From the Lord of hosts,
  God of Israel,
    I have declared to you.

[12] In anticipation.
[18] I.e., Judah.

C. WHAT LIES AHEAD FOR EDOM?

Vss. 11-12, as we learn from Gen. 32:3 and from the Septuagint version of vs. 11, is a prophetic oracle concerning Edom and in all likelihood the speaker, who is the same one as in vss. 1-10, "was famous beyond the borders of his own country." As Bewer suggests, "Watchman, what of the night?" simply means, with Edom now suffering under the might of Babylonian oppression, what lies ahead for it? [14] Is it freedom from Babylonian oppression or is it harsher domination and subjection? The answer seems to imply that the seer to whom this question is put is himself uncertain. At times freedom from the harsh heel of Babylon's ruthless power seems near at hand, and at other times yet harsher domination by that world power seems certain. It is as though he would say to Judeans who are seeking illumination, "Ask me later." Thus runs the oracle:

> 21:11 One is lifting up the voice from Edom
> The oracle concerning Edom
> One is calling to me from Seir[15]
> "Watchman, how far spent is the night?"
> "Watchman, how far spent is the night?"
> 12 The watchman said,
> "Morning comes
> And also night.
> If you would inquire, inquire!
> Return, come!"

D. AN ORACLE CONCERNING ARABIA

Vss. 13-17 compose an oracle concerning Arabia. It is spoken imaginatively to the caravans of a famous Arab tribe, the Dedanites, which, as we learn from Ezek. 27:20, traded "in saddle cloths for riding." They lodged in the thickets of Arabia, in the land of Tema, modern Teima, located in Northwest Arabia, which, as Bewer says, lay "east of the pilgrim route, midway between Damascus and Mecca." [16] Its inhabitants had the reputation of bringing bread and water to thirsty fugitives. It is the poet's firm conviction that within exactly one year as a hireling counts years—for a hireling works no longer than he must—the glory of the famed Ishmaelite tribe of Kedar, standing here, as in Deutero-Isaiah 42:11, for the nomads of North Arabia, will come to an end.

[14] *The Book of Isaiah,* 36.
[15] I.e., Edom; cf. Gen. 32:3.
[16] *The Book of Isaiah,* 57.

1. The Arabian Tribe of Dedan Flees to an Oasis in Arabia

In vss. 13-15, after the title, the prophet describes fugitives from war, fleeing without provisions into Arabia to escape from roving bands of warriors.

> 21:13 The Oracle concerning Arabia.
> In the thicket, in the steppe you shall lodge,
> O caravans of Dedanites,
> 14 O inhabitants of the land of Teima;
> Bring water to the thirsty,
> With bread for them, come to meet the fugitives.
> 15 For they have fled from before swords,[17]
> From before the drawn sword,
> And from before the bent bow,
> And from before the vehemence of war.

2. The Tribe of Kedar (Northwest Arabia) Will Come to an End

Vss. 16-17 are a prose note stating that within a year Kedar, an Ishmaelite
tribe famous for its bowmen and located to the northwest of modern Teima,
in the Hejaz in northwest Arabia,[18] will be wiped out, and the residue of its
archers will experience almost total annihilation.

21:16 For thus the Lord said to me, yet one year [strictly reckoned] like a hireling's years, and all the glory of Kedar shall end. 17 And the residue of the number of bowmen of the warriors of the sons of Kedar will be diminished, for the
Lord God of Israel has spoken.

E. THE IMMINENT JUDGMENT OF GOD UPON HIS ENEMIES

The underlying theme of ch. 34 is the imminent judgment of God upon
the world. The whole chapter from the literary point of view is brilliant. It
deals with finalities. There are in God's nature unrelenting, unaltering
qualities which neither prayer nor entreaty can move. The greatest power
in the universe is this inexorable will of God. When good clashes with evil,
although the Lord of all men and of history is defied, ultimately the will
of God will resolve the forces that disregard him and will prevail. The unknown author of this chapter was a poet of high order and at the same time
a profound thinker. He was keenly sensitive to the sound effects of Hebrew

---

[17] I.e., to escape from roving bands of warriors; Bewer, The Book of Isaiah, 57.
[18] Gray, op. cit., I, 361.

words, and as Muilenburg has demonstrated, "in every instance the important sounds are identical with the stress of thought." [19] The date is 540 just before the Second Isaiah.

1. A Call to the Nations for Attention

The first part of the poem (vss. 1-4) opens with a solemnizing call to the nations of the whole earth to give attention to their near-at-hand judgment by the Lord (vs. 1). The four sentences in vss. 2-9 that are introduced by "for," as Muilenburg points out, present the four main themes of the eschatological poem.

> 34:1 Draw near, O nations, so as to hear,
> And O peoples, give attention!
> Let the earth and that which fills it, hear;
> The world and all its produce.

2. The Wrath of the Lord Against the Nations

The first theme of the poem (vss. 2-4) is the wrath of the Lord against the nations of the earth. The divine fury is so great that the Lord has set the nations apart and has devoted them to be exterminated. Here is a picture of the *undoing* by the Lord of His own creation which he himself had pronounced good. The theme is introduced by the impressive word "For," which appears three more times in a similar context, and as Muilenburg notes, its fourfold expression (vs. 2, vs. 5, vs. 6e, vs. 8) introduces respectively the four main themes of 34:2-9.[20]

> 34:2 For the wrath of the Lord is against all the nations,
> And [his] fury is against all their host,
> He has doomed them,
> He has given them over for slaughter.
> 3 And their fatally wounded shall be cast out,
> And their corpses he shall cause to go up in their stench;
> And mountains shall flow with their blood.
> 4a And all the hills shall moulder away.
> 4b And the heavens shall roll up like a scroll;
> And all their host shall wither and fall
> 4c Like the falling of leaves from the vine,
> And like the falling of leaves from a fig tree.

[19] "The Literary Character of Isaiah 34," *Journal of Biblical Literature*, LIX, Part III, 346.

[20] *Ibid.*, 342.

3. The Sword of the Lord Against Edom

The second theme of the poem (vss. 5-6d) is the sword of the Lord, which is imaginatively conceived of as the agent of the Lord's ban against Edom. That nation is destined for the sword which drips with the blood of male lambs and goats and of the kidneys of fattened rams.

> 34:5 For you are intoxicated with fury;
>   The sword of the Lord and his denunciation is in the heavens;
>   Lo, upon Edom it shall descend,
>   Yes, upon a people of the sword of the Lord and his ban, for judgment.
> 6a-d The sword of the Lord is bathed with blood,
>   It has been anointed with blood and fat,
>   With blood of lambs and goats,
>   With fat of kidneys of rams.

4. A Great Sacrifice to the Lord

The third theme is a description of a great slaughter, a sacrifice to the Lord (vss. 6e-7), for which vss. 5-6abcd have prepared the way. The scene is set in Bozrah, the fortress city of Edom. A great slaughtering is depicted, wild oxen with fatlings and young bulls, so that the soil is saturated with blood and fat.

> 34:6e For the Lord has a sacrifice in Bozrah
>   Yes a great slaughtering in Edom.[21]
> 7   And wild oxen will go down with fatlings,
>   And young steers with mighty ones.
>   And their land shall become drenched with blood,
>   And its dust saturated with fat.

5. The Day of the Lord

The fourth theme (vss. 8-19) is a climax, a culmination, the day of the Lord. That day is viewed as one of vengeance, a time of the Lord's requital.

> 34:8 For the Lord has a day of vengeance,
>   A year of requital for the champion of Zion.
> 9   And her wadies shall be turned into pitch,
>   And her soil to brimstone.
>   And her land shall become

---

[21] Reading כארום with BH.

Burning pitch.
10 Neither by night nor by day shall it be extinguished;
Its smoke shall ascend forever.
From generation to generation it shall lie desolate.
With no one passing through it.

6. The Vacating of the Land of Human Occupancy

Vss. 11-15 compose the second part of this poem. They consist, as Muilenburg has shown, of four strophes of approximately six lines each with the final line, separated from the rest, forming the conclusion to the entire poem. In the opening of this section it is anticipated that pelicans, large fish-eating birds regarded as unclean, and porcupines, large gnawing animals, along with owls and ravens will take possession of the area. The Lord, stretching his hand over it, will vacate it of human occupancy, reducing its strongholds and palaces where formerly its nobles and captains had dwelt to mere haunts for jackals and farmyards for ostriches.

> 34:11 But pelicans and porcupines shall take possession of it,
> And great owls and ravens shall dwell in it.
> And the Lord will stretch over it
> A line of formlessness and stones of voidness.
> 12 And demons shall dwell in it,[22]
> But there shall not be any of its nobles,
> And no one there shall they call royalty,
> But all its captains shall be as nought.

7. The Effect of the Lord's Judgment

In vss. 13-15 is portrayed with considerable detail the effect of the Lord's judgment. The prophet paints a solemnizing picture—palaces abandoned, fortifications overgrown with weeds. We hear the weird cry of jackals and ostriches and the howling demons of the desert. There are no human inhabitants other than witches, and the closing picture is that of hungry, wild birds of prey who frequent ruins—each for itself. The prophet pictures the reduction of the productive rivers to burning pitch. There is here an implicit reminiscence of the fire and brimstone which destroyed the cities of Sodom and Gomorrah (Gen. 19:24-28) and which reduced them forever to uninhabited wastes.

> 34:13 And its fortresses shall grow up in thorns,
> Thistles and briers in its fortifications.

[22] Muilenburg, *JBL*, p. 356. Reading with BH יחיו ולא כח ישכו צירים וש, p. 655.

> And it shall become a habitation for jackals.
> It shall be degraded to a court for ostriches.
> 14 And demons[23] shall encounter jackals,
> And hairy demons each shall chance upon its fellow.
> Nought but night hags will repose there,
> And find for themselves a resting place.
> 15a There shall the owl make her nest and lay [eggs]
> And hatch out, and mother her young together
> In her shadow as a brood.
> 15b Yea, birds of prey shall assemble there
> Each will seek in vain for her mate.
> For the mouth of the Lord commands,
> And his spirit it is that has gathered them.

8. The Lord's Book of the Faithful

Vss. 16-17 have to do with the book of the Lord which contains the names of all who belong to him and are faithful to him. We sense here the controlling purpose of God, a purpose not negative but positive and constructive. As Muilenburg says, "The closing lines produce a marvelously healing effect, and one is able to read the poem again with renewed appreciation and understanding."[24] The Lord is caring for his own, everyone whose name is written in his book being precious to him. Having inherited the land, his people across the generations shall occupy it as their abiding residence.

> 34:16 Seek and read from the book of the Lord:
> Not one of them shall be lacking[25]
> For the mouth of the Lord[26] has commanded,
> And his spirit it is that shall gather them.
> 17 And he has cast a lot for them,
> And his hand has apportioned it to them by line;
> They shall take possession of it forever,
> For generation after generation they shall dwell in it.

F. THE FINAL INTERVENTION OF GOD IN DELIVERANCE AND BLESSING

In ch. 35 we have the counterpart of ch. 34. Isa. 34, as we have seen, deals with all nations and portrays the Lord's judgment upon them, with particular and detailed concentration upon Edom. In vivid contrast to this is 35: 1-10. Here, as S. B. Frost has rightly noted, "the New Age is so portrayed as

---

[23] Bewer: *The Book of Isaiah,* I, 89, note a-a.
[24] *Journal of Biblical Literature,* p. 356.
[25] Delete first four words of vs. 16c.
[26] Insert יהוה after mouth with BH.

"to counterbalance the woes of the threatened disasters." [27] Thus we have here a vision of an earthly paradise that has its foundation in the will and plan of God. With its accents of joy, encouragement, healing, and restoration it forms a vivid contrast to the immediately preceding terror-striking portrayal of what Scott has designated "the fearful end of the enemies of God." [28]

1. The Transformation of the Wilderness

In 35:1-2 is beautifully portrayed the transformation of the wilderness. The gates of new life are here opened to Judah. The language is symbolic but the meaning is clear. What was barren wilderness and dry desert will come alive with fertility and majestic beauty giving expression to the glory of the Lord.

> 35:1 The wilderness and desert shall rejoice,
> And the desert steppe shall sprout and send out shoots.
> Like narcissus (2) it shall abundantly sprout,
> And the steppe shall rejoice and bud.
> The glory of the Lebanon he will give to it,
> The majesty of Carmel and Sharon.
> My people shall see the glory of the Lord,
> The splendor of our God.

2. Behold Your God Will Save You

Judah is not sensitive to the majesty or splendor of God. However beautiful and luxuriant may be the districts of Carmel and Sharon Judah feels anything but strong. Its hands seem to droop in an awful sense of impotency. Its knees give way in exhaustion, and before their foreign masters, instead of being courageous, Judean hearts are full of fears. They are not conscious at all of God's concern for their cause. In their great need comes the message, clear and confident, that summons them to lift their spiritual vision so as to behold God and experience his presence and power, who will come not only to save them, but also to bring the divine vengeance upon their oppressors and divine compensation unto them because of their faith. Cries the prophet to his seemingly helpless people:

> 35:3 Strengthen the slack hands,
> And make firm the tottering knees.

[27] *Old Testament Apocalyptic*, p. 122.
[28] *Interpreter's Bible*, V, 354.

4 Say to the anxious of heart,
   "Be strong, do not be afraid!
Behold your God will come,
   Bringing vengeance;
The compensation of God
   He will bring,
   And He will save you."

3. Transformations That God Will Bring to Pass

In 35:5-7 the prophet pictures in concrete detail just what that compensation of God is and how it will manifest itself in the Judean community and in the domestic animal world. The blind shall see; the deaf shall hear; the lame, now fully healed, shall leap; the tongues of those who had been dumb shall utter thrilling cries of joy. In the desolate wilderness and in the dry desert veritable springs of water will burst forth. Hard, parched ground will be transformed into muddy pools and into springs of water. In those desolate haunts where formerly jackals made the region eerie with their unearthly howls, now herds of cattle will lie down in a comfortable enclosure of reeds and rushes.

35:5 Then the eyes of the blind shall be opened,
      And the ears of the deaf shall be unstopped;
   6 Then the Lame shall leap like an hart,
      And the tongue of the dumb shall cry for joy.
   For in the wilderness there shall break forth water,
      And torrents in the desert;
   7 And the scorched ground shall become a pool,
      And thirsty ground springs of water;
   In the abode of jackals herds shall lie down,
      An enclosure [it shall be] for reeds and rushes.

4. The Way of Holiness

In vss. 8-10 is described the highway to Zion. It has a name, "the Holy Way," and on it no one who is morally unclean will be permitted to walk. On that highway the traveler need have no fear of encountering lions or other wild beasts, for such will not be found there. Only the redeemed shall walk on that highway, those who have been ransomed from captivity and exile,[29] and they will come to Zion singing as they go, their heads up in joy unceasing, for no longer is their exultation and gladness lessened by sorrow and sighing.

[29] Scott, Interpreter's Bible, V, 360.

35:8 And a clean highway shall be there,
    And it shall be called "the Way of Holiness."
    No unclean thing shall pass over it,
    And fools shall not err in it.
9 No lion shall be there,
    And as for wild beasts, no one shall bring them up there;
    But the redeemed shall walk there.
10   And the ransomed of the Lord shall return,
    And come to Zion with a ringing cry[30]
    And [with] everlasting joy upon their heads,
    Exultation and gladness they shall attain,
    And sorrow and sighing shall flee away.

G. There Will Be an Altar to the Lord in Egypt

Isa. 19:16-22 is a prose supplement to 19:1-15 and dates from 540. These verses reflect the hopeful view of Judah that the day is coming when that nation will be a dominant world power, so mighty as to hurl Egypt into terror before what they believe to be the Lord's purpose of antagonism toward that nation. Yet there will be as many as five Egyptian cities that will speak the Hebrew language in their worship, swearing by oath their loyalty to Israel's God and thus acknowledging him as their Lord, whom they will worship with vows and offerings. Just as Israel has been disciplined by the Lord so will Israel be disciplined by chastisement, but will also be shown mercy. Israel will experience blows, but also will be blessed with healing.

19:16 In that day the Egyptians will be like women and will be terrified and will be in dread before the brandishing of the hand of the Lord of hosts which he will swing over them. 17 And the land of Judah shall become a reeling to the Egyptians; every one to whom it is mentioned will be in dread before the counsel of the Lord of hosts who counsels against him. 18 In that day there shall be five cities in the land of Egypt which speak the language of Canaan, and swear by the Lord of hosts; one of these will be called the City of the Sun.

19 In that day there will be an altar to the Lord in the midst of the land of Egypt and a pillar to the Lord beside its border. 20 And it shall be as a sign and a witness to the Lord of hosts in the land of Egypt. When they shall cry out to the Lord from before oppressors, he will send to them a saviour, and great shall be their deliverance. 21 And the Lord will become known to Egyptians and the Egyptians shall know the Lord in that day, and they shall serve as a sacrifice and an offering, and they will vow a vow to the Lord and they will pay it. 22 And the Lord will smite Egypt, smiting and healing, and they will return to the Lord and he will be interested on their behalf, for he will heal them.

[30] Of joy.

CHAPTER VI

The Second Isaiah (Part I–Isa. 40-48)
The Expanding of World Horizons

IT IS THE WELL-NIGH UNIVERSAL JUDGMENT OF OLD TESTAMENT SCHOLARSHIP THAT CHS. 40-55 OF THE BOOK OF ISAIAH WERE NOT WRITTEN BY ISAIAH, son of Amoz, but by an unnamed and unknown poet-prophet who is designated by scholars as Deutero-Isaiah, or the Second Isaiah. His prophetic activity dates from the time late in the Babylonian exile, which had extended from its earliest beginnings in 598 and 597 until 540 B.C. Throughout this period its was no longer Assyria that was the dominant world power of the Middle East, but Babylonia, with its capital at Babylon. Jerusalem and Judah had been destroyed by Babylonia, and Palestine lay in ruins. (Isa. 44:26b, 28b). The opening words of the Second Isaiah are a message of comfort and assurance. The wonderful new epoch that awaits the Judean exiles is due to the policy of Cyrus, the great Persian monarch, twice mentioned by name in the Second Isaiah (44:28; 45:1). As H. H. Rowley suggests, all of chs. 40-55 may be regarded as composed before the actual fall of Babylon, which took place in 538 B.C.[1] Soon Babylon will be overthrown and the exiles set free. These chapters may therefore be closely dated between 546 and 538 B.C. The anonymous author of 40-55 is one of the noblest minds among the prophets, and it is his messages that give our clearest concept of the most significant teaching of Old Testament prophecy—monotheism, the belief in the existence of but one God in all the world.

Two references to Cyrus, the Persian monarch, in 44:28 and 45:1 are our best evidence for dating this great section of prophetic writing (chs. 40-55) at *ca.* 540 B.C. There is no question that chs. 40-48 are homogeneous. Clearly, as Skinner says:

All the ideas cluster round the one central theme of Israel's approaching deliverance, and the consequences for mankind, which will grow from that. Certain leading topics—the inculcation of the sole deity of Jehovah, the polemic against

[1] *The Growth of the Old Testament,* p. 95.

138

idolatry, the argument from prophecy, the mission of Cyrus, the prediction of Babylon's fate, and the express designation of Israel as the servant of the Lord— are peculiar to these chapters, and are never resumed in the rest of the book.[2]

In chs. 49-55 the same author is at work, but we see that there is definite progress in his thought. He is looking ahead to the future, as Kittel says, and is concerned with "the gathering of the people of God, the future of Israel, the restoration and glorification of Zion, as the centre of the new kingdom of God." [3] It is to individual Israelites that the prophet here speaks. The selfishness and timidity of the people as a whole are dealt with in this portion.

A. THE NEW NOTE OF COMFORT

Vss. 1-11 of ch. 40 form a prologue to the homogeneous section. We sense at once a new note sounded in prophetic writing—the note of comfort. Jerusalem, here, in a sense, standing for the whole people of Israel, has suffered enough and has been adequately punished (vss. 1-2). We note three key words in the imperative tense which the unknown prophet sounds—comfort, speak, proclaim!

It is probably the prophets who are addressed, but no doubt the words of summons were intended also for the prophetically minded among the people as a whole who are now in exile. Here is a new and tender word in prophecy. Since 598 when first the outstanding leaders of the Judean community were taken as exiles to Babylon, and since 587 when the rank and file of the Judean people were carried off as exiles to "the waters of Babylon," these exiles have found it hard to sing the Lord's song in a pagan land. The prophet's opening words show his clear belief that God has intended the exile of his people as punishment, as adequate retribution for the sins the Judeans have committed. Then to the exiled Judeans comes the great word of comfort, of encouragement, and of hope. As George Adam Smith says: "It would be difficult to find in any language lips that first more softly woo the heart, and then take to themselves so brave a trumpet of challenge and assurance." [4] It is the glory of Israel's march toward restoration from exile that thrills the prophet's soul. As Smith has said, "Jerusalem, Zion, the cities of Judah, all mean Israel." [5] Cries the prophet to the prophets

---

[2] *The Book of the Prophet Isaiah,* pt. II, x.
[3] *Biblia Hebraica,* pp. xii-xiii.
[4] *The Book of Isaiah,* II, 75. Used by permission of Hodder & Stoughton, Ltd.
[5] *Ibid.,* p. 72.

and to the leaders of Judah, to all of the Lord's people who, although now in exile, are just at the point of return:

> 40:1 Comfort ye, comfort ye, my people:
> Says your God.
> 2 Speak to the heart of Jerusalem,
> And proclaim to her,
> That her time of hard service is ended,
> That her punishment has been accepted[6]
> That she has received from the hand of the Lord
> Double for all her sins.

1. Prepare the Way of the Lord

In vss. 3-5 the wilderness is the desert of desolation that stretches between Babylonia, where the exiles are, and Palestine. Just as it is the practice in the East to repair roads for a royal journey,[7] so Israel is to make ready the highway upon which her divine King will come. The Lord is returning to Palestine! There lies ahead a great renewal of that from which the Jews had been deprived during the exile. There is to be another exodus, this time from Babylon. The very fact of this imminent return will itself be, as Muilenburg says, a "final and decisive, universal and all-inclusive" revelation of the glory of God.[8]

> 40:3 Hark! One is crying:
> "In the wilderness, clear of obstacles,
> The way of the Lord;
> Make straight in the desert
> A highway for our God.
> 4 Every valley shall be lifted up,
> And every mountain and hill be brought low;
> And the hilly ground be made level,
> And the impassable territory, a plain:
> 5 And the glory of the Lord shall be revealed,
> And all flesh shall see together,
> That the mouth of the Lord has spoken."

2. The Prophet Hears God's Call to Preach God's Word

In vss. 6-8 the prophet is aware of an inner voice summoning him to preach. To his halting uncertainty as to what the burden of his message was

---

[6] As satisfactory.
[7] Skinner, op. cit., pt. II, 4.
[8] Interpreter's Bible, V, 428.

to be to mere men, who are seemingly as ephemeral as grass and their kind
deeds but temporary and transient, comes the command: Preach the word
which God gives you to say, his divine message.

> 40:6 A voice is crying, "Preach!"
> And I said, "What shall I preach?"
> All flesh is mere grass,
> And all its glory like the flower of the field;
> 7 Grass withers,
> Flowers fade:[9]
> 8b But the word of our God
> Stands forever.

3. Let the Herald Announce God's Coming

In vss. 9-11 the prophet addresses Zion-Jerusalem as the herald of good
tidings to the cities of Judah. The glad message is that the mighty God,
who is in command, will provide for exiled Israel with shepherdlike tenderness and concern. We have here, as Millar Burrows suggests, the origin of
the word "gospel." [10]

> 40:9 Get up upon a high mountain,
> You who are bringing good tidings to Zion;
> Lift up your voice with strength,
> You who are bringing good tidings to Jerusalem.
> Lift [it] up, be not afraid;
> Say to the cities of Judah,
> "Behold your God!"
> 10 Lo, the Lord God comes with strength,
> His arm ruling for him:
> Lo, his reward is with him,
> And his recompense before him.
> 11 He will tend his flock as a shepherd,
> He will gather the lambs in his arms,
> And carry [them] in his bosom;
> He will gently lead to a watering place and cause to rest,
> Those giving suck.

4. The Infinitude of God

In vss. 12-17 is portrayed the infinitude of God. In rhetorical questions
the prophet strives to bring before the despondent exiles the being of God
in his august nature. The majesty of the sea, the vastness of the heavens, the

---

[9] Deleting 8a, "Surely the people is grass," with DSS as a marginal comment.
[10] The Dead Sea Scrolls, pp. 21-23.

earth with its mountains and hills, all emphasize the height, depth, and power of the Lord's spirit. In comparison with him nations are as drops of water hanging from a bucket; islands are like fine dust; Lebanon, with its majestic cedars and its wild animals, is inadequate even for burnt offerings; and nations themselves to him are as nothing and worthless.

> 40:12 Who has meted out by handfuls the waters of the sea,
>   Or measured the heavens with a span,
>   And all the earth in a third of an ephah,
>   And weighed the mountains in scales,
>   And the hills in balances?
> 13 Who can measure the spirit of the Lord,
>   And what man of his counsel can make him known?
> 14 With whom did he consult that he might make him understand?
>   And cause him to know the way of justice?
> 15 Lo, nations are esteemed as a drop hanging from a bucket,
>   And are considered as mere dust on scales;
>   Islands are carried off like fine dust.
> 16 And Lebanon is not enough for fuel,
>   And its wild animals not sufficient for a burnt offering.
> 17 All nations are as nothing before him
>   And are accounted by him as naught and worthless.

5. How Describe the Character of God?

Isa. 40:18-20 presents the prophet's reflection upon what he has just said in vss. 12-17 about God's nature. How can the divine being be described? Can God be likened to an idol which merely human hands and skills make? In vs. 19 we see the process of making an idol, which Sidney Smith describes as follows: "On a metal figure [pesel] cast by the artificer, the gold- and silversmith proceeds to hammer out an idol." [11]

> 40:18 To whom then will you compare God,
>   And what likeness will you compare to him?
> 19 On a metal image cast by the artificer the gold- and silversmith proceeds to hammer a gold overlay "smelting bonds of silver." [12] 20 One who cannot afford such an oblation chooses excellent wood that will not rot, and secures a skilled artificer to set up an image that will not totter.

6. Can the Islands Predict What Will Happen?

In 40:21-24 the prophet appeals to mankind as a whole, to what they certainly already know and have long known. As Skinner says, "The two ave-

---

[11] Isaiah 40-55, pp. 12-13, 97, n. 85.
[12] I.e., pouring molten silver alloy into sockets to hold the figure upright.

nues by which the knowledge of God reaches the mind are reflection on the facts of nature, and history." [13] The prophet feels keenly the contrast between the vast wisdom of the Creator and the relative ignorance of mankind. To God, who dwells on high, how insignificant and impotent human beings must seem—even those who have achieved the dignity of rulers and judges (vss. 21-24).

> 40:21 Do you not know? Have you not heard?
> Has it not been declared to you from the beginning?
> Have you not discerned
> From the founding of the earth?
> 22 To him who sits above the vault,
> Are not its inhabitants like grasshoppers?
> He who stretches out the heavens like a curtain,
> Has spread them out as a tent to dwell in:
> 23 He who makes rulers into nothing,
> Judges of the earth he makes like chaos.
> 24 They were scarcely planted,
> Scarcely were they sown,
> Aye their stem had not
> Taken its root in the earth,
> When he blows upon them and they wither,
> And a storm wind whirls them off like chaff.

7. Who Is Comparable to God?

Isa. 40:25-27, as Skinner says, forms "a peroration of striking elevation." [14] The Lord is the speaker. Who is there that is comparable to God, a being who has created the well-nigh numberless stars and knows their names so that at his roll call each answers "Here"? Can such a God be uninformed regarding his people or ignore their divinely given rights?

> 40:25 To whom can you compare me that I am like,
> That I resemble? says the Holy One.
> 26 Lift up your eyes to the height,
> And see who hath created these:[15]
> He who brings out their host in full number,
> Who calls them all by their names;
> Because of the abundant might and strength of his power,
> Not one is lacking.
> 27 Why do you say, O Jacob,

[13] Op. cit., pt. II, 12.
[14] Ibid.
[15] I.e., yonder heavens, Cheyne, The Prophets, p. 251.

> And speak, O Israel,
> "My course of life is hidden from the Lord,
> And the right due me from God is disregarded?"

8. He Gives Power to the Faint

In 40:28-31, which section forms the seventh and climactic strophe of the chapter, the focus is on the character of the sovereign and eternal God, the untiring Creator of unfathomable understanding who gives power to the impotent and mounting strength to the weary. Stronger than the vigor of youth and the soaring strength of eagles is the renewed energy of those who wait for the Lord.

> 40:28 So do you not know?
> Or have you not heard?
> That the everlasting God, the Lord,
> Creator of the extremities of the earth,
> Does not faint and does not grow weary?
> And as for his understanding, it is beyond exploration.
> 29 It is he who gives power to the faint,
> And to those who have no vigor, he increases might.
> 30 Although youths faint and grow weary,
> And although young men may terribly stumble,
> 31 They that wait eagerly for the Lord shall change[16] their strength.
> They shall mount up on wings like eagles;
> They shall run and not grow weary,
> They shall walk and not faint.

B. The Lord Has Aroused Cyrus

In ch. 41 the prophet has to do with contemporary history in the person of Cyrus, the Persian monarch. As George Adam Smith says, "Whether of his own virtue, or as being the leader of a new race of men at the fortunate moment of their call, Cyrus lifted himself from the lowest of royal stations to a conquest and an empire achieved by only two or three others in the history of the world." [17] As prince of Anshan, a small state lying on the border between Elam and Persia, "a near neighbour of Babylonia to the east," in 550 B.C. he became lord of Media. As Smith says, "In the dust of Babylonia lay the scattered members of a nation, captive and exiled, a people civilly dead and religiously degraded; yet it was the faith of this *worm*

---

[16] For the better.
[17] *Op. cit.,* II, 173.

of a nation which welcomed and understood Cyrus, it was the God of this people who claimed to be his creator." [18]

1. Cyrus Is God's Instrument

It was Deutero-Isaiah's keen and God-illumined insight that saw in Cyrus, the Persian, an instrument which God was using on behalf of the exiles in Babylonia. Twice he utters his name (44:28 and 45:1). In 41:1-7 the amazing early career of that monarch is described.

In 550 B.C. Cyrus conquered Media; in 546 he overthrew Croesus, king of Lydia; and in 539 he captured Babylon. Ch. 41 opens with two imaginative debates, the first of which (vss. 1-7), is between the Lord and the nations. The prophet summons the coastlands and the nations to see if they can explain the rise of Cyrus (vss. 1-4), but he comes to the conclusion that it is God alone who is responsible.

> 41:1 Come silently unto me, coastlands,
> And as for nations, let them renew [their] strength;
> Let them draw near, then let them speak;
> Together let them approach for judgment.
> 2 Who has aroused him from the east,
> Whom victory meets at his every step?
> He gives up nations before him,
> And puts down kings.
> Aye his sword brings [them] down under him like the dust,
> With his bow they are driven about like chaff.
> 3 And he pursues them and passes through in peace;
> The path of his feet they do not perceive.
> 4 Who makes and does this,
> Calling into being the generations from the beginning?
> I, the Lord, first,
> And the last, I am he.
> 5 The coastlands have seen and are afraid;
> The ends of the earth trembled;
> They have drawn near and come.

A. THE RIDICULE OF MAN-MADE GODS

Vss. 6-7, as Muilenburg maintains, rightly belong here in the context of the response of the nations to the Lord's challenge.[19] The nations' resort to idols made by their own hands is here ridiculed. The prophet is pointing up the weakness of the nations in their feverish recourse to such nonentities.

[18] *Ibid.*, p. 119.
[19] *Interpreter's Bible*, V, 452.

How futile is the enterprise of idol making as here portrayed! We sense
vividly the sarcasm of the prophet.

> 41:6 A man helps his neighbor,
>   To his brother he says, "Be strong!"
>   7 And the craftsman encourages the goldsmith,
>   The forge-hammer making strong strokes;
>   Saying, "As regards the soldering, it is good!"
>   And he makes it firm with nails so it cannot be moved.

2. Israel Is God's Chosen Servant

In vss. 8-10 the prophet addresses Israel as the Lord's servant, chosen,
grasped, called by him to accomplish a unique mission. Here is the election
of Israel to be "a people holy to the Lord . . . out of all the peoples that are
on the face of the earth" (Deut. 14:2).

> 41:8 But you, Israel, my servant,
>   Jacob, whom I have chosen,
>   The offspring of Abraham who loves me;
>   9 Whom I took hold of from the ends of the earth,
>   Yes, from its borders I called you,
>   And I said to you: "You are my servant,
>   I have chosen you and not rejected you";
>   10 Do not be afraid,[20] for I am with you;
>   Do not be dismayed, for I am your God:
>   I will strengthen you, yes, I will help you;
>   Yes, I will support you with my right hand.

3. Israel Held Firmly by God's Hand

In vss. 11-13 the prophet, speaking in the name of the Lord, utters against
the nations the divine judgment. Shame and humiliation await the national
opponents of Israel, but Israel itself is held firmly by the Lord, who summons his people to a calm sense of security, to freedom from fear, and to
certainty of divine help.

> 41:11 Lo, they will be ashamed and humiliated,
>   All who are incensed against you;
>   They will perish,
>   All the men who are at war with you.
>   12 They will be as nothing, yes, as nonexistent,
>   The men who strive with you.

[20] Gaze about in anxiety.

13 For I, the Lord your God,
    Am holding you by your right hand;
    I keep saying to you, "Fear not,
    I will help you."

4. The Lord Is Israel's Redeemer

In vss. 14-16 to Israel, feeling like a worm—that is, debased, humble, help-less—God, taking the divine initiative, offers to make his people like a sharp threshing sledge—as Muilenburg describes it, "a heavy threshing board or drag, studded underneath with sharp stones or iron points," [21] the nation being here viewed as an instrument of judgment. Then having performed that mission, she will rejoice in God, whose characterizing feature is his holiness.

41:14 Do not fear, you worm, Jacob,
    You maggot, Israel.
    I will help you, says the Lord;
    Your Redeemer is the Holy One of Israel.
15 Lo, I will make you as a sharp threshing sledge,
    You shall thresh and pulverize the mountains,
    And the hills, just as you pile the chaff.
16 You shall winnow them, and the wind shall lift them,
    And the storm wind shall scatter them.
And you shall rejoice in the Lord;
    And you shall glory in the Holy One of Israel.

5. The Marvels of the Desert Journey

In 41:17-20, as is characteristic of the Second Isaiah, we have a lyrical description of the transformation of nature which, as Wheeler Robinson, by implication from Jer. 4:23-26 suggests, is to be taken "as more or less literal expectation." [22] Here is a lyrical interlude the mythical language of which bears witness to actually expected events.

41:17 When the poor seek for water but there is none,
    And their tongue is dry from thirst,
    I, the Lord, will respond to them,
    The God of Israel will not forsake them.
18 I will open rivers upon bare heights,
    And springs in the midst of valleys;

[21] *Interpreter's Bible*, V, 457.
[22] *Inspiration and Revelation in the Old Testament*, p. 29.

I will make the wilderness into pools,
    And the desert land into springs of water.
19 I will put cedars in the wilderness,
    Acacia and myrtle and olive trees;
I will put in the desert fir trees,
    Elm and box tree together.
20 In order that they may see and know,
    And perceive and ponder together,
That the hand of the Lord has done this,
    Yea, that the Holy One of Israel has created it.

6. The Lord Addresses the Idols as Good for Nothing

In 41:21-24 the Lord is presented as judge and as king of Israel, the nation being here designated as Jacob. The Lord is portrayed as the champion of justice. He calls upon the nation to draw near and present its case before him. Let God and his people look at each other and listen to each other. The Lord's judgment is that his people are detestable and good for nothing. It is an adulterated rebuke. Cries the prophet:

41:21 Bring on your case,
        Says the Lord;
    Bring near your arguments,
        Says the King of Jacob.
22 Let them draw near and declare to us,
        What will befall you.
    The former things, which have been until now, declare,
        That we may place them on our heart;
        Or declare to us the coming things.
23 Declare the things that are coming hereafter,
        And we shall acknowledge that you are gods;
    Yea, do something good or something evil,
        And let us look at each other,
        And let us listen to one another, and appear together.
24 Lo, your deeds are of nothing and are accounted as nothing;
        Something detestable one chooses in [choosing] you.

7. Cyrus Is an Instrument of the Lord

In 41:25-29 we have the second implicit reference to Cyrus and his forces, as by an amazingly victorious military campaign he comes into domination of the Middle East. As yet he is not mentioned by name, being designated "one from the east." The Second Isaiah is keenly aware of being the pioneer in proclaiming to indolent Zion a new and hopeful message.

41:25 I have roused up [one] from the north,[23] and he shall come,
 And from the place of sunrise he shall be called by his name;
 And there shall come petty rulers like clay,
 And he shall trample [them] as a potter tramples clay.
26 Who has declared from the beginning, that we might know,
 From before time, that we might say, "He is right."
 Indeed no one declares,
  Yes, no one proclaims,
  Furthermore no one hears your words.
27 I am the first to say to Zion, "Lo! indolent one!
 And to Jerusalem, "I give [you] glad tidings."
28 And I looked but there was no one;
 Yes, from them there was no counselor.
 I asked them that they bring back an answer.
29 Lo, all of them are worthless;
 And as for their deeds there are none;
 Their molten images are but wind and emptiness.

C. The Mission of Israel

1. The Lord's Chosen Servant

In 42:1-4 the theme is the servant's mission. The Lord chooses to lay hold upon his servant Israel and imbue him with his spirit so that he may bring about international justice. This the Lord will do unostentatiously and quietly, putting out no light in the nation however dimly it may be burning, but concentrating upon justice to and among nations. The Lord's servant will not lose his hopefulness or his energy until God's supreme objective shall have been attained—justice in the whole earth, whether on mainlands or on the islands of the sea.

42:1 Behold my servant, on whom I lay hold,
 My chosen one in whom my soul takes pleasure;
 I have put my spirit upon him,
 He will bring forth justice to the nations.
2 He will not make outcry or lift up his voice,
 And he will not cause his voice to be heard in the street;
3 A crushed reed he will not break,
 And a dimly burning wick he will not extinguish;
 To nations he will faithfully bring forth justice.
4 He will not grow faint,
 Or be crushed out or bruised,
 Until he has set justice in the earth;
 And given to the islands, as an inheritance, his law.

[23] The north is the region of mystery and the east the region of light. So Skinner, *op. cit.*, pt. II, p. 26.

2. The New Age in the Divine Purpose

In 42:5-9 the Lord, creator of the vast heavens and of the productive earth and giver of life to all human beings, speaks to Israel whom he, in his righteousness, has called into being. This people he has nourished in order that it might be his agent to open blind eyes and to release endungeoned prisoners. It is a great new epoch of life and of service that the Lord is at the point of opening to his people.

> 42:5 Thus says the Lord God,
>   Who created the heavens, and stretched them out,
>   Who spread out the earth and its produce,
>   Who gives breath to the people upon it,
>   And spirit to those who walk about in it:
>   6 I, the Lord have called you in righteousness,
>   And I have kept hold of your hand;
>   And I have guarded you and I have given you
>   As a covenant to the people,
>   As a light to the nations,
>   7 That you may open the eyes of the blind,
>   That you may bring out prisoners from the dungeon,
>   From the prison house, those who live in darkness.
>   8 I am the Lord, that is my name;
>   My glory I will not give to another,
>   Or my renown to idols.
>   9 As for past events, see, they have come into being,
>   And new things I am about to declare;
>   Before they spring forth.
>   I declare them to you.

3. Israel's "New Song"

In 42:10-13 we have a summons to Israel to sing a new song. It is to be a song of praise, glorying in the Lord's redemption of his people. The sea, the islands and their inhabitants, the wilderness and its cities, the swarthy tribes of nomads in the Arabian desert, and the cliff dwellers, all are summoned to shout the Lord's praise, to utter a roar as he goes forth to battle against his enemies.

> 10 Sing to the Lord a new song,
>   Yea, a praise song to him from the end of the earth!
>   Let the sea and its fullness thunder,
>   The islands and their inhabitants.
>   11 Let the wilderness exult, and its cities,
>   And villages and those who dwell in Kedar;

> And let those who dwell on the cliff give a ringing cry;
> From the top of mountains let them utter a roar.
> 12 Let them give glory to the Lord.
> And let the coastlands declare his praise.
> 13 The Lord goes forth like a warrior,
> As a soldier he stirs up zeal;
> Let him declare, yes, utter a roar,
> Let him show himself mighty over his enemies.

4. The Travail of the Lord

In 42:14-17, the third strophe in the poem, it is the Lord himself who speaks. Hitherto he has restrained himself in silence, but now, as though he were a woman in birth pangs, he goans as he lays waste bulwarks which have hitherto held the world secure. The picture is that of the Lord in travail. As Muilenburg says, "The figure of Yahweh's travailing has a profundity not easily discerned by modern minds. . . . they were the birth pangs of God." [24] It is this mighty being that now gets into action. He desolates mountains and dries up herbage, rivers, and pools. And here is the climax—forsaking them not, he will lead his blind people, guiding them through unfamiliar regions, transforming their darkness into light, and making straight the paths they should take. But how ashamed will those be who trust in lifeless, helpless idols as their gods!

> 42:14 Howbeit, I have been silent for a long time,
> I have been speechless, have restrained myself;
> Now, as one giving birth, I will groan, I will pant
> And I will gasp, together.
> 15 I will make mountains and hills desolate,
> And I will dry up all their herbage;
> And I will turn rivers to desert,
> And I will dry up muddy pools.
> 16 And I will lead the blind through a way they have not known,
> Through crooked places will I bring them.
> I will change the obscure regions, before their faces, to light,
> And make the crooked places straight.
> These are the things I will do for them,
> And I will not forsake them.
> 17 They will be ashamed,
> Who trust in idols,
> Who say to idols,
> "You are our gods."

[24] Interpreter's Bible, V, 473.

5. Israel, the Lord's Servant, Is Blind and Deaf

In vss. 18-25 the prophet maintains that although Israel, conceived of as the Lord's servant, has as its appointed task to make the deaf hear and the blind see, the nation itself is morally and spiritually blind to the Lord's purpose and meaning and deaf to his will. Accordingly it is the Lord's will, for the sake of consistency with his own righteous character and repute, to exalt and glorify the prophetic teaching (vs. 21). Israel views itself as despised, plundered, ensnared, and imprisoned, with no one concerned about its deliverance. Who among the Israelites will realize that it is God who has punished his people because of their disobedience and their sinfulness? Who among them will grasp the prophetic teaching and put it into action?

> 42:18 Would not the deaf hear?
>   Or do not the blind purpose to see?
>   19 Who is blind but my servant,
>   And deaf, like my messenger whom I send?
>   Who is blind like the one sent by me,
>   Or deaf like the servant of the Lord?
>   20 You have seen[25] many things, but you do not observe,
>   Opening your ears, but you do not hear.
>   21 The Lord is pleased, for the sake of his own character,
>   That he magnify the teaching, and make it glorious.
>   22 But this is a people despised and plundered;
>   All of them have been ensnared in holes
>   And have been hidden in prisons.
>   They have become as prey, with no one delivering them,
>   As plunder, but no one says, "Bring it back!"
>   23 Who among you will give ear to this?
>   Let him give attention and hear hereafter.
>   24 Who gave up Jacob to the spoiler,
>   And Israel to plunderers?
>   Was it not the Lord against whom we have sinned,
>   And in whose ways they were not willing to walk?
>   And they did not hearken to his teaching.
>   25 So he poured out upon him the heat of his anger
>   And the fierceness of battle;
>   And it set him ablaze on every side but he did not understand
>   And it burned him, but he did not lay it to heart.

D. ISRAEL'S CREATOR IS ALSO ITS REDEEMER

In 43:1-3b the prophet encourages his people in spite of their obduracy and unfaithfulness by the divine assurance that the Lord who created Israel

[25] So DSS.

will free the nation from bondage to Babylonia and the just penalties of its sin. Redemption of Israel, the naming of Israel, and the covenant with Israel, in which Israel is the recipient of the stipulated divine obligation and the Lord the initiator of the relationship, follow each other as the expression of God's character and purpose.

1. The Divine Initiative

We become aware in these verses of the divine initiative in dealing with Israel and a keen sense of divine responsibility, for as Borden P. Bowne said, "God is the most deeply obligated being in the universe." Israel is the recipient of the stipulated divine obligation and God is the initiator of the relationship. These two aspects of the situation follow one another as the expression of God's character, purpose, and activity.

> 43:1 But now, says the Lord
>   Who created you, O Jacob,
>   And formed you, O Israel:
>   "Fear not, for I have redeemed you;
>   I have called you by your name,
>   You are mine.
>   2 When you cross through the waters, I will be with you;
>   And through rivers, they shall not overflow you;
>   When you walk through fire, you shall not be burned;
>   And the flame shall not consume you.
>   3a For I am the Lord your God,
>   3b   The Holy One of Israel, your Savior.[26]

2. The Lord's Ransom of Captive Israel

In 43:3c-5a the prophet deals with the Lord's ransom of captive Israel. As Muilenburg says, "the mention of **Egypt, Ethiopia,** and **Seba** doubtless refers to their expected conquest by Cyrus. . . . the prophet had every reason to expect that Africa would be next in Cyrus' plan of world conquest. . . . Here Yahweh is to give the wealthy peoples in exchange for his beloved people, and it is a heavy price he is to pay." [27] It is God's mighty love of Israel, God's "own possession among all peoples" (Exod. 19:5), that motivates him.

> 3c I give Egypt to be your ransom,
>   Ethiopia and Seba[28] in exchange for you.

[26] So read with DSS.
[27] *Interpreter's Bible,* V, 482-83.
[28] Sabaeans.

> 4 Because you are precious in my eyes,
>   You are honored and I love you,
>   I will give coastlands in return for you,
>   And peoples in exchange for yourself.
> 5a Fear not, for I am with you.

3. The Imminent Return of Dispersed Israel

In 43:5b-9a is described the near-at-hand return of Israel, now widely dispersed, from east, west, north, and south to Palestine. It is God the Father gathering home his widely scattered people, his sons and his daughters who belong to him. As Muilenburg sensitively says, "Redemption and creation are the two final notes as they are the first of the oracle . . . addressed to the people who are [spiritually speaking] blind and deaf." [29]

> 5b I will bring your descendants from the east,
>   And from the west I will gather you;
> 6 I will say to the north, Give up!
>   And to the south, Withhold not!
>   Bring my sons from afar,
>   And my daughters from the end of the earth,
> 7 Everyone who is called by my name,
>   And whom I created for my glory,
>   Whom I formed and made."
> 8 Bring forth a people that is blind although they have eyes,
>   And deaf, although they have ears!
> 9a As for all the nations, let them gather themselves together
>   And assemble themselves as peoples.

4. Israel as the Lord's Witness to Monotheism

Then to this imaginatively gathered assembly comes the prophetic challenge of vss. 9b-12b. Who among the nations is alert to the meaning of transpiring events? Who among them really knows what is happening *now* in history as well as the true meaning of past events? Those to whom the prophet is speaking are at the same time both the Lord's witnesses and his servant. Here again in vss. 10b-11 is the clear proclamation of monotheism, as well as the sovereignty of God in history.

> 9b Who among them will declare this,
>   And will proclaim to us past events?
>   Let them present their witnesses and be justified,
>   Yes let them proclaim and say, "It is true."

[29] *Interpreter's Bible,* V. 485.

> 10 "You are my witnesses," says the Lord,
> "My servants whom I have chosen,
> In order that they may know and believe,
> And discern that I am he.
> No God was formed before me,
> And there shall be none after me.
> 11 I, I alone am the Lord
> And other than me there is no Savior.
> 12a I foretold and saved and proclaimed,[30]
> And not as a strange God among you;
> 12b And you are my witnesses, to my trusty ones[31]
> And I am God. 13 From the beginning I am He,
> And none can snatch [you] from my hand;
> I act and who can repulse it?"

E. Redemption by Grace

In 43:14-44:5 the theme, as Muilenburg states it, is Redemption by Grace.[32] Grace is the unmerited favor of God and proceeds toward man from his innermost heart. The Lord is sensitively characterized as Israel's "Redeemer" and as "the Holy One of Israel." There are here seven separate oracles: (1) 43:14-15, (2) 43:16-17, (3) 43:18-19, (4) 43:20-21, (5) 43:22-24, (6) 43:25-28, (7) 44:1-5.

1. The Imminent Fall of Babylon

The opening oracle 43:14-15 for the first time explicitly announces the fall of Babylon, which is viewed as preliminary to Israel's restoration. I follow in the last two lines of vs. 14 the R.S.V. The Hebrew text is quite uncertain.

> 43:14 Thus says the Lord,
> Your Redeemer, the Holy One of Israel:
> "For your sake I will send to Babylon,
> And break down the prison bars,
> And the shouting of the Chaldeans
> Will be turned to lamentations.
> 15 I am the Lord, your Holy One,
> The creator of Israel, your king."

2. The Lord Who Makes a Way Through the Sea

The second oracle (43:16-17) glorifies the Lord, who by making a way in the sea destroyed the Egyptian pursuers as the water at Moses' command

---

[30] Muilenburg, *Interpreter's Bible*, V, 490.
[31] So read with Duhm, *Das Buch Jesaja*, p. 491.
[32] *Interpreter's Bible*, V, 491.

came back "upon [them], upon their chariots, and upon their horsemen" (Exod. 14:26).

> 43:16 Thus says the Lord,
>   Who makes a way through the sea,
>   And a path through powerful waters,
>   17 He who leads out chariots and horses,
>   And a powerful army united together;
>   They lie down together not to arise,
>   They are extinguished, they go out like a wick.

3. Eyes Front

In 43:18-19, the third oracle, the prophet summons Israel to "eyes forward." Israel is not to look back to its now long-past deliverance from Egypt, but to "what is new," the restoration of Israel from the recesses of the earth. Across the desolate wastes of the desert, Israel is coming home! We are reminded here of the influential thought of Jer. 23:7-8, which without doubt was familiar to the Second Isaiah, in which he says, "Days are coming, says the Lord, when men shall no longer say, 'As the Lord lives who brought up the people of Israel out of the land of Egypt,' but, 'As the Lord lives who brought up and led the descendants of the house of Israel out of the north country and out of all the countries where he had driven them.' " God himself is represented as speaking:

> 43:18 "Remember not the former things,
>   And the things of old do not consider diligently.
>   19 Lo I am about to do what is new;
>   Just now it shall spring forth; shall you not know it?
>   Yes, I will make a way in the desert,
>   Paths through the desolate wastes.

4. Water in the Wilderness

In 43:20-21, the fourth oracle, the prophet says that even the nature of wild beasts will be transformed so as unconsciously to do honor to the Lord, who is here represented as speaking, and the Lord's own people— formed for himself—will utter praise to him.

> 20 "The beasts of the field shall honor me,
>   Jackals and their young shall sing.
>   For I will provide water in the wilderness,
>   Rivers in waste land,

> So as to give drink to my chosen people,
> 21 The people whom I have formed for myself,
> That they might utter my praise."

5. God Does Not Desire Burnt Offerings

In 43:22-24, the fifth oracle, the second Isaiah sharply and pointedly condemns Jacob (Israel) for its formal sacrificial offerings with their accompanying incense which the worshipers viewed as pleasing to God. God does not desire them or receive them as honoring him. Incidentally, we are here informed of the specific features of worship as it was carried on in the nation. It is not meticulous care regarding sacrificial offerings which the Lord desires. Such offerings do not relieve their sins with which God is so heavily burdened.

> 22 "For not *me* have you called upon, Jacob;
> And not of *me* have you grown weary, Israel!
> 23 You have not brought to *me* sheep for burnt offering,
> And with your sacrifices you do not honor *me*.
> And you have not made offerings such as befit *me*,
> And I did not weary you with frankincense.[33]
> 24 Not for me did you buy calamus,
> Or saturate me with the fat of your sacrifices.
> To the contrary, you burdened me with your sins,
> You wearied me with your iniquities."

6. Israel Has Broken Faith with God

In 43:25-28, the sixth oracle, the Second Isaiah represents God as speaking to his recalcitrant people. He strives to awaken their minds to reason. It is he and he alone who can blot out their sins, and this he desires to do. He is a reasonable God, longing to justify to his people the integrity and grace of his dealings, but Israel, the Lord's own people, has broken faith with him. The sin of the nation is deeply rooted. Jacob here stands for Israel, and a righteous God could deal now with his people solely in solemn justice. Denunciation, yes, defamation, had to be their lot.

> 25 I alone am he who blots out
> Your transgressions, and I do not remember any more your sins.
> 26 Inform me, let us enter into a controversy together;
> Recount to me, that you may justify yourself.
> 27 Your ancestral father [Jacob] sinned,
> And your rulers broke faith with me.

[33] So reconstructed according to DSS.

28 So Jacob I handed over to the ban
And Israel to defamation.

7. What Israel Is to Become in the Divine Intention

In 44:1-5 we have the seventh oracle, in which Israel is viewed in the ideal as a people formed and chosen by the Lord. The nation is called by the beloved designation, Jeshurun, "the upright one," which name stresses what Israel is to become in the intention of God. As one pours water upon vast, treeless plains so will the Lord pour his creative spirit upon his people, and they will acknowledge this unique relationship to him.

44:1 So listen now, Jacob,
And Israel, whom I have chosen!
2 Thus says the Lord who made you,
And who formed you from the womb, even your Helper:
"Fear not, my servant Jacob,
And beloved Israel, whom I have chosen.
3 For [as] I pour out water upon thirsty land,
And streams upon dry ground,
So will I pour out my spirit upon your descendants,
And my blessing will be upon your offspring.
4 And herbage will sprout up as in the midst of waters,
Like poplars along watercourses.
5 This one will say, 'I am the Lord's,'
And that one will call himself by the name, Jacob,
This one will write upon his hand, 'The Lord's,'
And he will entitle himself by the name of Israel."

F. THE TEACHING OF MONOTHEISM

1. There Is No God Besides the Lord

In 44:6-8 the Second Isaiah reasserts Israel's sole deity as being the Lord Yahweh. The prophet stands in awe before the Lord's incomparable being, and his bringing into existence that to which signs of old have pointed. The prophet challenges the truth of any signs other than those expressed through the medium of prophetic teaching. His hearers are themselves witnesses to the truth imparted to them by such reliable utterances of God's prophetic spokesmen as have asserted the sole Godhead of the Lord. The prophet speaks the Lord's message:

6 Thus says the King of Israel,
And his Redeemer—the Lord of hosts.[34]

[34] Delete with BH בל ירעתי.

> "I am the first and I am the last;
> And there is no God besides me.
> 7 And who is like me? Let him stand up and proclaim,
> And declare it, and lay it out in order before me!
> 8 Be not in dread and do not act arrogantly.
> Have I not from remote time proclaimed and announced it?
> And you are my witnesses! Is there a God
> Besides me, or is there a Rock other than me?"

2. The Folly of Idolatry

In 44:9-20 the prophet gives utterance to the most elaborate and remorseless satire on the folly of the worship of idols contained in the Old Testament. It falls into four divisions.

A. FRAIL HUMAN BEINGS MAKE IDOLS

In vss. 9-11 the prophet calls attention to the fact that those who make images of deity are themselves but frail human beings.

44:9a As for makers of idols, all of them deal in what is not real, and the things in which they delight are of no benefit, and as for their servants, they do not see and they do not know.

The issue of their actions—represented ironically as though it were designed—follows:

44:9b In order that they may be put to shame. 10 Who has fashioned a god or poured an idol, that is profitable for nothing? 11 Lo, all who worship it will be put to shame, and its craftsmen—they are mere men; let all of them gather together, let them stand up; they are in dread. All at once they are utterly ashamed.

B. THE PROCESS OF MAKING AN IDOL

In the second division (vss. 12-17) the process of making an image of deity is described. The idol maker is pictured fashioning an idol out of the wood of a tree—cypress, cedar, fir, or oak—and out of the same tree making a fire for melting and shaping iron metal into an idol. Out of wood from the same tree he builds a fire and bakes bread, roasts meat, and warms himself. Out of what is left he fashions an idol deity, then prays to it, calling upon the idol for deliverance! We sense the satirical irony of the prophet's words as he represents the idol worshiper growing faint and praying for deliverance to the god he himself has made.

44:12 A worker in iron sharpens it, and in the glowing coals with hammers fashions it, and makes it with his strong arm. He gets hungry and has no strength.

He has not drunk water and so becomes faint. 13 The carpenter stretches out a
measuring line. He marks it with a pencil; he fashions it with planes,[35] and with
a compass, draws it in outline, and shapes it like the figure of a man, like a handsome man to dwell in a house. 14 He goes and cuts down for himself a cedar,
or takes a cypress tree, or secures for himself an oak. He plants a fir tree and the
rain makes it grow. 15 Then it grows to be ready for a man to burn, so he burns one
of them[36] and becomes warm; yes, he makes a fire and breaks bread; he also fashions a god and prostrates himself before it. 16 Half of it he burns in fire, on its
coals he roasts flesh and eats it and is satisfied. And he becomes warm and says,
"Aha, I have become warm! I see the flame." 17 Then the rest of it he makes
into an idol and prostrates himself before it, and worships it and prays to it and
says: "Deliver me, for thou art my god."

C. THE SPIRITUAL BLINDNESS OF ISRAEL

In the third division (vss. 18-20) the prophet, sharply yet sadly, criticizes
his superficial people who seem utterly unaware of the shallowness of their
religious attitudes and rites and of the spiritual blindness of their eyes, as
from the same tree they both fashion a god and secure fuel for a burnt offering to him. We perceive the mingled sarcasm and humor, but also the deep
heart-sadness of the prophet as he sees with his own eyes how utterly inadequate is Israel's faith when the worshipers prostrate themselves before a
block of wood. How worthless and empty of reality is such worship!

44:18 They do not know nor do they discern; for their eyes have been besmeared
so that they cannot see. 19 And no one brings back in retribution to his mind,
and no one has the faculty of understanding, when he says, "Half of it I burned
in fire and with half I baked bread on its coals. I roasted flesh and have eaten;
and shall I make what is left over into an idol? Shall I prostrate myself before a
block of wood?" 20 Ah worthless shepherd! A heart which is deceived! They have
turned him away and he will not deliver his soul. Still he will not admit [it] and
say, "Is there not falsity in my right hand?"

D. THE LORD'S FORGIVENESS AND REDEMPTION OF ISRAEL

In the fourth division (44:21-22) the Lord speaks to Jacob (i.e., Israel)
in great tenderness, designating the nation "my servant," who has been
"formed" by him. The Lord pledges his abiding concern through the
prophet to his people. It includes his forgiveness and his redemption. God
has not forgotten his servant, and having thus forgiven the nation for all
its transgressions and sins, he calls upon Israel to turn to the Lord, the nation's redeemer.

[35] Literally, scraping tools.
[36] I.e., a fir tree.

21 Remember these things, O Jacob,
And Israel, for my servant are you;
I have formed you, you are my servant;
You are not forgotten by me.
22 I have blotted out, like a dark cloud, your transgressions,
And like a rain cloud, your sins.
Turn to me, for I have redeemed you.

3. The Glad Song of the Lord's Redemption

Isa. 44:23 is a glad song celebrating the Lord's redemption of his people. It brings the entire chapter to a peak of joy. The prophet's tender words rise in dramatic climax. They move from promise to the ecstatic joy of realization. It is the realization of the Lord's redemption of his people and his glorification in and by his people. The height of the heavens, the depths of the earth, the mountains, and the forests' every tree are summoned to sing the song of a redeemed people and of a Lord whose very nature and being is glorified in that redemption.

44:23 Give a ringing cry, O heavens, for the Lord has done it;
Raise a shout, ye depths of earth;
Break forth, ye mountains, with a ringing cry,
O forests and all trees in it!
For the Lord has redeemed Jacob,
And will be glorified in Israel.

4. Cyrus, a Servant of the Lord

In vss. 24-28 the Lord, the creator of heaven and earth and the Lord of human history, calls upon the mountains and the forests clothed with their trees to praise the Lord who is about to bring glory to his own being by the redemption of his now exiled people, Israel, through the instrumentality of Cyrus, the Persian. Here in vs. 28 is the first mention of Cyrus in Deutero-Isaiah. He is mentioned again in Isa. 45:1. These references to him give us a positive link with contemporary history which is of great importance, and they help us to see how an absolute foreigner to Israel played a historical role of vast importance to that nation and to mankind.

24 Thus says the Lord, your Redeemer,
Even he who formed you from the womb:
"I am the Lord, creator of everything,
Who stretched out the heavens by myself,
Who spread out the earth—

Who compares with me?
25 Who shatters the omens of the soothsayers,
   And makes fools of the diviner;
   Who turns back the wise in defeat,
   And makes their knowledge folly;
26 Who confirms the word of his servant
   And performs the counsel of his messengers;
   And keeps saying concerning Jerusalem, 'she shall be in-
   habited,
   And its desolations, I will raise them up.'
27 Who says to the ocean deep, 'Be dried up.'
   And thy rivers 'I will make dry';
28 Who says, as regards Cyrus, 'My servant,'
   'And all that I will, he will perform.' "

G. Cyrus as the Lord's Anointed One

In 45:1-3 we have the second and last specific reference in Second Isaiah to Cyrus the Great, founder of the Persian empire. In 44:28, as we have seen, he is represented as being designated by the Lord as "my shepherd," and in the present passage he is designated in vs. 1 as the Lord's "anointed." Cyrus was viewed by the Second Isaiah as being an instrument in the hands of God, who had grasped him by the right hand. Concerning the designation "his anointed," it is to be noted that this is the only place in the Old Testament, as Muilenburg points out, where "the ascription [is] applied to a foreign king or to anyone outside the covenant people. . . . Yahweh consecrates Cyrus as the mediator of his purpose and equips him as his instrument." [37] It is his mission to subdue many nations and to disarm them, and Cyrus, although he does not know Israel's God, will come into the realization that a power beyond his own universally admitted military prowess is working through him to achieve a divine objective. As H. Wheeler Robinson has finely said, "The human volition is taken up into the divine, without thereby losing its human quality." [38] Cyrus, although himself unaware of the fact, is destined to play his own distinct part in helping all mankind to know that *only one God exists,* and this is the most emancipating concept in religion. It is the God of all history who is represented as speaking to Cyrus:

45:1 Thus says the Lord to his anointed,
   To Cyrus, of whose right hand I have taken hold,
   To strike down nations before him
   And to loose the loins of kings,

[37] *Interpreter's Bible,* V, 522.
[38] *Redemption and Revelation,* p. 186.

To open doors before him
So that gates will not be shut:
2 "I will go before you,
And I will level the mountains,[39]
I will shatter gates of bronze
And I will hew down bars of iron,
3 And I will give to you treasures concealed in darkness
And hidden treasure from secret places,
In order that you may know
That I am the Lord, who calls you by your name,
The holy one of Israel."

1. Cyrus a Chosen Instrument of the Lord

In 45:4-8 the prophet continues speaking in the Lord's name to Cyrus, uttering the mighty truth that this monarch, although not himself a worshiper of the Lord, has none the less been chosen by him as his instrument and as one who is being equipped and used by him in such a reach of influence as will embrace all mankind. The accomplishment that Cyrus will achieve regarding Israel is intended by the Lord to teach all humanity that there exists no God other than the Lord. In Vs. 8 the prophet links together nature and history. To the life-giving showers from the skies above, the earth beneath gives response in fruitful growth, blossoming in salvation. But more! Righteousness which the Lord himself has created sprouts forth into constructive action.

45:4 For the sake of my servant, Jacob,
And Israel, my chosen one,
I have called you by your name,
I surname you although you do not know me.
5 I am the Lord and there is none besides,
Other than me, there is no God;
I will gird you, although you do not know me,
6 So that men may know, from the rising of the sun
And from its setting place, that there is none besides me;
7   I am the Lord and there is none else.
I form light and create darkness
Making peace and creating woe,
I am the Lord
Who does all these things.
8 "Shower, O heavens, from above,
And let the skies rain down righteousness;
Let the earth open,

[39] So DSS.

That salvation may sprout forth.
I the Lord have created it."

2. Prophetic Invective Against Judah

In 45:9-10 we come upon a type of utterance found often in the pre-exilic prophets. It is prophetic invective—that is, passionate denunciation—and nowhere else in Deutero-Isaiah do we encounter it. In vss. 9-10 we have a twofold denunciation of Israel's trifling objections to the Creator's doings. Both are introduced by the familiar "woe," a term used with great frequency by the prophets before the exile. We have here condemnation of Israel's finding fault with the Lord without adequate reason. The prophet utters no consequent judgment upon Israel, but the word "woe," often on the lips of pre-exilic prophets, carries with it a grave presentiment of disaster. Two woes are uttered. One is directed against the person who strives with the Lord, the one who made him, which struggle is as futile and as powerless as the strife of an earthen vessel with the potter who molded it (vs. 9). The other is against the child who asks his parents, "What are you begetting?" Clearly if a child asks his parents such a question he is overstepping his right—nor is the parent able to answer it if it were asked. Paul's words to the Christians in Rome help us understand these words when he says: "Will what is molded say to its molder, 'Why have you made me thus?' Has the potter no right over the clay, to make out of the same lump one vessel for beauty and another for menial use?" (Rom. 9:20-21.) Cries the prophet:

45:9a "Woe to him who strives with his maker,
   9b   A potsherd with the potter, him who formed the earth
   9c Does the clay say to him who fashions it,
          'What are you making?'
   10   Woe to him who says to a father, 'What are you begetting?'
          Or to a woman, 'With what are you writhing in travail?' "

3. Cyrus Aroused by the Lord

The prophet follows up the two denunciations with a prophetic oracle. Israel's trifling queries concerning her God lead to God's query of Israel (vs. 11). In vss. 12-13 he emphasizes that it is the creator God who has aroused Cyrus as the servant of the Lord's righteousness to bring about the rebuilding of Jerusalem and the setting free of the now scattered exiles.

11 Thus says the Lord,
     The Holy One of Israel, and his Creator:
   "Will you ask me for signs,

> And will you command me about the work of my hands?
> 12 I made the earth,
>   And created man upon it;
>   I with my hands spread out the heavens,
>   And I gave charge to all their hosts.
> 13 I have aroused him[40] to action in righteousness,
>   And I have freed all his ways from obstacles;
>   He shall build my city
>   And shall set my exiles free,
>   Not for a price and not because of a bribe,"
>   Says the Lord of hosts.

4. The Collapse of Pagan Religions

In 45:14-17 we have presented the Second Isaiah's conception of the world conquest which Cyrus is achieving under the leadership of the Lord of all human history. As Marti notes: "In this dramatic manner the collapse of pagan religions, and the splendor of Israelite religion is presented. Representatives from the nations confess that Israel's God is the sole God. None other exists." [41] By that God Israel will be saved. Israel is represented as being addressed by the Lord.

> 45:14 Thus says the Lord of hosts:
>   "Trafficers of Egypt and merchants of Ethiopia,
>   And Sabaeans, men of stature,
>   Will cross over to you and be yours.[42]
>   After you they will go in fetters,
>   And they shall worship your God,
>   And to you they shall intercede.
> 15 Surely with you is God, who hides himself
>   The God of Israel, a savior.
> 16 They are ashamed and even humiliated,
>   All who are incensed at him[43]
>   And makers of idols shall go into disgrace.
> 17 But Israel shall be saved by the Lord
>   With eternal salvation."

5. The Lord Is the Sole God

In 45:18-19 the Lord, Creator of the heavens and of the earth, as a place of order intended for human occupancy, is clearly the sole God in all exist-

[40] I.e., Cyrus.
[41] *Das Buch Jesaja*, p. 311.
[42] Omitting "in chains" as a gloss.
[43] So read with LXX.

ence. He is no secret or hidden being, but one who speaks his word in intelligible, reliable truth through his prophets.

> 45:18 For thus says
>   The Lord, Creator,
>   He [alone] is God,
>   Fashioner of the earth and its Maker,
>   He made it firm;
>   He did not create it a waste,
>   He formed it as a place to live in.
>   "I am the Lord and there is none else.
> 19 Not in secret have I spoken,
>   In a place of darkness,
>   I did not say to the descendants of Jacob,
>   'Seek me to no purpose.'
>   I am the Lord who speaks righteousness
>   Who declares what is right."

6. A Righteous God and a Saviour

In 45:20-21 the prophet, in the Lord's name, calls to the nations who thus far have escaped the divine judgment, but who, as idolaters, continue to pray to impotent nonentities. He invites them to draw near and present their case before him who, alone, belongs in the true category of deity and whose desire is that all mankind be saved.

> 45:20 "Gather yourselves together and come,
>   Draw near together,
>   You of the nations, who have escaped!
>   They have no knowledge, those who are lifting up
>   A tree as their idol,
>   And who keep on praying to a god
>   That cannot save.
> 21 Declare and draw near;
>   Yea let them counsel together;
>   Who has declared this from time past,
>   From ancient time has declared it?
>   Is it not I the Lord, and there is no other
>   God besides me,
>   A righteous God and a Savior;
>   And there is none besides me."

7. The Greatest Single Contribution of Prophetic Faith

In vss. 22-25 the prophet gives his clearest and most definite statement of monotheism, the greatest single contribution to mankind of Old Testament faith. With it he expresses his conviction that ultimately all mankind will bow in reverent faith before the Lord. The way to righteous and effective living is made clear in Israel's prophetic faith, and those who are incensed against the Lord shall come to shame. With vivid imagination the prophet represents the one Lord of the whole earth as calling to the extremities of his creation. The righteous God declares that he has sworn to a great certainty— indeed the greatest emancipating and unifying truth in religion—the existence of only one God in the entire world. But the prophet has a second great truth inspired with optimism. It is stated in terms of his own unique belief that every human being in the world will ultimately acknowledge his Lordship, and to every human being who has faith in the Lord there will come from that divine source righteousness of life and strength of character, while a sense of shame will fill the soul of those who are aflame with wrath against him. The chapter's last two verses breathe encouragement to Israel. Israel's righteousness rests in the dependence of every Israelite upon the righteous God. Those who had been enraged against him will come to him in penitence and shame, triumphing not in themselves but "in the Lord."

> 45:22 "Turn to me and be saved,
>   All extremities of the earth!
>   For I am God and there is no other.
> 23 By myself have I sworn,
>   There has gone forth in righteousness from my mouth
>   A word, and it shall not return:
>   For to me every knee shall bow down
>   And every tongue shall take an oath.[44]
> 24 'Only through [faith in] the Lord,' shall be said,
>   'Righteousness and strength
>   Shall come to him, but they shall be ashamed,
>   All who are incensed against him.
> 25 In the Lord all the offspring of Israel shall be justified and
>   shall glory."

H. GOD, THE MOST DEEPLY OBLIGATED BEING IN THE UNIVERSE

1. The Collapse of Babylonian Dominance

In 46:1-2 the Second Isaiah is concerned with strategic events that are taking place in the Middle East which were destined to issue in the collapse of the Babylonian dominance. Bel was originally god of Nippur and was conceived of as father of the gods and of men. He became identified with Mar-

---

[44] In solemn affirmation.

duk, chief deity of Babylon. Nebo was conceived of as son of Marduk and had in his control the tablets of destiny. His temple was located in Borsippa. The primary point the prophet is making is that these gods are impotent, are burdensome to the tired beasts that are loaded with their images, and have no power whatever to protect their Babylonian worshipers as they celebrate New Year's day, the time when the images of these deities were carried in solemn procession.

> 46:1 Bel bows down,
>   Nebo crouches,
>   Their idols are consigned to beasts and cattle;
>   They that should carry you are loaded
>   As a burden upon weary beasts.[45]
>   2 They stoop, they bow down together,
>   And they are not able to deliver a burden,
>   But their very selves go into captivity.

2. A God Who Bears Up His People

In vss. 3-4 the prophet of the only God who truly exists represents him as summoning his people Israel, whom he has borne from their very beginning as a nation and whom he will continue to lift, and carry, and deliver, unto old age—that is, as long as the nation exists. Here is a God who is the most deeply obligated being in the universe, who carries, lifts, bears, and delivers his people.

> · 3 Listen to me, house of Jacob,
>   And all that is left of the house of Israel,
>   Who have been carried from birth,
>   Who have been borne from the womb.
>   4 And even unto old age I am he,
>   And unto old age I will bear [him].
>   And I will carry and I will lift up;
>   And I will bear and I will deliver.

3. A Parody on Idolatry

In 46:5-7 Isaiah gives a classic parody upon the folly of idolatry. He pictures an idol worshiper in the typical process of making a god. From a lavish purse he takes out gold and silver; then he hires a skilled goldsmith who weighs out the necessary amount of these materials and molds them into the image of a deity before whom worshipers prostrate themselves in adoration.

[45] Bewer, *The Literature of the Old Testament*, V, 28.

God continues to speak, challenging his worshipers to see deeply into his own incomparable uniqueness of being, in vivid contrast to such man-made deities before whom they fall prostrate. We feel the sarcasm of the prophet in vs. 7 as the man-made idol is lifted by human hands, borne on human shoulders, and set in its place where it stands, powerless to move, and utterly silent before the desperate need of the worshiper, who cries out for help in his hour of trouble.

> 46:5 "To whom will you compare and liken me,
> And regard me as similar and comparable?
> 6 Those who lavish gold from a purse,
> And weigh out silver on the scales,
> Hire a goldsmith, and he makes it unto a god.
> They prostrate themselves, yea they worship.
> 7 They lift it up upon their shoulder, they carry it,
> And set it down in its place.
> There it stands, it cannot move from its place.
> Yes, one cries to it, but it does not answer,
> It does not save him from his distress.

4. The Former Things and the New Things

In vss. 8-11 the prophet renews his argument from prophecy, as Torrey suggests, urging his hearers to put themselves "on a secure foundation." He summons his people to look back over their own history to remember what God, the one and only divine being, has already done. These are "the former things," which he has made known from beginning to end, those which are in his mind and purpose for his people. This Israel must consider and re-call. But there are not only the former things which Israel must never forget. There are the new things in the Lord's purpose, "things not yet done." The bird of prey that God is calling from the east (cf. 41:2) is Cyrus, not an Israelite, but a Persian, and although unconsciously so, a man of God's counsel who will accomplish God's sovereign purpose.

> 46:8 "Remember this and put yourselves on a secure foundation.
> Bring back to mind your transgressions.
> 9 Remember the former things of old
> That I am God and there is none other;
> [I] am God and there is none like me,
> 10 Who declares the ultimate issue from the beginning,
> And from ancient times what have not yet been done,
> Saying, 'My counsel shall stand,
> And all that I please I will do,'

> 11 Calling from the east a bird of prey[46]
>   From a far distant land, a man of his counsel."

5. I Will Set Salvation in Zion

In 46:12-13 the prophet, in the Lord's name, addresses those in Israel who are still stubborn hearted and consequently far from deliverance at the Lord's hand. The Lord speaks words of grace and of good tidings. Deliverance is near. Zion, the Judean capital and religious center, is to be the recipient of the Lord's saving activity. It is God who on behalf of his covenant people Israel, whom he calls "my glory," is taking the initiative by bringing near as the manifestation of his saving grace "deliverance," and "salvation."

> 46:12 "Listen to me, you who are obstinate of heart,
>   Far distant from justification:
>   13 I will bring near my deliverance—it is not far off,
>   And my salvation—it will not delay;
>   But I will set salvation in Zion,
>   For Israel, [revealer of] my glory."

I. A Taunt Song Against Babylon

Isa. 47:1-15 is a taunt song which celebrates the coming humiliation and fall of Babylon. Muilenburg calls attention to it as "a superb example of the prophet's craftsmanship." [47]

1. The Fall of the Virgin, Babylon

Vss. 1-4 have as their theme "the fall of the virgin of Babylon." Babylon, once a regal capital now, in prospect, is dethroned and humiliated. Such degradation lies in the future. The poet pictures the present Babylon as a virgin, beautiful, delicate, and fastidious. Certain as he is of her imminent fall, speaking in the name of God, he commands the now regal Babylon to sit on the ground as a slave girl. The famed Chaldean capital is destined to disenthronement and degradation, to the status of female slaves who grind the grain.

> 47:1 Come down and sit upon the dust,
>   Virgin daughter of Babylon;
>   Sit upon the ground—not a throne,
>   Daughter of the Chaldeans!

[46] Cyrus.
[47] Interpreter's Bible, V, 544.

For never again will they call you
Delicate and dainty.
2 Take millstones and grind meal,
Remove your veil,
Strip off your skirts,
Uncover your legs,
Cross rivers.
3 Your nakedness shall be uncovered,
Yea, your disgrace shall be seen,
I will take vengeance,
I will spare no man,
Says your redeemer.
4 The Lord of hosts is his name,
The Holy One of Israel.

2. The Humiliation of Babylon

In vss. 5-7 Babylon, proud capital of the Chaldeans, is summoned by the
prophet to sit in humiliation, in silence and darkness. Forever she has lost
the right to be called Queen of Kingdoms. The Lord had been stirred to
wrath by his people Israel, and as a severe discipline he had brought them
under the Chaldean yoke. Babylon, however, had no interest in Israel and
no concern for its welfare, being driven solely by a tyrannical desire for international domination. It never occurred to the leaders of Babylon that the
one God of the whole world was using her as his agent and instrument of
judgment or that she had any relation whatever to the will of this supreme
Lord of all the earth. Thus the prophet interprets the Lord's rebuke of the
Chaldean capital.

47:5 Sit in silence, and enter into darkness,
Daughter of the Chaldeans;
For never again will you be called
"Queen of Kingdoms."
6 I have been wrathful with my people,
I defiled my property;
And I gave them into your hand,
You set no compassion upon them;
Upon the aged you made heavy—
Very heavy—your yoke.
7 And you said, "Forever I shall
Continue to be queen."
You did not put these things upon your heart;
You did not remember the following generation.

3. The Imminent Destruction of the Chaldean Nation

In 47:8-9 the Second Isaiah addresses the Chaldean nation which now is egotistical and self-confident regarding both her present and her future. That superficial nation is blind to the serious issue of contemporary events which are moving toward their inevitable climax for the Chaldeans, the final and irreparable destruction of that nation by the emerging world power, Persia, under Cyrus.

> 8 So now hear this, voluptuous one,
> Who art dwelling in security,
> Who says in her heart,
> "I am, and there is none besides;
> I will not dwell as a widow,
> And I will not experience bereavement."
> 9 There shall come to you these two things
> Suddenly in one day;
> The loss of children and widowhood.
> In full measure shall they come upon you,
> In spite of the multitude of your sorceries,
> And of the very great number of your magic spells.

4. You Have Trusted in Your Evil

In 47:10-11 the Second Isaiah claims that it is Babylon's dependence upon its famed knowledge and wisdom and the egotism implied by her attitude and conduct that has made inevitable and irreparable her destruction as a nation. Inescapable and sudden disaster which cannot be atoned for or propitiated awaits Babylon. Says the prophet:

> 47:10 For you have trusted in your evil;
> You have said, "No one sees me."
> Your wisdom, and your knowledge
> Has led you astray.
> And you said in your heart,
> "I am, and there is none besides me!"
> 11 But evil will come upon you,
> And you shall not know its dawn;
> Yes, disaster will fall upon you,
> And you shall not be able to propitiate it;
> Aye, it will come upon you suddenly,
> And you will not know how to charm it away.

5. The Prophet Challenges the Astrologers

In 47:12-13 the Second Isaiah portrays the sense of self-sufficiency of the Babylonian astrologers, who, as Muilenburg explains, "mapped . . . the

heavens into fields or constellations in order to forecast future events." [48]
Mockingly the prophet challenges these astrologers with their magical spells,
their incantations and charms, to take their stand ready for action.

> 47:12 Stand, pray, in your enchantments
> And in the multitude of your sorceries,
> With which you have labored from your youth;
> Perhaps you will inspire awe.
> 13 You have made yourself weary by the multitude of your
> counsels;
> Pray, let them stand up,
> And save you, they that divide the heavens,
> They who perceive with inner vision the stars,
> Those who at the new moon declare
> What shall come to you.

6. The Final Judgment Upon Babylon

In 47:14-15 the climactic theme is the final judgment upon Babylon, the
agent of which is to be Cyrus. Just as is the case in Amos 1:4, 7, 10, 12, 14
and 2:2, 5, fire is its most adequate symbol. No fire for comfort is this, but
such as embodies and expresses the doom which the righteous God is bringing upon Babylon. The closing verse leaves us in the atmosphere of help-
lessness and hopelessness for Babylon and for those nations who were her
vassals.

> 47:14 Behold they are as stubble,
> Fire will consume them;
> They cannot deliver themselves
> From the power of the flame.
> Not coals for warming themselves,
> A flame in front of which to sit.
> 15 Such to you are those with whom you have toiled,
> Who have bartered with you
> From your youth.
> They wander away,
> Each in his own direction.
> There is no one to save you.

J. THE REFINEMENT OF ISRAEL THROUGH SUFFERING

Isa. 48:1-22 brings to a close the first major section of the Second Isaiah
(40:1-48:22). The prophet's address is to the exiles whose lineage is traced

[48] *Ibid.*, p. 551.

from Jacob. In vss. 1-11 he directly addresses the nation, both Israel and Judah, and vindicates the methods by which the Lord has revealed himself and his truth to all Israel. While addressing the Lord's people on the one hand, as the house of Jacob and Israel and upon the other, as Judah, he is aware, as vs. 1 implies, that while such designations are not truly deserved, they represent a standard, an ideal, for all Israel.

The nation can now look back upon centuries of history and of prophetic revelation of God's purposes and acts. The Lord is dealing with a stubborn people whose neck is tough as an iron sinew, whose brow is obstinate and unyielding like bronze. The prophet emphasizes what the divine initiative has achieved, in spite of human obstinacy and stubbornness. Now Israel can look back through centuries and see what God has wrought and how the Lord's divine intent, uttered through prophetic insight and declaration, has now come into realization (vs. 7).

1. I Have Tested You in the Furnace of Affliction

The Lord's name, embodying his character, as the Second Isaiah interprets it, causes him to withhold his anger due to Israel's faithlessness lest the nation be destroyed. Rather will he "go into action" to refine Israel in the fire of suffering, and to test his people in "the furnace of affliction." It is due to God's own character that he will thus act. Motivating this divine intervention in history is "the glory of God," the very essence of his being. Calls the prophet:

> 48:1 Hear this, O house of Jacob,
>   Those who are called by the name of Israel,
>   Who have come from the loins of Judah;
>   Who swear by the name of the Lord,
>   And call upon the God of Israel,
>   2 Not in truthfulness and not by right,
>   But who call themselves "of the Holy City,"
>   And sustain themselves upon the God of Israel;
>   The Lord of hosts is his name.
>   3 "I have declared the past events from olden times,
>   They went forth from my mouth and I made them hear.
>   Suddenly I *did* them, and they came to pass.
>   4 Since I knew that you are stubborn,
>   That your neck is an iron sinew
>   And that your forehead is of bronze,
>   5 I declared [them] to you from of old.
>   Before they came to pass, I caused you to hear [them],
>   Lest you should say, 'My idol did them,

And my molten image commanded them.'
6 You have heard; you have seen all this;
    And will you not *perceive* it?
    From this time forth I will cause you to hear new things,
    And guarded things, but you did not know them.
7 *Now* they have been created and not from the remote past;
    Before today I did not let you hear them,
    Lest you should say, 'Lo, I knew them.'
8 Moreover you have not heard, nor have you even known;
    Indeed from the remote past your ears have not been opened.
    For I knew that you would deal very treacherously.
    Aye, calling you transgressor from the womb.
9 On account of my character I have continually deferred my
    anger,
    And for the sake of praise that will be paid me, I restrain [my
    anger] against you,
    So as not to destroy you.
10 Lo, I have refined you, but not like silver;
    I have tested you in the furnace of affliction.
11 On account of my name, I act;
    Yea, I will surely wait," [49]
    And my repute I will not give to another.

2. *The Spiritual Meaning of Contemporary History*

In vss. 12-16a the Lord, as Israel's creator, summons the nation of Israel
(his "called one"), designating it both as Jacob and as Israel, to listen to
him, the one and only God, creator of the world. He challenges the Judeans
to declare, if any among them can, the meaning of what is transpiring in
contemporary history (vs. 14a). In the prophet's mind is the amazing advance of Cyrus, the Persian, into lordship over the Middle East (vs. 15). The
only one who can accomplish this is Israel's Lord who loves Israel and is
using Cyrus as his instrument. With BH we rightly view vs. 16b, "and now
the Lord God sent me and his spirit," as a later addition to the text. We
stand here at a most significant moment in Israel's history.

48:12 "Listen to me, O Jacob,
        And Israel whom I have called!
        I am he, I am the first,
        Yea, I am the last.
    13 Yea, my hand founded the earth,
        And my right hand spread out the heavens;
        When I call to them,

[49] I.e., in expectation of the right moment. So rightly LXX.

> They stand up together;
> 14 Let all of you gather together and listen!
>   Who among them has declared these things?
>   The Lord loves me and will do my pleasure in Babylon,
>   And upon the offspring of the Chaldeans.
> 15 I, even I, have spoken, yea, I have called him,[50]
>   I have brought him and I will make his way prosperous.
> 16 Draw near to me and listen to this:
>   Not from the very first have I spoken in secrecy;
>   From time's being, I have been there!
> 16b And now the Lord God
>   Has sent me and his spirit."

3. The Lord's Compassion Upon Israel

In 48:17-19 the Lord's compassion upon Israel is expressed in words of rare beauty and depth. The passage opens with a cry of distress from the Lord over his people's neglect of his commandments.

> 48:17a Thus says the Lord, your Redeemer,
>   The Holy One of Israel,
> 17b "I am the Lord your God,
>   Who teaches you to profit,
> 18a Who leads you in the way you should go.
> 18b   You did not give attention to my commandments.
> 18c Then your peace would have been like a river,
> 18d   And your righteousness like waves of the sea;
> 19a And your offspring would have been like the sands,
>   And your descendants like grains of it;
> 19b Neither cut off nor destroyed shall be
>   Your name from before me."

4. "Go Forth From Babylon"

In 48:20-22 the prophet is athrill with joy. Cyrus, although not here mentioned, is opening the way for the exiles to return to Judah. A great new epoch of life is opening for Jacob—that is, for Israel. The Lord is behind historical events, redeeming his people Israel. Cyrus, as God's instrument, is opening the way for the return of those who since 587 have been under the harsh hand of pagan Babylon.

We feel the thrill in the prophet's words as he calls to the Judeans to flee from Babylon and to go back across the desert to Jerusalem. It is with a jubilant outburst of joy and of faith in a God who has not forgotten his people but will lead them in their long trek home, making provision for

[50] Cyrus.

their needs and sustaining them as they obey the summons home as uttered by the Lord. It is with a final burst of praise to the Lord, Israel's Redeemer of his people, that the chapter ends, but there is also a word of solemn warning (vs. 22) to the wicked. In the exodus from Egypt God sustained his people, giving them water from the rock. Now in this new exodus from Babylonian captivity he will likewise sustain his people. This provision is for God's people, however, not for those among them who are wicked.

> 48:20 Go forth from Babylon
> Flee from the Chaldeans.
> Announce with a voice of joy
> And publish this,
> Proclaim it
> To the ends of the earth.
> Say: "The Lord has redeemed
> His servant Jacob."
> 21 And they were not thirsty
> When he led them[51] through the wastes,
> Water from the rock
> He caused to gush forth for them.
> Yea, he broke open the rock
> And waters gushed forth.
> 22 But there is no welfare, says the Lord, for the wicked.

[51] Israel.

CHAPTER VII

The Second Isaiah
(Part II–Isa. 49-55, The New Israel) And Four Anonymous Passages

ISAIAH 49:1-55:13 COMPOSES THE SECOND MAJOR SECTION OF THE SECOND ISAIAH. THIS SECTION DATES FROM 538-536, AFTER THE FALL OF BABYLON BUT before the return of the exiles to Jerusalem.[1] It is primarily concerned with the redemption of captive Israel which was then scattered through Babylonia.

A. Exiled Israel Is Called to a New Mission

The first chapter of this section (49:1-26) deals with the Lord's call of his servant, Israel, conceived of as an entity. Aware now of this call, and that it reached back to Israel's beginnings as a people, the Lord speaks to the nations of the then known world. One realizes similarities here both to the call of Isaiah, son of Amoz, (Isa. 6) and to that of Jeremiah, son of Hilkiah, whose influence is apparent (cf. Isa. 49:5 and Jer. 1:5). As was the case with Jeremiah as an individual, so Israel, the nation, as a people has become aware of a direct call. Speaking of Israel's relation to God, the prophet says that Israel's call had come in the providence of God, even before it had become a people.

1. The Distinctive Nature of That Call

The distinctive nature of Israel's call, so deeply felt by the Second Isaiah, who is interpreting it, is that it was the *nation* Israel that was called to be God's servant through whom God himself was to be glorified. To glorify is to reveal the real essence, and in a unique sense Israel was destined to reveal God's glory. This is its one unique and distinctive mission. In spite of seeming frustration and much failure up until now (vs. 4a) Israel is here repre-

[1] R. H. Pfeiffer, *Introduction to the Old Testament*, p. 457.

sented as being made aware by the Lord of its "right" and its "reward," which is its mission. The prophet here speaks in the name of Israel:

> 49:1 Listen, O coastlands, to me;
>   And give attention, peoples from far away.
>   The Lord called me from the womb,
>   From the body of my mother, he has made mention of my
>   name.
>   2 And he has made my mouth a sharp sword,
>   He has hidden me in the protection of his hand;
>   And he made me as a selected arrow,
>   In his quiver he has concealed me.
>   3 And he said to me, "You are my servant, Israel,
>   By means of whom I will be glorified."

2. The Seeming Impotence of Discouraged Israel

Israel is both helpless and discouraged. The nation feels weak and inadequate to be the servant of the Lord. Thus far its toil has been fruitless (vs. 4). But now the prophet represents Israel as resting his case with God in relation to whom Israel is aware of being honored at the Lord's hands (vs. 5ef).

> 49:4   But I said, "I have toiled in vain,
>   And for what is worthless and fruitless.
>   My strength is at an end.
>   Nevertheless my right is with the Lord,
>   And my recompense is with my God.
>   5ef For I enjoy honor in the eyes of the Lord,
>   And my God has been my strength."

3. Israel's Mission Is to Be a Light to the Nations

In vss. 5abcd-6 a mission greater than merely the restoration of Israel as a unity here called "the tribes of Jacob" and greater than the preservation of Israel as a political entity is now given his people by the Lord. In one of the loftiest utterances of the entire Old Testament the Second Isaiah states that in the divine intent Israel is to be a bearer to the nations of the light and knowledge of God and of the fact and reach of his saving grace to the far ends of the earth. Not what Israel is to *receive* from the world, but what Israel is to *give to the world* is here lifted up before the nations of mankind.

49:5a And now, thus says the Lord,
   b   He who fashions me from the womb to be his servant,
   c To bring back Jacob to him,
   d   That Israel may be gathered to him;
   6 And now he says: "It is too trifling [a thing] to be my servant,
        To raise up the tribes of Jacob
        And to bring back the preserved of Israel;
        I will make you a light to the nations,
        That my salvation may extend
        To the extremities of the earth."

4. A Change in Fortunes Is at Hand

In 49:7, however, to the now despondent and self-deprecating Israel the prophet reveals the change of fortunes that is near at hand which will be wrought by the Lord and which will arouse the interest of kings and princes of the nations, who then cannot help acknowledging the superiority of Israel's God.

49:7 Thus says the Lord,
        Redeemer of Israel, and his Holy One,
     To one who despises himself,
        To the servant of rulers;
     "Kings shall see and arise;
        And princes shall prostrate themselves;
     For the sake of the Lord, who is faithful,
        The Holy One of Israel, who has chosen you."

5. Hope and Courage from God

In 49:8-9b to the dejected and self-conscious Israelites, now despondent under Chaldean domination and ground under that nation's heel, God brings hope and courage. He promises that the time is near when they will experience both his acceptance and his saving grace. Freedom from Babylonian bondage is at hand.

49:8   Thus says the Lord:
        "In a time of acceptance I have answered,
           And in the day of salvation I will help you.
        I will guard you and constitute you,
           As a covenant people,
        To establish the land,
           To give as an heritage the desolated properties;
        9a Saying to the captives, 'Go free!'
         b   And to those who are in prison, 'Come forth!' "

6. The Lord as Shepherd and Guide

In 49:9c-11 the prophet uses the beloved figure of shepherd and sheep, the shepherd representing the Lord, the sheep being his people. The hot journey across the desert from Babylonia, where the exiles now are, to their homeland, Judah, will be under the leadership and care of the Lord, who will make provision for their food and guide them to water springs in the desert. Every difficulty that now seems unconquerable and every mountain that now seems impossible to climb, under the Lord's creative strength and control will be brought within their power.

> 49:9c Upon all mountains they shall feed,
> 9d And upon all the bare heights shall be their pasturage;
> 10 They shall not be hungry and they shall not be thirsty,
> And the burning heat of the sun shall not strike them.
> For One who has compassion upon them shall lead them,
> And he shall guide them along springs of water.
> 11 And I will make every mountain into a way
> And my highway I will put in order.

7. A Hymn of Thanksgiving for God's Comfort

In 49:13 suddenly there is introduced a hymn of thanksgiving. The prophet calls to the heavens and the high places of the earth to cry out in joy because of the comfort and compassion which the Lord is about to bring to his afflicted people.

> 49:13 Sing, heavens; and rejoice, O earth.
> Let the mountains burst forth with a cry of joy!
> For the Lord has comforted his people,
> And will have compassion upon his afflicted ones.

8. God's Individualizing Concern for Zion

In 49:14-16 we are suddenly in an utterly different atmosphere. Zion, Jerusalem, is represented as feeling as though the Lord had forsaken her. In tender and comforting words descriptive of a mother's care for her nursing babe and her compassion upon a trustful son, the prophet reaches a climax. God is represented as giving expression to his individualizing concern for Zion, the political and religious capital of Judah, by having inscribed upon the palms of his own hands that precious word "Zion." Always present to the mind of the Lord are Zion's walls.

> 49:14 But Zion says,
> "The Lord has forsaken me,

Yea, my Lord and my God has forgotten me."
15 Can a woman forget her sucking child,
    So as to have no compassion upon the son who trusts her?
Yes, these may forget,
    But I will not forget you.
16 Lo, upon the palms of my hands I have inscribed you;
    Your walls are continually present to me.

9. The Coming Return of the Exiles

In 49:18, 12, 17, and 19, is pictured, in anticipation, the return of the sons and daughters of Zion as from exile they come back to Jerusalem, which now is still lying in ruins. The holy city, as vss. 17 and 19 portray, is to be restored by its builders (so read with the Dead Sea Scroll). The prophet clearly is optimistic regarding Zion's future.

18 Lift up your eyes round about and see;
    All of them have assembled themselves; they have come to
      you,
    As I live, says the Lord,
    Yea, all of them thou shalt put on as ornaments,
      Yea, thou shalt bind them on as does a bride.
12 "Lo, these shall come from afar,
    And lo, these from the north and west
    And these from the land of Syene.[2]
17 Your builders will speed up your ruined land
19   I devastated you, laid you waste,
    Razed you to the ground." [3]

10. The Repopulation of Zion

In 49:20-21 the prophet looks ahead to the time, now imminent, when Zion, barren of its populations since the beginning of the Babylonian exile, will be repopulated by these very exiles and their children, who will crowd the land to its capacity. With Cyrus a new day has dawned. It is he who has opened the way and behind Cyrus, although unrealized by him, is the Lord.

49:20 "The children born in the time of your bereavement
    Will yet say in your hearing:
    'The place is too narrow for me;
    Make room for me that I may dwell.'
21 And you will say in your heart

[2] Modern Aswan.
[3] Muilenburg, Interpreter's Bible, V, 575; following Torrey, p. 387, and DSS.

'Who has borne these to me?
I was childless and barren,
But who has brought up these?
Lo, I was left alone;
But as for these, whence have they come?' " [4]

11. The Lord's Signaling to the Nations

In 49:22-23 the prophet pictures the Lord signaling to the nations with his banner. They will respond, bringing the sons and daughters of Judah to the place where they truly belong, with the rulers of the lands of their exile opening the way for them to go home. We rightly understand vs. 23*b*, as Skinner suggests, as "an extravagant, but thoroughly Oriental metaphor of self-humiliation." [5]

49:22 For thus says the Lord,
  "Lo, I will lift my hands to the nations
    And to the peoples I will raise my banner;
  And they shall bring your sons in their bosom,
    And your daughters shall be carried on their shoulders
23 And there shall be kings supporting you.
  And their queens nursing you.
  With their faces to the earth they shall worship you.
  And they shall lick the dust of your feet.
  Then shall you know that I am the Lord.
  Those who wait for me will not be ashamed."

12. It Is the Omnipotent God Who Pledges Israel's Emancipation

In 49:24-26 the prophet rises to a climax as he represents the omnipotent God pledging the emancipation of Israel. Behind the prophetic word is the immeasurable and incomparable might of the Lord. Upon this the Second Isaiah directs attention. The passage closes with three great attributes which best characterize the Second Isaiah's conception of God.

49:24 Can the prey be taken from the mighty,
    Or can the captives of a tyrant be rescued? [6]
  25 For thus says the Lord God!
    "Yes, booty of the warrior will be taken
      And the booty of terrorizers will escape.
    Yet with your opponent I will contend
      And your sons I will deliver.
  26 And I will make your oppressors

---

[4] Reading ראלת with LXX.
[5] Skinner, *op. cit.*, pt. II, 108.
[6] So DSS, Syriac, and Latin.

> Eat their own flesh,
> And as with sweet wine, with their own blood
> They shall become drunk.
> Then all flesh shall know
> That I am the Lord,
> Your Savior, and Redeemer,
> The Mighty One of Jacob."

B. God's Hand Is Not Shortened

1. The Influence of the Prophet Hosea

In 50:1-3 we are aware of the influence of the pioneering concept of the prophet Hosea, whose basic pattern of thought was that of the Lord as husband and Israel as his wife. He has neither divorced his wife nor sold her into slavery because of her iniquities. Why has Israel been so unresponsive to the divine discipline? Certainly God's power, which can dry up rivers and seas, has not lost its capacity to deliver his exiled people.

As George Adam Smith says, with regard to the omnipotence of God, the Second Isaiah "expresses it in his favourite figures of physical changes and sudden reversions of the normal course of nature." [7] Thus the prophet speaks:

> 50:1 Thus says the Lord:
> "Where, now, is your mother's deed of divorce
> By which I sent her away?
> What creditor of mine is there
> To whom I have sold you?
> Lo, because of your iniquities were you sold,
> And because of your sins was your mother divorced.
> 2 Why did I come and there was no one?
> [Why] did I call with no one answering?
> Has my hand been shortened so that it cannot ransom?
> Or is there not in me strength to rescue?
> Lo, by my rebuke I dry up the sea,
> I make rivers a wilderness:
> Their fish stink from lack of water,
> And their beasts perish because of thirst.
> 3 I clothe the heavens with darkness,
> And I make sackcloth their covering."

2. The Intimate Experience of the Prophet with God

In 50:4-7 the Second Isaiah shares with his hearers in autobiographical fashion his own intimate experience of God through vigorous daily self-

[7] *The Book of Isaiah*, II, 408.

discipline. He permits us to gaze into his innermost soul. His gift of penetrating and inspiring speech is the result of a discipline of contact and con-
verse with God. We sense a vivid consciousness of the Presence, realized in
solitude and experienced daily morning by morning. It changed his rebellion
into spiritual receptivity and moral courage. He ceased resisting the divine
impulses and, with dedicated devotion, set his face to his mission. He is perfectly confident of the vindication God will give him in the presence of his
adversaries and is sensitively aware of the power of God pulsating through
his soul. Thus he speaks:

> 50:4 The Lord God has given me
>> The tongue of those who have been taught,
>> So as to know how to revive the weary
>>> With a word.
>> Morning by morning he arouses my ear
>>> So as to hear like disciples.
> 5 And I was not rebellious,
>> I did not turn away backwards.
> 6 I gave my back to those scourging,
>> And my cheeks to those plucking out the beard.
>> My face I did not hide
>>> From insults and spittle.
> 7 For the Lord God will help me;
>> Therefore I shall not be humiliated;
>> Therefore I have set my face like flint,
>>> And I know that I shall not be ashamed.

3. The Lord God Will Help Me

In vss. 8-9 the prophet challenges his adversaries to conduct a suit against
him and is confidently sure that the Lord will take his side against his opponents, who are comparable to a moth-eaten garment.

> 50:8 My vindicator is near, who will dispute with me?
>> Let us stand up together.
>> Who is judge of my cause?
>>> Let him draw near to me.
> 9 Behold the Lord God will help me;
>> Who is he that will condemn me as guilty?
>> Lo, all of them will wear out like a garment;
>>> Moths shall eat them.

4. The Contrast Between the Faithful and the Godless

In vss. 10-11 the prophet, with a penetrating note of challenge, lifts into
vivid contrast on the one hand, those who are faithful to the Lord, listening

to and heeding prophetic counsel, and on the other, those who, without God's presence in their lives, walk in darkness. Those who are without God are imaginatively described as kindlers of fire, but the fire they are kindling will itself consume them. They will perish in its flames. The essential nature of evil character and conduct is that it is self-destructive. Cries the prophet:

> 50:10 Who among you fears the Lord?
> [Who] listens to the voice of his servant?
> Who walks in darkness
> And has no light.
> Let him trust in the name of the Lord,
> And lean upon his God.
> 11 Behold, all of you are kindlers of fire,
> Who set brands alight! [8]
> Walk by the light of your fire,
> And by the brands you have kindled!
> This will come to you from my hand:
> You shall lie down in torment.

C. Pride in a Noble Ancestry

In the first portion of 51:1-16 are words of encouragement and cheer to those of exiled Israel who, although timid, are nonetheless faithful. It opens in vss. 1-3 with a lesson from Israel's earliest history. Israel began with Abraham, who was called by the Lord, and his wife Sarah, the parents, as it were, of the nation. Here is the expression of great pride in a noble ancestry and at the same time a word of good cheer for the now scattered and homeless exiles.

1. Look to the Rock From Whence You Were Hewn

> 51:1 "Listen to me, you who are in pursuit of deliverance,
> You who seek the Lord;
> Look to the rock from which you have been hewn,
> And to the quarry from which you were dug.
> 2 Look to Abraham your father,
> And to Sarah who bore you;
> For as but one, I called him,
> And I blessed him and multiplied him.
> 3 For the Lord grieves over Zion;
> He is moved to pity over all her ruins,
> And he will make her wilderness like Eden.

---

[8] So read with Syriac.

> Exaltation and gladness will be found in her,
> Thanksgiving and the voice of song."

2. The Spread of the True Faith of Israel

In 51:4-5 the prophet predicts the spread of the true religion, the worship of the Lord God, to the end of the earth. The prophet calls all Israel to attention, to draw near and to listen to what will issue from the divine will. The Lord himself speaks:

> 4 "Draw near to me, my people,
>   And as for the tribes, let them listen to me,
> For instruction goes forth from me,
>   And my ordinance, as a light to nations.
> 5 Suddenly I will bring near my deliverance,
>   My salvation will go forth like the light,
> And my arm will govern the peoples,
>   Coastlands will wait for me,
>   And for my arm they hope."

3. Let Israel Lift Its Vision From the Temporal to the Eternal

In 51:6-8 the prophet calls his people to lift their vision from earth to heaven, from the temporal to the eternal. Let them gaze at the glorious stars and think of their creator. It is from him that Israel will experience salvation, something that is eternal like the righteous being of God. The prophet is speaking to a people who carry God's law and his testimony regarding what is right in their hearts. Consequently let Israel, now in exile, be unmoved at the scorn and abusive insults of men, keeping in mind that these revilers are themselves comparable to garments that have been destroyed by moths and cockroaches. The righteousness and salvation of Israel's God, directed as it is toward them, his people, will make for their permanence as a nation—past, present, and future.

> 51:6 Lift up your eyes toward heaven,
>   And look at the earth beneath;
>   For the heavens will be dissipated like smoke,
>   And the earth will wear out like a garment.
>   Those dwelling on it shall die like maggots;
>   But my salvation shall be forever,
>   And my righteousness shall not come to an end.
> 7 Listen to me, you who know what is right,
>   A people with my law in their heart;

Do not be afraid of the reproach of men,
And do not be dismayed at their reviling words.
8 For the moth will eat them like a garment,
And a cockroach will consume them like wool;
But my righteousness will be forever,
And my salvation to generation after generation.

4. A Call Out of Vast Need to the Mighty God

In 51:9-11 the prophet utters an intensely earnest appeal to the Lord. It is a human call out of desperate need to the mighty God to intervene on behalf of his people. The prophet is familiar with the mythology of the Middle East and presents a Hebrew version of it. This in itself is source material of great importance. Rahab (vs. 5) was a mythical sea monster. "The dragon," "Sea," and "The great deep" are here used to suggest the awful void that existed before the creation of the world. Here is Oriental mythology, well known to many of the prophet's hearers and used to depict a God of unapproachable might. In 10b there is an implicit reference to the Exodus but *now* the God of Israel's redemption from Egyptian bondage is bringing his scattered people back to Zion. Exultant and increasing joy is to displace the sadness, which since its exile to Babylon has been Judah's lot as a people. If it remains loyal that nation will abide across the generations— past, present, and future.

51:9 Rouse thyself, rouse thyself, put on strength,
Arm of the Lord;
Rouse thyself as in days of old,
The generations of the ancient past.
Is it not thou that didst shatter Rahab,
Who didst pierce the dragon?
10 Is it not thou who didst dry up the sea,
The waters of the great deep;
That didst make the depths of the sea a way
For the redeemed to cross over?
11 And the ransomed of the Lord will return,
And come, with a ringing cry, to Zion;
And joy eternal shall be on their heads;
Exultation and gladness shall increase,
Sorrow and sighing shall flee away.

5. The Lord Answers the Passionate Cry of His People

51:12 I, I am he who comforts you.
Who are you that you are afraid

Before mortal man who dies, and mere human beings,
Who are made like grass?
13 And have forgotten the Lord who made you,
Who stretched out the heavens
And laid the foundations of the earth?
And you are in continual dread all day long,
Because of the wrath of the oppressor,
When he sets himself to destroy.
And where is the rage of the oppressor?
14 He who is stooping[9] shall be speedily released,
So he shall not die in the pit [10]
And his food shall not be lacking.

6. I Have Put My Words in Your Mouth

In 51:15-16 the prophet represents the mighty God himself as speaking to his people. It is the majestic creator, Israel's Lord. Clearly the prophet is familiar with Jer. 31:35f, a passage which emphasizes the fixed order of the sun, moon, and stars. In words that recall the prophet's earlier utterance (49:2) this section closes with a great and challenging message, the mission of the nation of Israel as the Lord's servant, a mission of vast import. As Muilenburg says: "The new heaven and earth are set within a framework of the people of revelation . . . the unique relationship between God and Israel becomes clear." [11]

51:15 "For I am the Lord your God,
Who arouses the sea and makes its billows roar—
The Lord of hosts is his name.
16 And I have put my words in your mouth,
And I have hidden you in the shadow of my hand,
Stretching out the heavens,
And laying the foundations of the earth,
And saying to Zion, 'You are my people.' "

D. A New Epoch of Hope

In 51:17-23 there opens to Judah a new epoch of hope.

1. Stir Yourself, Arise, O Jerusalem

In vss. 17-18 the prophet speaks to Jerusalem, which to him, no doubt, is the most beloved city in the world. At her destruction at Chaldean hands

---

[9] That is, under a burden.
[10] I.e., Sheol.
[11] Interpreter's Bible, V, 601.

she had drunk to the dregs the cup of the Lord's wrath. He strives to awaken Jerusalem, to arouse her from her stupor, she who has suffered staggering blows. Now that the historical situation is at a great new turning point she needs leadership, but among all her sons there is no one to grasp her hand in eager helpfulness and to give her people hope and courage. Cries the prophet:

> 51:17 Stir yourself, stir yourself,
>   Arise, O Jerusalem,
>   You who have drunk from the hand of the Lord
>   The cup of his wrath;
>   The cup which causes reeling,
>   You have drunk, you have drained.
> 18 There is no one to be a guide for her
>   Among all the sons she has borne;
>   And there is no one to strengthen her hand,
>   Of all the sons she has reared.

2. The Tragic Disaster of Jerusalem's Fall

In 51:19-20 is portrayed the tragic disaster of Jerusalem's fall in 587 to the Babylonians. Two things are emphasized: (1) The devastation of Jerusalem —those who had experienced it knew all too well the ravaging of the whole land of Judah, climaxing in the fall of the capital city. (2) The awful destruction by famine and sword that put an end to the Judean state. The dead sons of Judah are evidence of the divine rebuke. Says the prophet:

> 51:19 These two things have befallen you,
>   Who will condole with you?
>   The devastating and the shattering, and the famine and
>   the sword.
>   Who will comfort you?
> 20 Your sons have swooned away,
>   At the head of all the streets they lie,
>   Like an antelope in a snare;
>   They who are full of the wrath of the Lord,
>   The rebuke of your God.

3. The Lord's Reversal of Judah's Fortunes

In 51:21-23 the chapter reaches its climax. The Lord knows that his afflicted people have drunk to the depths from the cup that has caused them to stagger. Now it is God himself who is taking the initiative. The word "Behold" (vs. 22) is important. Those who have caused the suffering to Judah are to experience such a reversal of fortunes as will cause those suffering and those responsible for the suffering to change places. The mighty God takes from the trembling hand of his people the "cup of staggering," "the bowl of my [i.e., the Lord's] wrath" and hands it to Judah's tormenters, Judah's afflicters. This climactic utterance leaves us with the deep realization not only of the divine initiative but of divine justice and fairness and above all of God's enduring concern for his people.

> 51:21 Therefore, pray hear this, afflicted one,
> You who are drunken, but not from wine:
> 22 Thus says your Lord,
> Who pleads the cause of his people:
> "Behold, I have taken from your hand
> The cup of reeling;
> The cup of my wrath
> You shall not drink any more.
> 23 But I will put it into the hand of your tormentors,
> And of those who afflict you,
> Who have said to your soul,
> 'Bow down, that we may pass over';
> And you have made your back like the ground,
> And like a street for them to pass over."

E. The Lord's Call Upon Zion to Loosen the Bonds of Its Captivity

Isa. 52:1-2 is a song of Zion which contrasts vividly with the previous chapter's lament over Zion's dishonor and disgrace. The prophet speaks directly to Zion. He summons the inhabitants of the holy city from which they had been taken into exile, freed now from the presence of uncircumcized pagans, to return and dwell there as honorable residents.

1. Put On Your Strength, O Zion

> 52:1 Awake, awake, put on
> Your strength, O Zion;
> Clothe yourself with beautiful garments,
> O Jerusalem, the holy city;
> For not again shall there enter into you
> The uncircumcised and unclean.
> 2 Shake yourself free from dust, and arise;
> O captive Jerusalem;

> Loosen the bonds from your neck,
> O captive daughter of Zion.

2. The Lord Opens a New Epoch of His Redemptive Captivity

In 52:3-6 the prophet utters an oracle of the Lord in which he deals with the impossibility of the payment of the tribute of silver to dominant foreign powers in order to set captive Israel free. Tracing swiftly the boastful foreign domination of Israel, first by Egypt and then by Assyria—both conceived of as harsh, yet needed, discipline—suddenly the prophet is aware that the Lord is entering into a new redemptive activity which will make clear to his people that he is still their God.

3 For thus says the Lord: "You have been sold for nothing, and you cannot be redeemed by silver." 4 for thus says the Lord God: "My people went down to Egypt, at the first, to dwell there, and Assyria oppressed them in anger. 5 But now, what do I find here," says the Lord, "that my people have been taken away undeservedly, with their rulers boasting over him," says the Lord, "and continually, all the day, my name is spurned. 6 Therefore my people will know my name in that day that I am he, the one who is speaking. Behold me!"

3. The Glad Herald of the Good Tidings of the Lord's Redemption

In 52:7-10 the prophet imaginatively pictures a messenger rapidly approaching, for he is the bearer of good tidings which herald a new epoch of peace and salvation for Zion. The watchmen on Zion's walls, seeing him come, call aloud with voices stirred with good news that the Lord is returning to Zion! The very desolations of Jerusalem are summoned to break forth with the good news that the Lord, compassionate toward his people, and in the sight of all the nations, even those at the earth's extremities, is making manifest their salvation.

> 52:7 How beautiful upon the mountains
>   Are the feet of him who bears good news,
>   Who heralds peace, who preaches good tidings,
>   Who proclaims salvation,
>   Saying to Zion,
>   "Your God reigns!"
> 9 Hark, your watchmen lift up their voice,
>   Together they give a ringing cry of joy;
>   For eye to eye they see
>   The return of the Lord to Zion.
> 8 Break forth, sing together,
>   Desolations of Jerusalem;

> For the Lord has comforted his people,
> And will redeem Jerusalem.
> 10 The Lord has laid bare his holy arm
> Before the eyes of all the nations;
> And all the extremities of the earth shall see
> The salvation wrought by our God.

4. The Lord's Call to a New Exodus

In 52:11-12 the prophet summons the Lord's people to a new exodus, now not from Egypt, but from Babylon—and now deliberate and planned, not a flight from oppression such as centuries before Israel had experienced in Egypt. This significant move is to be a holy undertaking, a deliberate action, unhurried and with no fearful, hasty flight such as had characterized the exodus from Egypt (Exod. 12:11; Deut. 16:3). Moreover, as the exiles leave Babylon they are to realize that before them, as it were, blazing the trail and in protection bringing up the rear is Israel's invisible, but living and powerful God! Thus the prophet summons his people:

> 11 Depart! Depart!
> Go forth from there!
> Do not touch an unclean thing;
> Go forth from its midst, purify yourselves,
> You who bear the vessels of the Lord.
> 12 For not in trepidation, shall you go out,
> And not in flight, shall you go,
> Because the Lord will go before you,
> And your rear guard is the God of Israel.

F. ISRAEL AS THE SUFFERING SERVANT OF THE LORD

In 52:13-53:12 the theme is the Lord's Suffering Servant. There are five strophes in this portion, and, as Muilenburg says: "The dramatic power of the poem as a whole is almost overwhelming." [12] In 52:13-15, the first strophe, the Lord introduces his servant. It is Israel, his people, whose tragic fate of captivity at the ruthless hand of Babylonia had seemed truly appalling. Israel is here personified as an individual whose painful experience of exile has amazed and dismayed even the pagan nations of the Middle East, startling and astonishing them. The Lord speaks first.

1. The Lord Introduces His Servant, Israel

52:13 Behold, my servant acts prudently;
He shall be high and lifted up, and greatly exalted.

[12] *Ibid.*, p. 615.

14 Even as many were appalled at him—
    Because his appearance was marred beyond human semblance,
    And his form beyond that of human beings—
15 So shall many nations be amazed;[13]
    Because of him, kings shall shut their mouths,[14]
    For that which had not been told them they shall see;
    And that of which they have not heard, they shall diligently consider.

2. Nature of the Servant's Suffering

The second strophe (53:1-3) opens with a characteristic question which expresses the prophet's amazement at an almost incredible insight that has come to him from the Lord. It is the servant which is the center of attention, Israel—lacking in any splendor, making no brilliant appearance, indeed despised by mankind, yet nonetheless God's servant.

53:1 Who could have believed the report that has reached us?
    And the arm of the Lord—to whom has it been revealed?
2 For he[15] grew up before us like a sapling,
    And like a root out of dry ground;
He had no form and no splendor,
    And no appearance that would make us desirous of him.
3 He was despised and forsaken by men;
    A man of pain and acquainted with sickness;
And like one before whom one hides one's face,
    He was despised, and men did not esteem him.

3. The Redemptive Power of the Vicarious Suffering of Israel

The third strophe (53:4-6) gives us one of the profoundest concepts in the Old Testament, vicarious suffering—one who does not deserve it suffering on behalf of another. The servant has been made humbly aware by the very nation whom they had thought the Lord himself was punishing that the suffering of Israel in exile is not meaningless or powerless, but startling, gripping, and above all, redemptive in its results. Here is a deep insight, one of the most moving in the Old Testament. The prophet represents the nation Israel as speaking forth his great revelation from God in the reverent awe. The "he" is the servant; the "we," "our," and "us" the rank and file of people that compose the nation. The great truth that leads us into the very heart of God, the redeemer, follows:

[13] Caused to leap in joyous surprise.
[14] I.e., in astonishment.
[15] I.e., Israel.

53:4 But in fact it is our sicknesses he has carried,
      And as for our pains, he has borne them;
      But we thought of him[16] as stricken,
         Smitten by God, and afflicted.
   5 But he was pierced because of our transgressions,
         Crushed because of our iniquities;
      Chastisement leading to our welfare was upon him,
         And by blows inflicted upon him, healing has come to us.
   6 All of us, like sheep, have wandered about;
         We have turned, each to his own way;
      And the Lord has caused to light upon him
         The iniquity of all of us.

4. Harsh Treatment of Israel Borne in Silence

In 53:7-9 the Second Isaiah continues to portray the servant's suffering—the servant as the people Israel—bearing its harsh treatment silently while experiencing extreme humiliation. By the "rich" (vs. 9) is probably intended, as in the case with the prophets (cf. Jer. 17:11), something synonymous with the wicked, as Muilenburg says.[17]

   7 He was treated harshly and afflicted,
         But he did not open his mouth;
      Like a sheep borne along to slaughter,
         And like a sheep before its shearers
            Is dumb, so he did not open his mouth.
   8 By coercion and without justice he was taken off;
         And who inquires after his posterity,[18]
      That he was cut off from the land of the living,
         [That] because of the transgression of my people he was
            struck down to death?
   9 And they made his grave with the wicked,
         And with the evildoers at his death,
      Notwithstanding that he had done no violence,
         And no deceit was in his mouth.

5. The Purpose of God for His Suffering Servant

In 53:10-12 is expressed the purpose of God for his people, which the prophet holds at the center of his theology. It is the climax of the entire poem. Along with this, however, there is the more concrete thought of the destiny of the servant as conceived in the Lord's purpose and as it is to be

---

[16] I.e., Israel.
[17] *Interpreter's Bible*, V, 627.
[18] *Ibid.*, p. 170.

manifested in the future generations of Israel. We sense here a climactic intensity in the mind and spirit of the Second Isaiah. More specifically we see the redemptive mission of Israel as bearing the sin of many, making many righteous, and interposing on behalf of sinful members of society.

> 53:10 Yet it pleased the Lord
> To crush him, and he defiled him;
> When he shall have brought to pass the trespass offering of
> his soul,
> He shall see his posterity, and shall prolong his days;
> And the cause of the Lord shall prosper in his hands.
> 11 After the travail of his life,
> He shall see light[19] and be satisfied;
> And by his knowledge shall my righteous servant
> Make many righteous.
> And he shall bear the burden of their iniquities.
> 12 Therefore I will divide to him the many as a portion,
> The countless he will share as booty.[20]
> Because he poured out his soul unto death,
> But was reckoned among those transgressing against them,
> Yet he bore the sin of many,
> And interposed for the transgressors.

6. The Significance of the Suffering Servant to Christians

We have been dealing with teaching that has to do with Israel, the Israel that was then in exile but soon to be back in the homeland. But this is a passage (52:13-53:12) of great significance to Christians as well as to Judeans. How did the early Christian community employ, interpret, and use it?

We have our answer in Acts 8:30-35, where we see at once that the early Christian Church, as interpreted by Philip, applied the suffering servant to Christ. He was "as a sheep led to slaughter"; he was as "a lamb dumb before the shearer." Philip's questioner (Acts 8:34), the eunuch, asked, "About whom, pray, does the prophet say this, about himself or about some one else?" Then Philip opened his mouth, and beginning with this scripture he told him the good news of Jesus.

Mui¹enburg deals carefully and sensitively with the interpretation of this climactic servant of the Lord passage (53:10-12). Says he:

Like Hosea and Jeremiah and the other tragic sufferers of Israel, the servant of

---

[19] So read with LXX.
[20] *Interpreter's Bible*, V, 631.

the Lord finds his ultimate and intensely personal fellowship with the Lord whose servant he was. . . .

It is a matter of major importance to understand how the covenant community employed this poem, how it interpreted it, and when it made use of it. For the Christian community this passage has a supreme significance: it depicts the life history of the Lord. The church is not disturbed over discrepancies between the O. T. portrait and the N. T. reality. . . .[21]

G. The Thrilling Message of Comfort

Ch. 54 consoles Israel with a message of comfort. The opening words are directed to Zion which is now desolated.

1. Zion Is Summoned to Sing!

We become aware of the Second Isaiah's deep and throbbing joy which he strives to impart to his people. In vss. 1-3 we delight in his mighty hope for a great future that is now imminent for the Lord's exiled people. They will have a large and spreading population which will transform the broad areas of cities which now lie desolate.

> 54:1 "Sing, O barren one, who has not borne;
>   Break forth into singing and cry out, you who have not
>   travailed in birth!
>   For the children of the desolate one will be more
>   Than the children of her that is married, says the Lord.
>   2 Enlarge the place of your tent,
>   And stretch out the tent curtains of your dwellings;
>   And do not refrain, lengthen your tent cords,
>   And fasten your tent pegs.
>   3 For you will break over [your borders]
>   And your descendants will dispossess the nations,
>   And you will cause the desolate cities to be inhabited."

2. Your Redeemer Is the Holy One of Israel

In 54:4-5 the Second Isaiah views the whole pre-exilic period of Israel's life as the time of its infidelity toward its Lord and the period of Israel's widowhood is the period of its exile. So now Israel is summoned to forget the shame of its sinful past, for Israel's Creator is related to his people as a husband to his wife, and this Creator, Redeemer, and Lord is not only Israel's God, but is the Lord of the entire world.

> 4 "Fear not for you shall not be confused by guilt;
>   And do not be humiliated, for you shall not be ashamed;

[21] Ibid.

> For you shall forget the shame of your youth,
>> And the reproach of your widowhood you shall remember no
>> more.
> 5 For your Maker is your husband,
>> The Lord of hosts is his name;
>> And your Redeemer is the Holy One of Israel,
>> He is called the God of all the earth."

3. A God of Righteous Judgment but of Loving Compassion

In 54:6-8 the prophet beautifully combines the God of righteous judgment with the God of loving compassion, and while his judgment was, as it were, but momentary, his compassion that leads to Israel's redemption is the outflow of a continuing, never-ending love. In vs. 6 we are aware of the influence upon the Second Isaiah of the prophet Hosea.

> 54:6 "For as an abandoned wife,
>> And as one grieved in spirit, the Lord has called you,
>> And as a youthful wife, though you were cast off,"
>> Says the Lord, your God.
> 7 "For but an insignificant moment I forsook you,
>> But with great mercies I will gather you.
> 8 In a flood of anger, I hid my face for a moment from you,
>> But with everlasting mercy I will have compassion on you."
>> Says the Lord, your Redeemer.

4. God's Covenant of Peace Will Not Be Violated

In 54:9-10 the prophet takes his people, in memory, back to the days of Noah (Gen. 8:21f), when, after the destructive flood was over, the Lord solemnly swore that as long as the earth would last never again would such destruction fall upon it. So now the Lord takes a sacred oath that divine love, peace, and compassion toward his people would never be withdrawn.

> 54:9 "As with the waters of Noah,
>> Just as I swore that the waters of Noah
>>> Would not again flood the earth,
>> So have I sworn not to be wrathful
>>> Against you any more or to rebuke you.
> 10 Though the mountains should be removed,
>> And the hills be greatly shaken,
>> My mercy shall not depart from you,
>>> And my covenant of peace shall not be violated,"
>>> Says the Lord, who has compassion on you.

5. God's Assurance to His People of a Secure Future

In 54:11-13, in the name of the Lord the prophet proclaims tender, compassionate, and loving words to his storm-tossed people, assuring them of a secure and dependable future and bringing to them not merely strength and firmness, but well-nigh inexpressible beauty.

> 54:11 "Poor one, storm-tossed, not comforted,
> > Lo, I am laying your pedestal with precious stones,
> > And your foundations with sapphires.
> 12 And I will make your pinnacles of ruby,
> > And your gates of sparkling stones,
> > And at all your borders beautiful stones.
> 13   All your sons shall be taught of the Lord,
> > And great will be the welfare of my builders.
> > In righteousness you shall be established."

6. The Future Welfare of the Sons of Israel

In 54:14-15 the prophet emphasizes Israel's righteousness, freedom from oppression and from terror which oppression creates, as assuring the future welfare of the sons of Israel. The Lord will so protect his people that Israel will not be attacked except by a nation that quarrels with God.

> 54:14 "Right and sound shalt thou settle thyself! [22]
> > Thou shalt be far from oppression,[23]
> > Thou need'st not fear;
> > And from terror, for it shall not come near you.
> 15 Lo, should any stir up strife, it is not from me,
> > Whosoever stirs up strife against you
> > Shall fall away unto you." [24]

7. The Lord Will Not Permit His People to Be Destroyed

In 54:16-17 the prophet thinks of the Lord who creates the smith that he may produce weapons as instruments of the divine will, but who will not permit his people Israel to be destroyed. It is the Lord himself who is represented as speaking.

> 54:16 "Lo, it is I who create the artificer,
> > Who blows upon the charcoal fire,

[22] G. A. Smith, op. cit., p. 426.
[23] BDB, p. 955.
[24] Cheyne, The Prophecies of Isaiah, II, 57.

And brings into being a weapon as his work.[25]
And it is I who created the destroyer to destroy;
17 Any weapon that is devised against you shall not prosper,
And every tongue that rises against you in judgment,
You shall condemn as guilty.
This is the assigned portion of the servants of the Lord
And their vindication from me, says the Lord."

H. ISRAEL WILL BECOME A WITNESS OF GOD'S STEADFAST LOVE

Ch. 55 is the climax of the Second Isaiah's message, and it is athrill with the glad note of the consolation of Israel. It is closely related to the prophet's opening call to comfort (40:1-2) and brings his entire message to a magnificent climax.

1. God's Gracious Invitation

The opening verses (55:1-5) are a gracious invitation of the Lord to his people, and every one of them is included. The prophet makes it clear that it is not money that the Lord wants from his people in order that they may be sure of his blessing. They cannot buy their way into his kingdom. What God desires is an attentive ear and a spirit in harmony with the eternal covenant which he is making with his people so that Israel will become a witness of the Lord's steadfast love most clearly manifested in David's royal career, who was, as Muilenburg states it, "in some sense at least a mediator between Yahweh and [Israel]." [26] Three specific terms the Second Isaiah uses to express Israel's mission—witness to, leader of, and commander for the peoples. Calls the prophet:

55:1 "Ah! Let every one who is thirsty come to the waters;
And he who has no money come, buy and eat,
Buy wine and milk without price.
2 Why do you weigh out silver for what is not bread?
And why do you toil for what does not satisfy?
Listen carefully to me, and eat what is good,
And take delight in the spiritual blessing of your soul.
3 Incline your ear, and come to me,
Listen, that your soul may live;
I will make with you an eternal covenant,
The sure mercies of David.
4 Lo, I have made you[27] a witness to the nations,
A ruler and commander of peoples.

[25] *Ibid.*
[26] *Interpreter's Bible,* V, 645.
[27] Israel.

> 5 Behold nations you do not know will call, and endow you,
> And nations who have not known you will run to you,
> Because of the Lord your God,
> And of the Holy One of Israel, for he has glorified you."

2. Seek the Lord While He May Be Found

In 55:6-9 the prophet calls upon his people to seek the Lord and emphasizes the supremely significant fact that Israel need not seek him in vain, for he is available and not far away, but near. We are reminded of the words:

> Closer is He than breathing
> And nearer than hands or feet.

If all Israel will find him, that nation must lift up mind and heart and think in terms of God's thoughts and God's ways of dealing, for these tower above merely human thoughts and aims as the heavens tower above the earth.

> 55:6 "Seek ye the Lord while he may be found,
> Call upon him while he is near;
> 7 Let the wicked abandon his way,
> And the unrighteous man his purposes;
> And let him turn to the Lord,
> For he will have compassion upon him,
> And to our God,
> For he will abundantly pardon.
> 8 For my thoughts are not your thoughts,
> And your ways are not my ways,
> Says the Lord.
> 9 For as the height of the heavens above the earth,
> So are my ways higher than your ways,
> And my purposes than your purposes."

3. The Lord's Word Will Accomplish His Purpose

In 55:10-11 our prophet represents God as still continuing the utterance which began at vs. 8. The Lord compares his living word as spoken by the prophet to rain and snow, which he, as creator, sends from the skies to make the soil moist and fertile so that it will carry out his intention of providing both seed for further sowing and bread for human consumption. God's word will not fall short of his intention for it.

> 10 For just as the rain and the snow come down from heaven,
> And do not return there, but water the earth,

> And make it bring forth and sprout,
> And give seed to the sower and bread to the eater,
> 11 So shall my word be which goes forth from my mouth;
> It shall not return to me without effect,
> But will accomplish that in which I take delight,
> And will prosper in that for which I have sent it.

4. The Joy of Liberation from Babylonian Exile

In 55:12-13 the prophet thrills with joy as he anticipates his people's liberation—now not from Egyptian bondage, but from Babylonian exile—with the mountains and hills breaking forth into song and with trees of the field applauding the great release. Desert thorns and briers will be displaced by cypress and myrtle trees. The record of this great deed of the Lord's deliverance of his people will be a permanent memorial to him which shall never be destroyed. The Second Isaiah ends his prophetic message in the mood of joy and peace, hope and triumph.

> 55:12 "For with joy you shall go out,
> And in peace shall you be led forth;
> The mountains and the hills shall break forth before you into singing,
> And all the trees of the field shall clap their hands.
> 13 In place of the thornbush, cypress trees shall grow;
> And in place of the desert plant, the myrtle tree shall grow up;
> And they shall be to the Lord as a sign,
> And as an everlasting memorial which shall not fail."

I. Four Anonymous Passages After the Second Isaiah

1. The Future Worship of the Lord by Ethiopia

Isa. 18:7 is a prose comment certainly dating as late as after 540, from one who, under the influence of Second Isaiah (45:14), anticipated the future acceptance by Ethiopia of the worship of the Lord.

18:7 In that time gifts shall be borne to the Lord of hosts from a people, tall and of polished skin, aye from a people dreadful from that time and onward; a nation mighty, but trodden down, whose land rivers divide, to the place of the name of the Lord of hosts, Mount Zion.

2. Emerging Monotheism

In 19:23-25 we have what Bewer designates "a triple religious alliance of Egypt, Syria and Israel." It refers to Egypt of the Ptolemies, Syria of the

Seleucids, and Israel of the author's own day. The anonymous author of these three verses looks ahead to the time when these three nations, although rivals from the national point of view, will be owned and acknowledged by the Lord and accounted by him as his worshipers.

19:23 In that day there will be a highway from Egypt to Assyria, and the Assyrians will go into Egypt and the Egyptians into Assyria, and the Egyptians will worship with the Assyrians. 24 In that day Israel will be a third with Egypt and with Assyria, a blessing in the midst of the earth, 25 which the Lord of hosts utters, saying, "Blessed be Egypt, my people, and Assyria, the work of my hands, and Israel, my inheritance."

Here is emerging monotheism, one God for all the nations of mankind. As Scott finely says:

The final pair of promises breathes a more generous air than almost any other picture, in the eschatology of postexilic prophecy, of the relationship of Judah to foreign peoples. Egypt, the ancient oppressor, and Assyria, the cruel conqueror, will share the highway of Zion's restoration (cf. 11:16) and will be united with Israel as equal members of the chosen people.[28]

3. The Future of the Lord's Regenerate People

Isa. 4:2-6, as A. S. Peake says, "on grounds of style, ideas, and imagery" are probably post-exilic, dating after 540.[29] The theme is the future of the regenerate community of Israel. The anonymous prophet who wrote these words is deeply concerned because of the obscenity and corruption of the post-exilic Judah of his day. He is not a pessimist, however. Now the Judean community, "the sprout of the Lord," is foul and obscene, a condition which springs largely from the corrupt character of the young women of Jerusalem—"the filth of the daughters of Zion." Only God himself, who acts in part in the spirit of destruction, but always in the spirit of justice, can cleanse such bloodstains from Jerusalem. He alone is able to remove from the Judean people that moral corruption which is now destroying anything that is good in the nation. As in the wilderness days before Israel became a nation the Lord is still to his people as "a pillar of cloud by day and a flame of fire by night" and as a shade from burning heat and as a protection from the downpour of rain.

When the Lord shall have dealt with Judah as only a just God whose acts are based on moral principles must do, his washing off of the filth of Zion's

[28] *Interpreter's Bible*, V, 282.
[29] *A Commentary on the Bible*, p. 439.

daughters and of the bloodstains of Judah's capital city will be succeeded by his continuous hovering over his beloved Mount Zion as the protector, shelter, and Savior of his people. Thus writes this post-exilic thinker.

4:2 In that day the sprout of the Lord will be beautiful and glorious, and the fruit of the land majestic and beautiful, for the escaped remnant of Israel. 3 And the survivors in Zion, and those set free in Jerusalem, will be called "holy to him," everyone who is recorded unto life in Jerusalem. 4 When the Lord shall have washed off the filth of the daughters of Zion and shall have cleaned from its midst the bloodstains of Jerusalem, by the spirit of justice and by the spirit of destruction, 5 Then the Lord will come over the whole extent of Mount Zion, and over its sacred assembly, [as] a cloud by day and smoke and brightness of flaming fire by night; for over all the glory there will be a canopy and a booth. 6 And he will be as a shade from the heat and as a shelter and place of protection from flood and from rain.

4. A Promise to the Remnant

In 28:5-6 the verses are inserted by a later writer, after 540, who is familiar with the speech of Isaiah but whose militarism really clashes with the hopes of our prophet. Isaiah is utterly opposed to Judah's dependence upon such military strength as is expressed in vs. 6. Says this anonymous later writer, from about the time of Ezekiel:

> 28:5 In that day
>> The Lord of hosts will be
>> As a crown of honor,
>>> And as a symbolic headband of beauty
>>>> To the [purified] remnant of his people;
>> 6 And as a spirit of justice
>>> To him who sits as judge,
>> And of might to those who turn back
>>> The battle at the gate.

CHAPTER VIII

The Third Isaiah

I SA. 56-66 IS THE NEXT MAJOR SECTION OF THE BOOK OF ISAIAH. OLD TESTA-
MENT SCHOLARS, TO DIFFERENTIATE THESE CHAPTERS FROM CHS. 40-55, HAVE
designated them the Third Isaiah. As we have already noted, the differentia-
tion of these chapters from chs. 40-55, the so-called Second Isaiah, goes back
to the pioneering work of Bernhard Duhm, who in his commentary on
Isaiah, *Das Buch Jesaja,* contends convincingly that the difference in historical situation which the chapters seem to presuppose from that of chs. 40-
55 argues for a later date.[1] We cannot rightly refer to the writer of chs.
56-66, as it is practically certain that these chapters have more than one
writer. Of this we can be certain, however: The religious life of Israel in
the decades which follow the beginnings of the return from exile in 538,
its problems and its practices, are here presented in concrete manner. The
return of the exiles, anticipated in Isa. 40-55, has taken place in chs. 56-66.
The Jewish community is in Jerusalem. In this section we become aware
of a new sense of the importance of established forms of worship as bringing
to the community spiritual coherence. For here the cultus is more important
than political government, and it is the worshiping community that is at
the center of concern.

A. The Jewish Community in Jerusalem
1. In the Restored Community There Is Place for the Eunuch

In 56:1-57:21, the opening words of Third Isaiah, we are aware at once
of the difference in background of this section from that of chs. 40-55. The
Jews with whom the prophet is concerned are no longer in exile; they and
their children are now upon their own soil, enjoying freedom from foreign
domination and influence both in politics and in religion. The return anticipated and incited by the Second Isaiah has been achieved to considerable
degree. In politics and in religion, after nearly fifty years, Israel is free from

---

[1] Julius A. Bewer, in *The Literature of the Old Testament,* considers Duhm's book "an
epoch-making book, greatly advancing the critical understanding, full of originality, depth
of insight and sympathy, the greatest commentary on Isaiah in any language." P. 446.

foreign government. Cyrus, the great Persian, has been in the Lord's hand,
an instrument of his will that Israel return to its beloved homeland. To a
very considerable extent the Jews and their sons and daughters, who since
587 B.C. had been exiles, have returned to Israel and are enjoying the new
freedom.

We at once become aware that a rival community exists in their midst,
probably the Samaritans. We are informed by 56:3 that there are now in
the restored Israelite community foreigners who have become worshipers of
Israel's God. Also, as vs. 4 informs us, there are eunuchs, emasculated men,
who have joined the Jewish community of worship although in their own
self-consciousness they definitely need to be assured of their rightful place
within Jerusalem's walls and of an honorable participation in the Temple
worship. Although these unfortunate members of society, who had to a
large extent been servants in a foreign court, had been bereft of the power
to create a posterity, the prophet encourages them with the assurance that
if they give assent to the responsibilities made articulate in the Jewish law
they will win acceptance from the Lord himself, and the dignity of a worthy
and abiding repute in the community of Israel will be theirs.

2. In the Restored Community There Is a Place for Foreigners

Likewise foreigners who have become worshipers of Israel's God are acceptable, as are their offerings, in the Judean worshiping community, and
the restored community of Judah will be enriched by people from many
nations.

56:1 Thus says the Lord:
    "Observe justice and do righteousness,
    For my salvation has drawn near,
    And my righteousness will be revealed.
  2 O the happiness of the man who does this,
    And of the son of man who lays hold on it,
    Keeping the Sabbath, so as not to profane it,
    And withholding his hand from doing any evil!"
  3 And let not the foreigner who has joined himself to the Lord
    Say, "The Lord has completely separated me" [from his peo-
    ple];
    And let not the eunuch say,
    "Behold, I am a dried-up tree."
  4 For thus says the Lord:
    "As regards the eunuchs who observe my sabbaths,
    And who choose that in which I delight,

And hold firmly to my covenant,
5 I will give them entry into my house,
  And within my walls, a monument and a memorial,
Better than sons and daughters;
  I will give them eternal fame,
    Which shall not be cut off.
6 And the foreigners who have joined themselves
  To the Lord, to be his servants
And to bless the name of the Lord,
  And those who keep the sabbath not profaning it,
    And who support my covenant—
7 I will bring them to my holy mountain,
  And I will make them joyful in my house of prayer;
Their whole burnt offerings and their sacrifices they shall offer,
  With acceptance, upon my altar;
For my house shall be called
  A house of prayer for all peoples.
8 Says the Lord God,
  Who gathers the banished of Israel,
I will yet gather his exiles
  To those [already] gathered to him."

3. Corrupt Leadership in the Judean Community

In 56:9-57:2 the prophet's words vividly reflect cultic and social conditions in the Jewish community so far as leaders of worship and the rank and file of worshipers are concerned. His foremost interest is with the leaders of the community who should be quick to see community needs. His criticism of them is severe. Because they are so lacking in knowledge and alertness regarding community protection he dubs them "blind watchmen," dogs that cannot see, so do not bark, but they have fierce appetites that are never satisfied. These have surrendered their spiritual commission to their own desire for gain and to their fierce appetites for strong drink; nor do they have any concern for improvement in character. So when righteous men die because they are unprotected by their leaders and when those who are truly merciful are, by death, removed from the human scene, there is utter indifference to the moral and spiritual welfare of the community and no one seems to care.

56:9 All wild beasts of the field, come and eat,
  And all wild beasts of the forest,
10 His watchmen are blind,
  None of them have knowledge;
  All of them are dumb dogs,

They cannot bark;
Sleeping seers,
Who love to slumber.
11 And the dogs are of fierce appetite;
They do not know satiety.
They have all turned, each to their own way,
Each to his own plunder.
12 "Come," [they say] "let us get wine.
Yet, let us fill ourselves with strong drink;
And may today and tomorrow be like this,
Exceeding great in abundance!"
57:1 So righteous men continue to perish, and no man
Takes it to heart;
And merciful men are removed,
With no one taking heed.
2 But before the face of evil, the righteous man perishes,
And peace comes;
They rest in their beds,
Everyone who walks in his integrity.

4. Immorality and Corruption in the Judean Community

In 57:3-8 the reference is to the immorality of the Canaanite nature cults, including sexual intercourse. The phrase "ease themselves under oaks," as J. A. Montgomery suggests, is connected with the divine amours.[2] Also a phase of this cult was child sacrifice, carried on in the wadies. Here is both reproof and threat, and at the same time, information regarding specific immoral cultic acts that were being performed in the name of religion. The mountains and hills were the places where such immoral rites were perpetrated, under the shade of oaks, poplars, and terebinths (cf. Hos. 4:12b-14; Jer. 2:20-25; 3:2).

57:3 And as for you, draw near hither,
Sons of a sorceress,
Offspring of an adulterer, and committers of adultery.
4 With whom have you behaved amorously?
Against whom have you widened your mouth,
Have stretched out your tongue?
Are you not children of transgression,
Seed of corruption,
5 You who ease yourselves[3] under oaks,
Under every luxuriant tree;

[2] "The New Sources of Knowledge" in the Ugaritic texts in connection with the divine amours.
[3] I.e., sexually.

Slaughterers of the children in the wadies,
Under the clefts of the cliffs?
6 Among smooth stones of a wady is your chosen life;[4]
They, they are your allotment;
Also you have poured out to them a drink offering,
You have offered cereal offerings.
7 Upon a mountain, high and lofty,
You have set your bed;
And you go up there,
to sacrifice.
Shall I not take vengeance for these things?
8 And behind the door and door-post,
You have set up your phallus image;
For, deserting me, you have uncovered your bed and offered up;
You made wide your bed;
That you might be cut off from them.
You have loved their bedchamber;
And you have increased your fornication with them;
You have looked on nakedness.[5]

5. Corrupt Pagan Rites in Worship

In 57:9-10 the Third Isaiah designates amazing intensive and persistent
exertions of a cultic nature, using oils and perfumes by which the idolatrous
worshipers sought to make sure of contact with deity, more particularly the
Canaanite god Melek, sending down envoys thus equipped even to Sheol, the
land of the dead, where dwelt the gods of the underworld to consult them.

57:9 And you drenched yourself with oil in honor of Melek,
And you multiplied your perfumeries;
And you sent your envoys far distant,
And you showed abasement even to Sheol.
10 You wearied of the length of your way,
But you did not say, "There is no hope!"
You found renewal of your strength,
Therefore you did not feel weak.

6. The Futility of Idolatrous Rites

In 57:11-13 the prophet, speaking for the Lord, raises a very natural
question, Who are these pagan gods that the Israelites cringe before them
in cowardly terror yet do not fear him who, alone, should awaken in them
holy awe? (Vs. 11). The Lord can keep silent no longer. Only he has the

[4] I.e., of idolatrous habit; BDB, p. 324, and Ginsburg in JBL, p. 59.
[5] Transferring this clause from the end of vs. 6 with BH.

power to declare mankind righteous. Their religious assemblies, with their loud lamentations of distress, are as powerless to influence him as chaff before the wind. The sole source of refuge for Israel is not in pagan deities but in the Lord, and abiding residence in Jerusalem, the hill of Zion, is possible only for those who seek his protection and help. God speaks through the prophet to his people:

> 57:11 And whom did you dread and fear
>   That you failed me,
>   And me you did not remember?
>   Yet did I not put these things upon your heart?
>   And have I not long kept silent,
>   So that you do not fear me?
> 12 I will tell of your righteousness
>   And your deeds
>   But they will not benefit you, when you cry out in distress.
> 13   Will your idolatrous practices save you?
>   Aye, a wind will lift up all of them,
>   A breath will carry them away
>   But he who seeks refuge in me shall possess the land,
>   And shall inherit my holy mountain.

7. *The Wrath of God Toward His People Is Both Punitive and Redemptive*

In 57:14-21 the prophet speaks gracious words in the name of the high and holy God who lives in the hearts of the truly penitent to revive and encourage them. The wrath of God toward his sinful people is not primarily punitive, but redemptive. It is to awaken the spirit of life, available now even to those who have been guilty of forsaking their Lord, for that which proceeds from God is not persistent wrath, but forgiving grace. Moreover his wrath is also disciplinary, intended to awaken repentance. In God's dealings with his people his deepest desire is to heal their hurts and to arouse in them the spirit of thanksgiving. It is peace of mind and heart that God would create, but just as the tossing sea casts up mire, so are the wicked in Israel, as it were, casting up mire and mud. For such citizens within the nation there can be no peace.

> 57:14 And one⁶ shall say, "cast up, cast up a highway, free the way of obstacles,
>   Remove stumbling blocks from the way of my people."
> 15 For thus says the high and exalted one

⁶ Israel.

Who abides forever, and holy is his name:
"I dwell in the high and holy place,
And with the contrite and lowly in spirit,
To quicken the spirit of the lowly,
And to revive the heart of the contrite.
16 For I will not contend forever,
And not forever will I be wrathful;
For the spirit proceeds from me,
And it is I who have created the breath of life.
17b But he went apostate in the way of his heart;
I have seen his ways
17a Because of the iniquity of his unjust gain I was very angry,
And I smote him, hiding myself;
But he went on in the way of his apostate heart.
18 I have seen his ways, but I will heal him and give rest to him;
And I will reward him with comforts, and for those mourning him,
I create thanksgiving[7]
19 Peace, peace to those afar and near.
20   But the wicked are like the tossed-up sea;
21 For it cannot show quietness, but its waters heap up mire and mud.
There is no peace, says my God, for the wicked."

8. The Prophet Is Summoned by God to Declare to the People Their Sins

Fasting, the voluntary practice of abstinence for a time from food and
drink, occupied an important place in ancient Israel. The intent of it was
to lessen the hold upon the Lord's people of the physical in order to exalt
the spiritual element in personality. In 58:1 the prophet is aware of an
impelling impulse from the Lord summoning him to action. He is to "call"
in a loud, clear voice and to publish to Israel—here designated as the Lord's
people and as the house of Jacob—their transgressions and their sins. The
people of Israel appear to be very devout; they observe the externals of religion, delighting to draw near to God and seeking daily contact with him.
They seem to be intensely religious, but the Lord knows how superficial
their worship really is. When they complain that their fasting and repres-
sion of sexual impulses have seemed to win no response from the Lord (vs.
3) the prophet puts his finger on the difficulty. This abstinence is not as
unto God. There is no consecration that sincerely flows out of it toward
him. As Skinner says: "the fasting made them as irritable as Arabs in the
month of Ramadan; it produced a quarrelsome temper which even led to

[7] Literally, fruit of life.

violence." [8] So their prayers which accompanied this fasting do not reach
the ear of God.

It is God who is thus represented as summoning the prophet to action:

> 58:1 "Call aloud, do not refrain,
>   Lift up your voice like a trumpet;
>   And declare to my people their transgression,
>   And to the house of Jacob, their sin.
>   2 Yet me they seek daily,
>   And they delight in the knowledge of my ways,
>   As [though it were] a nation which did righteousness
>   And had not abandoned the judgment of its God.
>   They ask of me righteous judgments,
>   They delight in the approach to God."

9. The Fast as Practiced by the Judeans

While they have sought the Lord through fasting, self-affliction, and lamentation their souls have not really made contact with him. This abstinence has not led to fellowship with God but has made them quarrelsome
and contentious with one another. The only fast God chooses to honor (vs.
5) and with which he is pleased is that in which the suppliant humbles his
own soul and through abstinence represses sensual impulses.

Isa. 58:3a is a question growing out of disappointment that their fasting
has not seemed to bring a divine response. The prophet answers (3b-4)
that their fasting is not a spiritual act of humbling and afflicting themselves
before God with the hope of receiving the divine cleansing and forgiveness
(cf. Lev. 16:30). They are not honestly concerned about learning the divine
will and submitting to the righteous judgments of God. Since their abstinence, through fasting, has made them contentious and quarrelsome their
prayers do not reach his ear at all. Thus the people question the Lord (vs.
3a), and the prophet answers (vss. 3b-4):

> 58:3a "Why have we fasted, but thou hast not seen?
>   Why have we afflicted our souls, but thou dost not know?"
>   3b Behold, in the day of your fast you pursue your own business
>   And you exact all the pledges in your hand.
>   4 See, it is for strife and contention that you fast,
>   And to strike the poor with the fist.
>   You do not fast as you are doing today
>   To make your voice heard in the height of heaven.

[8] Skinner, *The Book of the Prophet Isaiah*, pt. II, 182.

10. The Kind of Fast That Pleases God

In vss. 5-7 the prophet interprets negatively, but also positively, the kind of fast and the purpose of fasting that the Lord himself conceives and accepts. It is not a negative attitude, but a positive humbling of the soul in meekness and humiliation before God in honest, sincere penitence. It is the loosening of fetters of oppression imposed by wicked men wherever in human society that oppression manifests itself. Every yoke of human bondage is to be snapped. In its place must arise social concern—honest solicitude for human beings who are in any kind of bondage, for the hungry, for the oppressed, for the rebellious, and for those who are themselves causing rebellion.

> 58:5 "Is *such as this* the fast which I choose,
>   A day when a man humbles his soul;
>   Is it to bow down his head like a bulrush,
>   And spread on sackcloth and ashes?
>   Is it *this,* which you call a fast,
>   And a day pleasing to the Lord?
> 6 Is not *this* the fast which I choose,"
>   Says the Lord:
>   "To loosen the fetters imposed by the wicked,
>   To unfasten the thongs of the yoke-bar,
>   And let the oppressed go free,
>   And that you snap every yoke?
> 7 Is it not to break your bread to the hungry,
>   And that you bring the rebellious to your house,
>   That when you see the naked you clothe him,
>   And do not hide yourself from your own kindred?"

11. The Rewards of Ethical Spiritual Fasting

In vss. 6-9b the prophet portrays what will result as the rewards of such positive and ethical spiritual fasting. One reward will be light upon life's way, which will break forth like the sun on a glorious Palestine morning. Another will be speedy restoration of the exiles to their beloved homeland. The prophet personifies righteousness and the glory of the Lord, the one blazing the trail, the other, as a protection bringing up the rear guard. Thus God will be sensitive to their prayers and will himself answer the petitions addressed to him.

> 58:8 Then your light shall break forth like the dawn,
>   And your recovery shall spring up speedily;
>   And your righteousness shall go before you,

With your rear guard the glory of the Lord.
9ab Then you shall call, and the Lord will answer;
    You shall cry out for help, and he will say, "Here am I."

12. Corrections in Judean Conduct Will Bring Light Into Darkness

In 58:9cd-10 we have a series of radiant promises conditional, to be sure, upon the favor of God. There are specific corrections that need to be made in the conduct of the Israelites. There must be no oppression of a fellowman. There must be no scornful contempt or gesture of it either felt or expressed toward any human being. Generous provision of food for the hungry and sympathetic attention to the needs of those afflicted will transform the darkness of selfish unconcern into the glorious sunlight of constructive and specific helpfulness. Such lives the Lord will guide, and in accordance with their souls' desires he will bring to them fulfillment, physical strength, and vigor. They will have such influence as will be comparable to the watering of a garden by springs that never go dry. Jerusalem still stands in the ruins that Babylon had brought about, "ancient ruins" they now seem to be. But Israelites to whom the prophet was speaking will return to repair the now shattered foundations of a long and prized past.

58:9cd If you remove oppression from your midst,
        The pointing of the finger, and slander,
10   If you bring out your bread to the hungry
        And satisfy the desire of the afflicted,
        Then shall your light come forth in darkness
        And your darkness will be as noon day.

13. The Noble Names That God Will Give His Obedient People

In vss. 11-12 the prophetic picture comes to its climax. God will be Israel's constant guide and satisfying provider, making them strong, joyous and productive. He pictures Israel, yet to be restored, its deepest desires met, rebuilt upon the ruins of Judah, there to be a dependable foundation for generation after generation of productive living. Two noble names they will be given across the future centuries.

58:11 And the Lord will guide you continually,
       And he will satisfy your soul in scorched regions,
       And you shall be like a watered garden,
       And like a spring, the waters of which do not fail.
12 And your sons shall build up the ancient ruins;
       The foundations of generation after generation.

> And you shall be called "Repairer of the breach,"
> "Restorer of ruins for habitation."

14. The Central Importance of the Observance of the Sabbath

In 58:13-14 the central concern of the prophet is the observance of the sabbath, an institution of prime importance in Israel, which was inaugurated by Moses (Exod. 20:8) and which, during the entire exilic period when the Israelites were in foreign lands, could be and was largely observed by them. If they take delight in sabbath observance as a sincere way of exalting the Lord's character, his words, and his ways religion will not be a burden but a delight, and they will live in dignity with a sensitive appreciation of their heritage, which goes far back to Abraham, Isaac, and in a unique sense, to Jacob (Gen. 28:12-14).

> 58:13 "If you turn back your feet from profaning the sabbath,
>   From carrying on your own business on my holy day,[9]
>   And call the sabbath exquisite delight,
>   And the holiness of the Lord, [thus] honored;
>   And honor it by not going your own ways,
>   By not doing your own pleasure or uttering idle words,
>   14 Then you shall take exquisite delight in the Lord,
>   And I will cause you to ride upon the high places of the earth,
>   And I will feed you with the inheritance of Jacob, your father,
>   For the mouth of the Lord has spoken."

B. The Lord Takes It Upon Himself to Intervene

1. It Is Human Wickedness, Not Lack of Divine Power That Separates from God

In 59:1-8 the prophet sets himself to meet the pessimistic view of many within the community of Israel (vs. 1) that the Lord is powerless to save his people. He makes it clear that there is no lack of power on the Lord's part, but it is the wickedness of the Judean community that is responsible for its separation from God (vs. 2). In vss. 3-8 in vivid language he describes to them in considerable detail and concreteness how their wickedness manifests itself.

> 59:1 Behold,
>   the hand of the Lord has not become powerless, so that it cannot save,
>   Or his ears dull, so that he cannot hear;

[9] Muilenburg, Interpreter's Bible, V, 685.

2 But your iniquities have been making a separation
  Between you and your God,
And your sins have hidden his face
  From you, so that he does not hear.
3 For your hands are defiled with blood
  And your fingers, with iniquity;
Your lips speak falsehood,
  Your tongue utters injustice.
4 No one enters suit justly,[10]
  And no one pleads in honesty;
Trusting in falsehood, and speaking lies,
  They conceive mischief and bring forth trouble.
5 They hatch out adders' eggs,
  And they weave the spider's web;
He who eats of their eggs will die,
  And that which is crushed will hatch into a viper.
6 Their spider threads will not become garments;[11]
  And men will not cover themselves with what they make,
Their deeds are works of iniquity,
  And acts of violence are in their hands.
7 Their feet run to evil,
  And they hasten to pour out innocent blood;
Their deeds are schemes of iniquity,
  Violence and shattering are in their highways.
8 They do not know the way of peace,
  And justice is not in their course of action;
Their paths they have twisted for themselves,
  No one who walks in them knows peace.

2. The Resultant Moral Collapse in Their Community Life

In 59:9-15ab the prophet describes the results of such wickedness in the life of the community. There is no evidence of justice and righteous living in their manner of life. Instead there is darkness and calamity, through which men grope and stumble. In solemnized imagination the prophet hears the groans of oppression in the community where justice and salvation are far from being expressed in human relations. The people do not need to be informed of their sins. Transgression and deceit, crooked dealings man to man, the forsaking of religious principles, and falsehood—all are rampant. Imaginatively the prophet describes the community corruption—justice is driven back; righteousness stands a long way off; truth is stumbling; and honesty and straightness of conduct are utterly impotent. Rebellion, back-

[10] *Ibid.*, p. 688.
[11] I.e., machinations of the wicked.

sliding, oppression—these characterize the Judean community. In vivid, unforgettable pictures (vss. 14-15a) the moral and religious collapse of the
community is portrayed. And if anyone tries to turn from evil conduct to
good he only makes himself a target for corrupt men to aim at with intent
to destroy. Cries the prophet:

59:9   Therefore, justice is far distant from us,
       And righteousness does not overtake us;
       We look [expectantly] for the light, but lo, darkness,
       For brightness, but we walk in calamity.
10   We grope like blind men, for a wall,
       We feel like one who has no eyes;
       We stumble at midday as in twilight,
       Among the lusty [we are] as dead men.
11   We groan like bears, all of us,
       And we moan aloud like doves;
       We look for justice, but there is none;
       For deliverance, but it is far distant from us.
12   For our transgressions have become many in thy sight,
       And our sins testify against us;
       For our transgressions are with us,
       And as for our sins, we know them:
13   Transgressing and acting deceitfully against the Lord,
       And turning away from following our God,
       Speaking crookedness and apostasy,
       And uttering words of falsehood from the heart.
14   So justice has been driven back,
       And righteousness stands far off;
       For truth has stumbled in the streets,
       And honesty is unable to enter;
15a And the truth has become lacking,
15b   And he who departs from evil makes prey of himself.[12]

3. The Lord Intervenes

In 59:15c-17 the Lord, seeing the desperate situation in which his people
seemed impotent and astounded that no human being was shouldering the
responsibility to intervene on behalf of the community, takes it upon himself. Among the great passages of Holy Scripture is this which shows how
God cares for his people. He is here presented as appalled that there was
no one in the community of Judah upon whom he could depend, who
would intervene on its behalf. So God, with the divine initiative, takes upon
himself the responsibility and enters upon a saving activity which is of

[12] The Interpreter's Bible, V, 690.

supreme importance. He it is who, when the need of his people was unspeakably great, intervenes in their behalf. Clothed with garments of divine vengeance, wrapped in a mantle of fury against every evil, the Lord takes the initiative.

> 59:15c The Lord saw with his own eyes, and knew
>   That there was no justice.
>   16 And he saw that there was no man,
>   And he was appalled that there was no one intervening;
>   So his own arm gave him victory
>   And his righteousness sustained him.
>   17 And he put on righteousness as a breastplate,
>   And salvation as a helmet upon his head;
>   And he clothed himself with garments of vengeance,
>   And he wrapped himself with zeal like a robe.

4. God Comes as Redeemer to Those Who Turn From Transgression

In 59:18-20 God is revealed as the Lord who compensates or who makes a suitable reward; to his enemies it is wrath, and we feel this keenly in vs. 18. To those who turn from transgression to righteousness, however, it is recompense—that is, suitable return or reward. From east to west the name and character of the Lord will be forever known as one who rewards righteousness and punishes evil.

> 59:18 As Lord of recompense, recompense he will pay,
>   Wrath to his adversaries, requital to his enemies.[13]
>   19 And they shall see from the west the name of the Lord,
>   And his glory from the rising of the sun;
>   For he will come like a pent-up stream,[14]
>   With the breath of the Lord driving it on.[15]
>   20 "And as redeemer he will come to Zion,
>   And to those who turn from rebellion in Jacob,"
>   Says the Lord.[16]

5. The Lord's Covenant with His People Abides in Force

It is vs. 21 that seems to bring the first major section of the Third Isaiah to a close. It is likely that it was added by the compiler of the Isaianic prophecies. It emphasizes the Lord's covenant with his people and the

---

[13] Delete, with Cheyne, *The Prophecies of Isaiah*, II, 86, as lacking in LXX "To the isle he will pay back recompense."
[14] *Interpreter's Bible*, V, 695.
[15] So BDB, p. 630.
[16] So Cheyne, *op. cit.*, p. 87.

permanence of that covenant in abiding power, as it will be passed down across the generations of Israel.

59:21 "And as for me, this is my covenant with them," says the Lord: "my spirit, which is upon you, and my words which I have put in your mouth, shall not depart from your mouth or the mouth of the offspring of your offspring," says the Lord, "from now even forever."

C. THE GLORY AND GREAT HAPPINESS OF FUTURE ZION

In chs. 60-62 there is one connected theme, the glory and great happiness of Zion of the future. At once in ch. 60 we become aware that we are in a different spiritual climate from that of ch. 59. There the wickedness of the Judean community was the center of attention. Men grope their way through spiritual darkness and calamity. The community is corrupt; the forces of righteousness are impotent. At the end, however, the Lord himself in mighty power intervenes on behalf of his people and as Redeemer comes to Zion and makes with Zion an eternal covenant (59:20-21). These verses become an excellent transition to the thrilling joy of chs. 60-62.

1. Nations Shall Come to Your Light

In 60:1-3 in glad, glowing words the Third Isaiah gives an imaginative description of Zion with God's glory shining upon her as she arises from her despondency and discouragement, attracting other nations and their monarchs by the glory of her light. To Zion the prophet speaks:

> 60:1 Arise, shine; for your light has come,
>   And the glory of the Lord has risen upon you.
>   2 For behold, the darkness shall cover the earth,
>   And a heavy cloud, the peoples;
>   But the Lord shall rise upon you,
>   And his glory shall be seen upon you.
>   3 And nations shall come to your light
>   And kings to the brightness of your dawning.

2. The Return of Dispersed Judeans to Zion

In 60:4-7 the prophet paints an imaginative picture of the restoration of the diaspora, the dispersed Judeans, from distant places. He pictures the return to Zion, the sons walking, the daughters being carried. The exiles themselves will be thrillingly happy. To restored Israel will come by sea-borne commerce the riches of the nations, and caravans of camel bedouins will come from the tribe of Median, of the area east of the Gulf of Akaba;

and from Sheba, in southwest Arabia, a region famous for trade, will come flocks of sheep. Kedar, a tribe of nomads in the North Arabian desert, and Nebaioth, most likely as Nelson Glueck suggests, the Nabateans,[17] will offer themselves, as it were, as animals for sacrifice. In the Temple, yet to be restored, such offerings will dignify the Lord's house. Cries the prophet:

> 60:4 Lift up your eyes round about, and see;
> All of them assemble themselves, they come to you;
> Your sons they shall bring from afar,
> And your daughters shall be carried by a nurse.
> 5 Then you shall see and be radiant,
> And your heart shall be in awe and expanded [with joy];
> Because the abundance of the sea shall be turned toward you,
> The wealth of the nations they shall bring[18] to you.
> 6 A multitude of camels shall cover you,
> Young camels from Midian and Ephah;
> All those from Sheba shall come.
> Gold and frankincense they shall bear.
> And they shall gladden with praises of the Lord.
> 7 All the flocks of Kedar shall be gathered to you,
> The rams of the Nabateans shall minister to you,
> They shall come up acceptably upon my altar,
> And I will beautify my house of prayer.

3. God Has Glorified You

In 60:8-9, to the awed and thrilling question, "Who are these?" the Lord answers that the very isles are stretching out toward Zion and the great commercial vessels that ply the entire length of the Mediterranean Sea to Tarshish in southern Spain are bringing to Zion her exiled sons, who bring with them as offerings to honor their Holy God the gold and silver which they have earned in exile. Cries the prophet:

> 60:8 Who are these that fly like a cloud,
> And like doves to their lattices?
> 9 Galleys shall be gathered to me,
> Ships of Tarshish first,
> To bring my sons from afar,
> Their silver and their gold with them,
> For the name of the Lord your God,
> And for the Holy One of Israel,
> Because he has glorified you.

[17] The Other Side of the Jordan, pp. 13, 40-41.
[18] Reading וכיאו with BH.

4. Wealth From the Nations for the Rebuilding of Zion

In 60:10-12 the prophet is concerned with the rebuilding of Jerusalem's walls, a project which will be participated in by foreigners and their kings as well as by Judeans; that, not in forced submission but in voluntary, international co-operation, thus acknowledging the clear evidence the return of the Judeans gives regarding Jerusalem's spiritual authority. The gates of Jerusalem will not be closed. It is the Lord who speaks:

> 60:10 And foreigners shall build up your walls,
> And their kings shall serve you;
> Although I smote you in my wrath,
> In my favor I will have compassion on you.
> 11 Your gates shall be open continually;
> Neither day nor night shall they be shut;
> So as to bring to you the wealth of the nations,
> With their kings led in procession.
> 12 For the nation and the kingdom which do not serve you
> Shall perish and the nations shall be utterly desolate.

5. The Contribution of Lebanon to the Glory of Zion

In 60:13-16 is portrayed the contribution that Lebanon will bring to the restoration of Zion. The next generation of those who oppressed Zion will contribute to her restoration. Lebanon's contribution will be her famous cypress, pine, and cedar trees (so LXX) which will beautify the sanctuary on Mount Zion. Thus the sons of those who had oppressed Zion will honor it, and restored Israel, enriched by commerce with the nations, shall come into a new awareness of the Lord and a new joy in him. To Zion the prophet gives three great and abiding designations (vs. 14), and the Lord pledges to his people everlasting excellence, and commerce with the nations will pour in its produce and its wealth.

> 60:13 The glory of Lebanon shall come to you,
> Cypress, elm, and pine together,
> To beautify the place of my sanctuary;
> And I will make the place of my feet glorious.
> 14 And humbly there shall come to you, bowing in homage,
> All the sons of those who have spurned you.
> And they shall call you City of the Lord,
> Zion, the Holy One of Israel.
> 15 Instead of being forsaken,
> And hated with no one passing through,

> I will make you an everlasting excellency,
> An exultation generation after generation.
> 16 And you shall suck the milk of nations,
> And you shall suck the breasts of kings,
> And you shall know that I, the Lord, am your Savior
> And your redeemer, the mighty one of Jacob.

6. Zion's Anticipated Splendor and Stability

In 60:17-18 is described, in anticipation, restored Zion's progress in material splendor and national stability. Gold, silver, bronze, and iron, symbols of the Lord's spiritual presence, will replace respectively, bronze, iron, wood, and stones. Zion's walls and gates will be given spiritual designations.

> 60:17 Instead of bronze I will bring gold,
> And instead of iron, I will bring silver;
> And instead of wood, bronze,
> And instead of stones, iron.
> And I will make your magistrates peaceful
> And your rulers righteous.
> 18 Violence shall not be heard any more in your land,
> Havoc or shattering within your borders;
> But you shall call your walls Salvation,
> And your gates Praise.

7. The Lord Will Be Israel's Everlasting Light and Glory

In 60:19-20 the theme "the glory of God in Zion," which this chapter introduced, comes back to the prophet's mind as the climax of the poem. The best characterization which the prophet can give of the glory of the Lord is light ineffable, light that cannot adequately be described. He uses "sun" and "moon" in his description, but it is such a sun as never sets and such a moon as is never withdrawn. Mourning is a thing of the past.

> 60:19 And the sun shall not exist anymore
> To give light by day,
> Nor will the brightness of the moon
> Give light to you;
> But the Lord will be your everlasting light,
> And your God, your glory.
> 20 Your sun will not set anymore;
> And your moon will not withdraw itself;
> For the Lord shall be your everlasting Light,
> And the days of your mourning shall be ended.

8. Inhabitants of the New Jerusalem Will Be Participants in Salvation

In vss. 21-22 the prophet pictures the future glory of Israel, the people of the Lord. All the people of the new Jerusalem will be righteous in the sense, as Volz suggests, of "participating in salvation." [19] Their hold upon the land will be perpetual and will reflect glory upon their God. As Henry Sloan Coffin says: "Here is nationalism, but nationalism under God for the enlightenment of all peoples." [20] The prophet is concerned here with the whole nation. And the closing sentence, as Muilenburg says, "must be read as the climax of all the other climaxes of the poem." [21]

> 60:21 And as for your nation, all of them shall be participating
>   in salvation[22]
>   They shall possess the land forever,
>   A branch of my planting,
>   The work of my hands,
>   That I may be glorified.
>   22 The least one shall become a thousand,
>   And the insignificant one a powerful nation;
>   I am the Lord;
>   In its time I will hasten it.

D. THE GLAD TIDINGS OF SALVATION TO ZION

There is a single theme in ch. 61, the glad tidings of Salvation to Zion. This chapter holds a significant place for the Christian because, as Luke 4: 16-19 informs us, Jesus read Isa. 61:1-2a at the synagogue in Jerusalem on the sabbath day when "he stood up to read." It is significant that, although his own teaching was based upon the Old Testament scriptures, he stopped where he did and thus omitted 61:2b "and the day of vengeance of our God." This shows that he was aware of the limitations of the Old Testament, for to Jesus there was no place for vengeance in religion and certainly not in the character of God.

1. The Spirit of the Lord Is Upon Me

In 61:1-3 we have the content of "the good tidings" which the prophet felt inwardly impelled to utter. We note the verbs which he uses to describe his own awareness of and reception of the Lord's message: "is upon me,"

[19] So Volz; cf. Muilenburg, *Interpreter's Bible*, V, 707.
[20] *Ibid.*
[21] *Ibid.*
[22] So read with Volz; cf. *ibid.*

"has *anointed me* to bring good tidings," "*to bind up*," "*to proclaim*," "*to comfort*," "*to give*." The prophet is aware that it was the Lord's intention that he should thrill people who desperately needed it with "good news," "good tidings." We are in one of life's holiest revelations regarding how God works through men and, specifically here, how God grants transformation from depths of despair to the heights of joy. Those who had been carried into captivity—they and their descendants—are to have their mourning turned into joy, their dullness of life with its sense of mission gone transformed into a joyful awareness of such a mission as will exalt the glory of the Lord.

> 61:1 The spirit of the Lord God is upon me,
>   Because the Lord has anointed me
>   To bring good tidings to the meek;
>   To bind up the broken in heart,
>   To proclaim liberty to the captives,
>   And the opening of the eyes to the blind;
>   2 To proclaim the year of the Lord's favor,
>   And the day of vengeance of our God;
>   3 To comfort all who mourn over Zion—
>   To give them a turban in place of ashes,
>   Oil of joy in place of mourning,
>   The mantle of praise instead of a dull spirit;
>   That they may be called instead oaks of righteousness,
>   The planting of the Lord that he may be glorified.

2. Israel's Recovery of National Prosperity and Dignity

In 61:4-5 the recovery of prosperity and dignity as a nation on the part of Israel is anticipated. Foreigners will attain to insight regarding the plan of God and Israel's part in it, and they will become servants of Israel in the capacity of shepherds, plowmen and vinedressers.

> 61:4 And they shall build up the ancient ruins,
>   Former desolations they shall raise up;
>   And they shall repair desolate cities,
>   The wastes of generation after generation.
>   5 And foreigners shall stand and tend your sheep,
>   And the sons of foreigners will be your plowmen and your
>   vinedressers.

3. Israel's Restoration and Increase of Spiritual and Material Pre-eminence

In 61:6-7 the prophet anticipates for restored Israel pre-eminence both spiritual and material.

> 61:6 But you shall be called priests of the Lord,
>   It shall be said concerning you, "You are servants of our
>   God";
>   You shall eat of the wealth of nations,
>   And in their riches you shall honor yourself.
> 7 Instead of your shame you shall have a double portion,
>   And instead of reproach you shall rejoice in your lot;
>   In your land you shall possess a double portion;[23]
>   Joy everlasting shall be yours.

4. The Lord's Eternal Covenant With Israel

In 61:8-9 is affirmed the character of the Lord and the faithfulness of the Lord to Israel as manifested by his eternal covenant with them and the spiritual quality of Israel's descendants, which will win honorable repute and acknowledgment on the part of the nations. It is the Lord who is here represented as speaking:

> 61:8 For I the Lord love justice,
>   I hate robbery and injustice;
>   And I will faithfully give them their reward,
>   And I will make an eternal covenant with them.
> 9 And their descendants shall be known among the nations,
>   And their offspring among the peoples;
>   All who see them shall acknowledge them with honor,[24]
>   That they are the offspring whom the Lord has blessed.

5. An Exultant Hymn of Praise to the Creator of Righteousness

The chapter comes to its climax in vss. 10-11 with an exultant hymn of thanksgiving and praise to the Lord. The prophet here speaks as one of the representatives of Zion. He is stirred to deep joy. God's righteousness protects and inspires him. In the Judean community Israel's restoration, recovery, and righteous dealings will be clearly evident to the surrounding nations.

> 61:10 I will exultantly rejoice in the Lord,
>   My soul shall rejoice in my God;
>   For he has clothed me with the garments of salvation,
>   With a robe of righteousness has he covered me,
>   As a bridegroom makes ready a turban,
>   And as a bride decks herself with her jewels.
> 11 For as the earth sends forth its shoots,

[23] So read with DSS.
[24] Cf. BDB, p. 648.

> And as a garden causes what is sown in it to sprout,
> So the Lord will cause righteousness to sprout forth,
> And praise in sight of all the nations.

E. THE MESSIANIC PEOPLE

1. Zion as a Crown of Beauty in the Hand of the Lord

In 62:1-3 the theme centers in the people who may rightly be called the messianic people. Beloved Zion (vss. 1-3) is thought of, as vs. 3 suggests, as a crown of beauty in the Lord's hand. We are aware as we read that the author has brilliant literary power as he concentrates upon the mission of his people as the Lord had taught him to understand it. The prophet cannot keep silent until Zion shall have achieved such righteousness of character as will make her comparable to a torch which the pagan nations will see and by which they will be spiritually illumined. As we read these words we must sense that not realization of, but passionate expectancy for the dignity, greatness, and moral beauty of his people is stirring in the prophet's soul. Cries the prophet:

> 62:1 For Zion's sake I will not be silent,
>   Yes, for the sake of Jerusalem, I will not keep quiet,
>   Until her righteousness goes forth like brightness,
>   And her salvation like a torch that is burning.
> 2 And nations shall see your righteousness,
>   And all the kings your glory;
>   And you shall be called by a new name
>   Which the mouth of the Lord shall designate.
> 3 And you shall be a crown of beauty in the palm of the
>   Lord,[25]
>   And a royal turban in the hand of your God.

2. The Covenantal Marriage of God to His People

In 62:4-5, in terms of a human marriage wherein a man marries a virgin, the prophet uses the bride-bridegroom relationship to interpret the new covenantal "marriage" between Israel, which at the moment feels forsaken by its God, and the Lord, who, as it were, taking a new initiative, "marries" Israel, rejoicing in deep joy as though he were the bridegroom and Israel were his bride. Says the prophet:

> 62:4 You shall not be called any more Forsaken,
>   Not any more will your land be called Desolate;

[25] Reading וְאָנִיף instead of וְאָנוּף.

> But you shall be called Hephzibah[26]
> And your land Beulah[27]
> For the Lord takes delight in you,
> And your land shall be married,
> 5 For as a young man marries a virgin,
>   So shall your sons marry you,
> And as the bridegroom rejoices over the bride,
>   So will your God rejoice over you.

3. Watchmen on Zion's Walls Pray for Jerusalem's Welfare and Influence

In 62:6-7 the prophet represents watchmen as stationed by the Lord on the walls of Zion. They are to "put the Lord in remembrance" day and night, and because of their very importunity they are to keep the desperate needs of Jerusalem, their holy city, so steadily before him that the Lord, moved by their intense intercession, will go into action and make Jerusalem an object of praise on the part of the whole earth.

> 62:6 Upon your walls, O Jerusalem,
>   I have set watchmen;
> All the day and all the night
>   Continually they shall not be silent;
> You who keep causing the Lord to remember,
>   Let there be no rest to you,
> 7 And give him no rest
>   Until he establishes,
> Yea, until he makes Jerusalem,
>   A praise in the earth.

4. Judeans Will Enjoy the Product of Their Own Toil

In 62:8-9 the Lord pledges to insure that corn and wine, which the Judeans will cultivate, shall not be consumed by Judah's enemies, but by the Judeans themselves. Their labors provide it and gather it, to be consumed, probably, as Deut. 12:17 ff. and 14:23 indicate, in the sanctuary.

> 62:8 The Lord has sworn by his right hand
>   And by his strong arm:
> "I will never again give your grain
>   As food for your enemies,
> And foreigners shall not drink of your wine
>   Over which you toiled;
> 9 But those who garner it shall eat it,
>   And praise the Lord,

[26] My delight is in her.
[27] Married.

> And those who gather it shall drink it,
> In the courts of my sanctuary."

5. Behold Your Salvation Is Coming

In 62:10-12 the prophet has had awakened within him an overwhelming longing for the return of the exiles to Jerusalem and Judah. Thousands of festival pilgrims were there in Jerusalem, and to them the prophet speaks. The gates are the gates of Jerusalem. He uses warm and telling words as now he speaks to all Jewish exiles everywhere in the entire Middle East, although only his immediate hearers are within reach of his voice. Their salvation is at hand. The difficulties of return are great, but God's reward for them, while not made concrete, is held before them as a challenge. The terms the prophet uses to indicate the Lord's concern for them are "The holy people," "The redeemed of the Lord," and those now being "Sought out" and challenged to return to Jerusalem, "a city not forsaken." The last two lines of vs. 11 are a quotation from the Second Isaiah (40:10).

> 62:10 Go through, go through the gates,
>   Free from obstacles the way for the people;
>   Build up, build up the highway,
>   Free it from stones,
>   Lift up a banner over the nations.
> 11 Behold, the Lord has made proclamation
>   To the end of the earth:
>   Say to the daughter of Zion,
>   "Behold your salvation is coming;
>   Lo, his reward is with him
>   And his recompense before him."
> 12 And they shall be called "The holy people,"
>   "The redeemed of the Lord";
>   And you shall be called "Sought out,"
>   "A city not forsaken."

F. The Two Poles of Third Isaiah's Message

In 63:1-6 we have a passage that reveals a nearness of relationship both with 59:15c-20 and 61:2. In the former passage when "the Lord saw with his own eyes and knew there was no justice," he took the initiative and intervened, "in wrath to his adversaries, requital to his enemies" (59:18bc), and, as the prophet is convinced, "as redeemer he will come to Zion, and to those who turn from transgression in Jacob." In the latter passage in addition to the proclamation of "good tidings to the meek," he is to proclaim "the day of vengeance of our God" (61:2*b*). Here we see the two poles of the Third Isaiah's message, redemption and judgment. Israel, as the Lord's people, from beginning to end is responsible to him. There is keen and sensitive imagination here; there is also drama.

Moreover in this passage we see that the Third Isaiah is at one with his prophetic predecessors in his view of Edom, the capital of which is Bozrah, as the very embodiment of enmity toward God. Here is eschatology—that vital phase of Judean thought that is concerned with finalities. Evident also is imagination—vivid, striking, and gripping. But greater still, there is manifest faith in a God of strength and of vindication who is morally justified in his every judgment and, at the same time, in a God of salvation, deliverance, and redemption. This is vivid prophetic imagination in the service of a mighty faith.

1. *God Took It Upon Himself*

The prophet, in his mind's eye, sees one approaching, marching along in strength, his raiment red with blood. The prophet asks, "Who is this?" God himself, in his almighty saving power, answers. To the further question, "Why the redness of his raiment?" a redness like that spattered on the garments of those treading grapes, the answer reveals to us the sense of responsibility and the loneliness of God, who, seeing the overwhelming need of his people for one who cared for them enough to intervene, yet seeing none who did thus care, *took it upon himself.* In the loneliness of divine vision and the supreme consciousness of responsibility and obligation to his own human creation, yet unaided by them, he alone brings the divine judgment. The prophet's technique in this passage is to raise a question, then answer it, putting his words into the Lord's mouth.

> 63:1 Who is this who is coming from Edom,
>   In crimsoned garments from Bozrah!
>   This one adorned with his raiment,
>   Marching on in the might of his strength?
>   "It is I, speaking in fidelity,[28]
>   Mighty to save."
>   2 On what account is your raiment red,
>   And your garments like one who treads in a winepress?
>   3 "I have trodden the winepress alone,
>   And of my people, there was no one with me;
>   And I trod them down in my anger

[28] S. Smith, *Isaiah 40-55,* p. 484.

> And I trampled them in my wrath;
> And their blood is spattered upon my garments,
> And all my garments I have stained."

2. God's Own Arm Wrought Redemption and Salvation

In 63:4-6 the Lord's answer continues, in which the prophet announced a day of the Lord, a day of universal judgment, but the reverse side of that judgment is the vital, positive, and ultimate contribution of the Lord, "redemption." This is wrought by the divine initiative. The sole source of redemption is God.

> 63:4 "For a day of vengeance is in my heart,
> And my year of redemption has come.
> 5 And I looked, but there was no one to help;
> And I was appalled that there was no one sustaining;
> So my own arm wrought for me salvation,
> And my wrath—it supported me.
> 6 And I trod down peoples in my anger,
> And I shattered them in my wrath,
> And I poured out their life blood on the ground."

G. The Prophet's Intercessory Prayer for His People

In 63:7-64:10 is the prophet's intercessory prayer on behalf of Israel. As Muilenburg says, here "our prophet identifies himself with the life and fate of his people. . . . The words are born in the agony and travail of the prophet for his people. . . . They are Israel's autobiography in man's loftiest and deepest language." [29]

1. Not an Envoy or Messenger, but a Savior

In 63:7-10 there is a look back across the generations of Israel's history, wherein the prophet recalls the mercies of the Lord—his greatness and goodness, and specifically, his compassion and lovingkindness are emphasized. To Israel the Lord himself became a Savior, not an envoy on a mission, but a continuing presence whose love and compassion redeemed his people and bore them. Their rebellious spirit so grieved him, however, that his compassion changed into emity and antagonism. Thus the prophet speaks:

> 63:7 I will recount the lovingkindnesses of the Lord,
> The songs of praise of the Lord,
> According to all which he has dealt out to us,

[29] *Interpreter's Bible*, V, 729.

His great goodness to the house of Israel
Which he has dealt out to us in accordance with his compassion,
And according to his great deeds of kindness.
8 For he said, "Surely they are my people,
Children who will not deal falsely!"
So he became to them as savior,
From all their affliction.
9 No envoy was it, or messenger,
[But] his own presence saved them.
In his love and in his compassion
He redeemed them;
And he bore them and carried them
All the days of old.
10 But they were rebellious and they grieved
His holy spirit;
So he turned into an enemy to them,
He himself fought against them.

2. The Recall of the Wonderful Days of Israel's Beginnings

Isa. 63:11-14 takes us back to the unforgettable wonders that Israel had experienced in its past history. The prophet seeks to turn back the readers' thoughts vividly to the great days of their nation's very beginning when Moses, the Lord's servant, was their leader, with the Lord himself at Moses' right hand and his spirit in Moses' soul (Num. 11:17). It was the Lord who called Moses to become shepherd of Israel, the Lord's flock. They were led by the Lord's spirit, and by his mighty power he opened the waters of the Red Sea before them and led the Israelites through them into a wonderful new epoch of experience as God's people, which reflected glory upon the character of God.

63:11 Then they remembered the days of old,
Of Moses his servant.
Where is he who brought up from the sea
The shepherd of his flock?
Where is he who put in their midst
His holy spirit?
12 He who caused to go at Moses' right hand
His glorious arm?
Cleaving the waters before them,
To make for himself an enduring name,
13 Leading them on through the deeps;
Like a horse in the desert,
They did not stumble.

> Like cattle that go down into a valley,
>   The spirit of the Lord guiding them on.[30]
> 14 So thou didst lead thy people,
>   So as to make for thyself a glorious name.

3. Hold Not Back Thy Pity for Thou Art Our Father

In 63:15-19a the prophet turns from the glorious days of Israel's past history to the critical present, wherein Israel's need for the Lord's help is very great. He appeals in strategic intensity for the presence and solicitude of the Lord, who, to the prophet, seems to be unconcerned and unresponsive. He desires that the Lord should not only see the need of his people, but respond to that need and turn to the help of his people who are his servants and to whom the tribes of Israel belong. Now it seems to the prophet that the Lord does not claim his people as his "servants," his "tribes," nor does the Lord seem concerned about his own sacred precincts where once the Temple stood. It appears now as though Israel could never have been the Lord's people, ruled spiritually by him. We feel the deep sincerity and the passionate intensity of the prayer which the congregation now prays.

> 63:15 Look down from the heavens and see
>   From thy high and holy abode.
>   Where are thy zeal and thy might?
>   The yearning of thy heart, and thy compassion?
>   Hold not thy pity back,
> 16   For thou art our Father!
>   Although Abraham does not know us
>   Nor does Israel acknowledge us;
>   Still thou, O Lord, art our Father,
>   Our redeemer from eternity is thy name.
> 17 Why dost thou make us err, O Lord, from thy ways?
>   Why dost thou harden our heart from fear of thee?
>   Turn for the sake of thy servants,
>   For the sake of the tribes thou dost possess.
> 18 For a little while thy holy people possessed thy sanctuary;
>   Our adversaries have desecrated thy holy place.
> 19 We have become like those from of old over whom thou
>   didst never rule,
>   Like those who have not been called by thy name.

[30] S. Smith, *Isa. 40-55*, 491.

4. A Longing Prayer for the Intervention of God

In 64:1-5b the prophet lifts to the Lord a passionate prayer filled with intense longing that he will intervene on behalf of his people. Let him rend the heavens and come down, making mountains quake as though in awe before his majestic presence and bringing fire which consumes brushwood and makes water boil. Let those nations which are now at enmity with the Lord's people become aware of God's almighty power as he accomplishes, on their behalf, that for which they had not even dared to hope. Let them tremble before him as wax melts before fire. In such vivid, down-to-earth pictures the prophet prays for the Lord to intervene and thus reveal to all enemies of righteousness his immeasurable power. Already this has been evidenced in the awesome events which Israel has experienced—such as the perilous exodus and the wilderness wanderings. Since these mighty events of Israel's past—"from of old"—no human being has ever seen such a God of action, whose very accomplishments on behalf of and through Israel reveal his abiding uniqueness. While working directly from the Hebrew text (63:19b-64:12), we follow the verse numbering as presented in the R.S.V. (64:1-5b).

> 64:1 O that thou wouldst rend the heavens, that thou wouldst come down,
> From before thy face the mountains would quake—
> 2 As when fire enkindles brushwood,
> As when fire brings water to boil—
> So as to make thy name known to thine adversaries,
> Till before thee nations might tremble!
> 3 When thou didst fearful things, which we did not expect,
> Thou didst come down; at thy presence the mountains quaked.
> 4 From of old, men have not heard,
> Eye hath not seen, and ear has not heard
> Of a God save thee, who works for those who wait for him.
> 5a If only thou wouldst meet [with kindness] those doing righteousness!
> And who are remembering thy ways!

5. We Have Sinned Against Thee

In vss. 5cd-7 we are aware of a sudden change in mood. Here is sincere, deeply earnest confession of guilt. The prophet is conscious of the need for the spirit of penitence. With keen spiritual sensitivity he is aware of sin, of iniquity. He is conscious of a sense of separation from God, spiritual hunger, for fellowship with him is gone. God's presence is not felt. The community had surrendered to iniquity and was in its power.

64:5cd Lo, thou wast wrathful for we had sinned against thee.
     Yea, from of old we had transgressed, and shall we be saved?
6   Until we have become as one unclean, all of us,
     And like a soiled garment, all our righteous deeds.
     And we languished as a leaf—all of us,
     And our iniquity swept us off like the wind.
7   With no one calling upon thy name,
     Rousing himself to lay hold upon thee.
     For thou didst conceal thy face from us
     And didst deliver us into the power of our iniquity.

6. Thou Art Our Father: Wilt Thou Restrain Thyself?

The climax of the prayer (vss. 8-12) is a deeply earnest supplication to the Lord opening with a recognition of God as the Father of the worshipers. He turns to the suggestive figure of speech that Jeremiah had used: Israel is the clay; God is the potter (Jer. 18:1-6). He will fashion Israel if Israel will grant him freedom to mold his people as he wills to do. Let the Lord not be angry because of Israel's iniquity. Let him remember that Israel is his people. It is his "holy cities," Zion chief among them, that lie destroyed. Zion's once beautiful Temple is now in ruins, burned by fire, its precious Temple possessions—such as the altar—destroyed, and beloved Jerusalem has been reduced to ruins. How can God restrain himself from intervening? How can he refrain from action on behalf of his people in their desperate need?

64:8 Yet O Lord, thou art our Father;
     We are the clay, and thou art our potter;
     We are all the work of thy hand.
9   Be not exceedingly angry, O Lord,
     And do not remember our iniquity forever.
     Behold, look, I pray,
     For all of us are thy people.
10   Thy holy cities have become a wilderness,
     Zion has become a wilderness
     Jerusalem, the object of a curse.
11   Our holy and beautiful house,
     In which our fathers praised thee,
     Has been burned by fire,
     And all our precious things have become a desolation.
12   Wilt thou, in face of these things, restrain thyself?
     Wilt thou keep silent, and sorely afflict us?

H. God Is Available but His People Call Not Upon Him

In 65:1-25 the prophet is concerned with two parties within the community of Israel that differ sharply the one from the other. In vss. 1-2 he interprets the attitude of the Lord toward his people who have forsaken the religious principles which, through the prophets, Israel had been taught. The Lord has waited in vain for his apostate people to return in loyalty to him. The prophet represents the Lord himself speaking, expressing his availability and his eagerness to help, but also describing the people's utter lack of concern regarding his will for them. The Lord speaks (vss. 1-2):

> 65:1 I was available to be inquired of by those who did not ask me;
> I was available to be found by those who sought me not.
> I said, "Here am I, here am I," to a nation which did not call upon my name.
> 2   I spread out my hands all day long to a stubborn and rebellious people,
> Who walk [in] the way that is not good, following their own ideas.

1. Paganized Features of Israel's Worship

In 65:3-5 the prophet gives some features of the paganized worship which his people are carrying on, a worship with rites abhorrent to the Lord. These are what is taking place in sacred gardens which, as Skinner suggests, are roof gardens "where sacrifices were sometimes offered to false gods." [31] The sitting among the graves (vs. 4) was intended as a way of receiving oracles from the dead, as there they pass the nights. To all Semites, as William Robertson Smith points out, this rite was abhorrent.[32] As Skinner says: "The whole passage is unique, and furnishes a startling revelation of a state of things without parallel in the Old Testament." [33] Says the prophet, speaking for God:

> 65:3 A people who provoke me to anger, to my face, continually,[34]
> Who sacrifice in the gardens, and burn incense on the roof tiles;
> 4 Who sit in tombs and lodge in vaults;
> Who eat the flesh of swine and broth in secret places;
> 5 Who say, "Keep to yourself, come not near me, lest I make you taboo!"
> They are smoke in my nostrils, a fire that keeps burning all day.

[31] *Op. cit.*, pt. II, p. 235.
[32] *Op. cit.*, pp. 218, 290 ff., 351.
[33] *Op. cit.*, pt. II, p. 235.
[34] *Interpreter's Bible*, V, 747.

2. The Lord's Retaliation Because of His People's Idolatrous Conduct

In 65:6-7 the Lord pledges himself to retaliation because of such conduct by a judgment upon these idolaters such as they deserve because of their own guilt and that of their fathers. The Lord speaks:

> 65:6 Lo, it has been written before me!
>   "I will not keep silent until I have paid back the
>   recompense of
>   7 Their guilt, together with the guilt of their fathers,"
>   says the Lord,
>   "Who have burned incense upon the mountains and
>   insulted me upon the hills.
>   I will measure out their recompense and I will pay
>   it into their bosom."

3. God Will Not Destroy His Loyal Servants

In 65:8-10 the prophet turns in a more tender vein to the Lord's own true servants, and his words suggest that they will escape the judgment of God. They are, as it were, the new wine in cluster—that is, the nation as a whole, growing to ripeness and bringing blessing to mankind. The judgment of God is careful and honest, and his power it is, above all, which will bring to fruition in his vineyard the healthy grapes. So out of the offspring both of the northern (Jacob) and southern (Judah) sections of Israel will come worthy descendants who will raise sheep in the fertile maritime plain of the Sharon, the northern part of it from near Carmel to Joppa from six to twelve miles in breadth, and will care for cattle in the valley of Achor, "one of the valleys running up into the mountains from the Jordan depression, somewhere near Jericho." [35]

> 65:8 Thus says the Lord:
>   "Just as when new wine is found in the cluster,
>   And one says, 'Destroy it not for a blessing is in it.'
>   So I will do with respect to my servants,
>   I will not destroy them all.
>   9 But I will bring offspring out of Jacob,
>   And from Judah, the heir to my mountains;
>   And my chosen ones shall possess them,
>   10 And Sharon shall become a pasture of flocks,
>   And the Valley of Achor a resting place for herds,
>   For my people, who shall have sought me out.

[35] Skinner, op. cit., pt. II, 236.

4.. The Lord's Solemn Judgment upon Those Who Forsake Him and Forget Zion

In 65:11-12 the prophet announces the solemn judgment that is destined for those who are forsaking the Lord and letting Zion, the Lord's holy hill, be erased from their memory. Gad and Meni, rendered in the R.S.V., respectively, as Fortune and Destiny, as Muilenburg says, "were probably gods of fate." [36] Gad is a Syrian deity, meaning luck or fortune, and Meni is an Arab deity meaning fate. [37]

> 65:11 But as for you who are forsaking the Lord,
> You are forgetting my holy hill,
> You who set a table for Luck (Marduk),
> And who fill up mixed wine unto Destiny (Fate);
> 12 I will destine you to the sword,
> And all of you will bow down to the slaughter;
> Because, although I called you, you have not answered,
> I spoke, but you did not listen,
> But you have done what is evil in my eyes,
> And have chosen that in which I take no delight."

5. A Fourfold Oracle of Judgment and Blessing

In 65:13-14 in a fourfold oracle of judgment the Lord contrasts his own dealings with his servants that are truly loyal, with the way he must deal with those that are corrupt.

> 65:13 Therefore, thus says
> The Lord God,
> "Lo, my servants shall eat,
> But you shall go hungry;
> Lo, my servants shall drink,
> But you shall thirst;
> Lo, my servants shall rejoice,
> But you shall weep.
> 14 Lo, my servants shall sing
> From joy of heart,
> But you shall cry out from mental pain,
> And from a crushed spirit, you shall wail."

6. God Shall Call His Servants by a New Name

As a consequence the corrupt citizens of Judah will leave behind them a curse, but the loyal servants who worship the true God and swear by him

[36] *Interpreter's Bible*, V, 751.
[37] G. A. Smith, *op. cit.*, II, 498, n. 2.

(vs. 16) will be given a new name corresponding to their transformed character, and with their former distresses forgotten, they will bless themselves by the true God.

> 65:15 And you shall leave your name to my chosen as a curse,
> And the Lord God will put you to death;
> But his servants he shall call by a new name,
> 16 So that he who blesses himself in the land shall bless himself
> By the true God;
> And he who takes an oath in the land shall swear
> By the true God;
> Because the former distresses shall be forgotten,
> And shall be hid from my eyes.

7. God Is Creating a New Heaven and a New Earth

In 65:17-19 the prophet, with mighty faith in the creator God, in vivid, clear pictures, portrays a new age which the redemptive acts of God are bringing into being. This new creation will be such as will thrill Jerusalem with happiness and the heart of God with exultation. Although Jerusalem is now a sad and desolate ruin, it will become a source of joy, and its inhabitants, the Lord's people, will be radiant and never again will be heard there the sobbing of those who are in distress.

> 65:17 "For behold, I am creating a new heavens
> And a new earth;
> And the former things shall not be remembered
> Nor shall they come to mind.
> 18 But be glad and rejoice forever
> Because of what I am about to create;
> For lo, I am creating Jerusalem
> And its people, an exultation!
> 19 And I will rejoice in Jerusalem,
> And will exult in my people;
> And no one shall hear in it any more the sound of weeping
> Or the cry of distress."

8. A Late and Obscure Gloss

Vs. 20 is rightly viewed by Torrey and Kissane as a late gloss.[38] As Muilenburg says, "The language is reminiscent of late Jewish apocalyptic." [39] As Skinner notes, "The impression of the thought is unaccountably laboured

[38] See also Muilenburg, *Interpreter's Bible*, V, 755.
[39] *Ibid.*

and obscure." [40] I follow in part George Adam Smith in the translation of
this verse.[41]

> 65:20 No more shall there be from thence,
>   A suckling of days,
>   Or an old man who does not fill out
>   The days of his life,
>   For a child shall die a hundred years old;
>   Whoever fails of the hundred is accursed.

9. Features of Life in the Messianic Community

In 65:21-25 the prophet is describing, in anticipation, what life will be
like in the messianic community of Judah. George Adam Smith calls attention to the change of meter in this passage "to longer equal lines." [42]
The prophet anticipated the inhabitants' having a long-lived hold upon
the soil, enjoying the fruit of their own labor. The source of lines 2 and 4
in vs. 25 is the messianic passage in 11:7, 9. The third line of vs. 25, "and
dust shall be the serpent's meat," as Skinner says, is an allusion to Gen.
3:14.[43] These lines were probably inspired by the prophet's brooding upon
what Jerusalem and its inhabitants will experience in that wonderful era
that awaits Judah. Building for a future and the enjoyment of the product
of their own labor is the keynote. Permanent hold upon the soil is a second
feature. The security of the children they will bring into the world is a
third. A fourth is the ready response of God when they pray to him. The
major theme of life in the eagerly anticipated community of the future will
be peace in the world of men, and in the animal world as well. The climactic
feature in Mount Zion, the holy center of Judah's life is the reign of peace
and goodwill among Judah's inhabitants, who will live in gracious relation-
ships where the injury or destruction of one by the other will utterly cease.
Duhm is probably right in rejecting as a gloss the half-sentence in the fifth
line of vs. 25, "and dust shall be the serpent's food" [44] (65:25c).

> 65:21 "And they shall build houses, and dwell in them;
>   And they shall plant gardens and eat their fruit.
>   They shall not build and another inhabit;
>   They shall not plant and another eat.
>   22 For as the days of a tree shall be the days of my people,

[40] Skinner, op. cit., pt. II, p. 241.
[41] Op. cit., II, 502.
[42] Ibid.
[43] Op. cit., pt. II, p. 242.
[44] See also Skinner, ibid.

And my chosen ones shall enjoy the work of their hands.
23 They shall not labor in vain,
And they shall not bear children for sudden calamity:
For they shall be the offspring of those blessed of the Lord,
And their children with them.
24 And it shall be, before they call, I will answer;
While they are still speaking, I will hear.
25 The wolf and the lamb shall graze together,
And the lion shall eat straw like the ox;
They shall not do an injury or destroy,
In all my holy mountain," says the Lord.

I. The Third Isaiah Stands in the Line of Purest Prophetic Tradition

The most likely date of Isa. 66:1-24 is within the period 538 to 520 B.C. As James D. Smart has demonstrated, vss. 1-6 date to the time of the rebuilding of the Temple under the instigation of the prophet Haggai.[45] The Third Isaiah, the author of these words, clearly reveals (vss. 1-2) that he is opposed to the dependence of Israel upon any kind of purely external cultus for the bringing of better days to the Judean people. We are aware here that he stands in the line of purest prophetic tradition as manifest particularly in Amos 5:21-25; Hos. 6:6; Isa. 1:11-17; and Mic. 6:1-8.

1. Humility of Spirit and Sensitivity to the Prophetic Teaching

In Isa. 66:1-2 the Third Isaiah emphasizes that what God wants above every other human quality are humility of spirit and sensitivity to the true word of God as uttered by his spokesman. As Skinner says, "the only worship acceptable in his sight is that which proceeds from a humble, contrite and reverent spirit." [46]

66:1 Thus says the Lord:
"The heavens are my throne,
And the earth my footstool;
What kind of house is it which you will build for me?
And where is my resting place?
2 For all these things my hand has made,
And all these things are mine," says the Lord:
"But to this man I show regard, to him who is humble,
And stricken of spirit and who trembles at my word."

[45] *A New Interpretation of Isaiah*, pp. 420-24.
[46] *Op. cit.*, pt. II, 243.

2. The Debasement of the Sacrificial Cult

In vss. 3-4 is vividly described the situation wherein the sacrificial cult has lost any spiritual quality it might have had on the part of reverent worshipers and has become utterly debased and corrupt. The first half of each line, respectively, describes a sacrificial act such as the slaughter of an ox, the sacrifice of a lamb, the presentation of a cereal offering, and the making of a memorial offering of frankincense. The second half of each line, respectively, represents the debasement of sacrifice "by syncretism with corrupt pagan practices," [47] such as murder, the breaking of a dog's neck, the offering up of swine's blood, and the blessing of an idol. Just as these syncretizers have "chosen their own ways," paying no heed to the Lord's call to them, so the Lord will choose affliction for them.

> 66:3 "He who slaughters an ox is like him who kills a man;
>> He who slaughters a lamb for sacrifice is like him who breaks the neck of a dog;
>> He who offers up a cereal offering is like him who offers the blood of swine;
>> He who makes a memorial sacrifice of frankincense is like him who blesses an idol.
>> Yea, these have chosen their own ways,
>> And their souls delight in their detestable things;
> 4 I also will choose wanton dealing inflicted on them,
>> And I will bring upon them their terrors;
>> Because, when I called, no one answered,
>> When I spoke they gave no heed;
>> But they did what was evil in my eyes,
>> And they chose that in which I take no delight."

3. The Mocking Profanity of the Godless in the Judean Community

In 66:5-6 the prophet presents a sharp contrast between, on the one hand, the sincere worshipers in the Jerusalem community, who were sensitive to and receptive of God's word and on the other hand, their corrupt brethren who in mocking and in utter insincerity had taken upon their profane lips a prayer that the Lord's glory might be heightened and that they might themselves see it. These insincere and godless people will themselves be humiliated. In vivid imagination the prophet seems to hear the wrathful voice of God proceeding from the Temple (vs. 6) in solemn in-

[47] Muilenburg, Interpreter's Bible, V, 762.

dignation "rendering recompense"—that is, requiting judgment upon
these his enemies.

> 66:5 Hear the word of the Lord,
> You who tremble at his word:
> "Your brethren who hate you have said,
> Who exclude you for the sake of my name,
> 'May the Lord get himself glory,
> That we may see your joy';
> But they it is who will be ashamed.
> 6 The sound of uproar from the city!
> A voice from the Temple!
> The voice of the Lord, rendering
> Recompense to his enemies."

4. The Birth Pangs of the New Zion

In 66:7-9 the prophet teaches what he passionately believes awaits Israel.
He uses the metaphor of birth to suggest the new people which Zion is to
become. There will take place a sudden, swift, marvelous, and hitherto un-
heard of increase in Jerusalem's population, like the birth of a nation in
a day. There will not be, on the part of God, any weakness in his accomplishment of this on behalf of his people. He will not bring the new Israel
to the point of birth and then forsake her. He who begets the new Israel
will follow through until that new Israel shall be born. Says the prophet:

> 66:7 "Before she was in labor, writhing in travail,
> She gave birth;
> Before birth pangs came upon her,
> She was delivered of a male child.
> 8 Who has heard the like of this?
> Who has seen such things as these?
> Shall a land be born in one day?
> Or shall a nation be born in an instant?
> For as soon as she writhed in travail
> Zion brought forth her sons.
> 9 And I, shall I bring to birth, but not cause to bear?" says the
> Lord your God.
> "Or shall I the begettor, restrain birth?" says your God.

5. The Summons to the Lovers of Jerusalem to Rejoice

In 66:10-11 the prophet summons all lovers of Jerusalem and those whose
hearts mourn over her to rejoice with her. Zion is represented (vs. 11) as

a mother, her breasts being bountifully supplied with milk for her sons and daughters, from which they may suck, draining them in exquisite delight.

> 66:10 "Be thou glad, Jerusalem, and rejoice in her,
>   All who love her;
>   Be glad with her, exalting,
>   All who are mourning over her;
>   11 That you may suck and be satisfied,
>   From her consoling breasts;
>   That you may drain out and take exquisite delight,
>   From the abundance of her glory."

6. The Promise of Prosperity to the New Jerusalem

In 66:12-14 the prophet, in the Lord's name, promises the new Jerusalem and her inhabitants prosperity which will be derived from the wealth of foreigners. Jerusalem will experience God's comfort, but the enemies of the Lord, his indignation.

> 66:12 For thus says the Lord:
>   "Lo, I am extending to her prosperity like a river,
>   And the wealth of the nations like an overflowing stream,
>   13 And their sucklings shall be carried on her hip,
>   And fondled upon the knees.
>   14 And you shall see, and your heart shall rejoice;
>   And your whole being shall flourish like green grass,
>   And it shall be known that the hand of the Lord is with his servants,
>   And his indignation is against his enemies."

7. The Manifestation of the Lord in Worldwide Judgment

In 66:15-16 is described imaginatively the sudden and majestic manifestation of the Lord in fire and tempest as he comes to take vengeance upon his enemies. It is a worldwide judgment that is here anticipated and is to be expressed by fire and sword.

> 66:15 "For lo, the Lord will come like fire,
>   And his chariots like a storm-wind,
>   To pay [as recompense] in the heat of his anger,
>   And his rebuke in flames of fire.
>   16 For by fire the Lord will enter into judgment with all
>   the earth,
>   And by his sword with all flesh,
>   And the slain of the Lord will be many."

8. Ceremonies of Purification

In 66:17 we have, as Muilenburg suggests a verse which "is composed as a link between vss. 1-16 and vss. 18-24. . . . The allusion [go into the gardens] is doubtless to the lustrations [i.e., ceremonies of purification] preliminary to the cultic practices in the gardens." [48]

66:17 "As for those who consecrate themselves and those who purify themselves for [worship in] the gardens, following a leader in the midst, they who eat swine's flesh and swarming things and mice—their deeds and their thoughts will come to an end together," says the Lord.

9. Declaring God's Glory Among the Nations

In 66:18-21 is described, in anticipation, the extension of the knowledge and power of the Lord to all outlying nations and their consequent surrender—not forced, but voluntary—to the Israelites who are in exile among them. The Lord is represented as the speaker.

66:18 "And I am coming to gather all the nations and tongues and they shall come and see my glory. 19 And I will perform a miracle among them, and I will send from them fugitives[49] to the nations, to Tarshish,[50] Put[51] and Lud,[52] Mesheck and Rosh Tubal and Javan[53] to the isles far away which have not heard of my fame and have not seen my glory; and I will declare my glory among the nations. 20 And they shall bring all your brethren[54] from all the nations, as an offering to the Lord, upon horses, and in chariots, and in litters, and upon mules, and upon dromedaries to my holy mountain Jerusalem," says the Lord, just as the Israelites bring the mean offering in a clean vessel to the house of the Lord. 21 "And I will also take some[55] of them for priests and for Levites," says the Lord.

10. The Abiding Permanence of the Worshiping Community

Isa. 66:22-23 is in poetry, vs. 24 in prose. Here the book of Isaiah rises to a magnificent climax. These verses stress the abiding permanence of the blessed, restored community of the new era which the Lord will create. Its descendants and the dignity of their name will abide just as surely as the new heaven and the new earth which the Lord will bring into being. In the story of creation, "[the Lord] rested on the seventh day from all his

[48] *Ibid.*, p. 769.
[49] I.e., survivors of the Judgment (vs. 16).
[50] Tartessus in southern Spain.
[51] So LXX.
[52] African peoples, cf. Gen. 10:6; Ezek. 30:15.
[53] Tribes living south and southwest of the Black Sea.
[54] I.e., Jews.
[55] Gentiles.

work which he had done" (Gen. 2:2), and because of this "'God blessed the seventh day and hallowed it (Gen. 2:3).'" So in the new creation sabbath after sabbath all mankind are to worship before the Lord.

> 66:22 "For just as the new heaven and the new earth
> Which I am making
> Shall remain before me," says the Lord;
> "So shall your descendants and your name remain.
> 23 And it will be from new moon to new moon,
> And from sabbath to sabbath,
> All flesh shall come to worship before me,"
> Says the Lord.

Vs. 24 almost certainly comes from another hand. Although the place is not indicated, it is most likely that the valley of Hinnom is intended, "at the foot of Mount Zion where the contemporaries of Jeremiah built the high places of Topheth for human sacrifice.[56] According to Jer. 7:32, "the days are coming . . . when . . . it will . . . be called . . . the valley of Slaughter: for they will bury in Topheth, because there is no room elsewhere."

24 "And they shall go forth and look on the dead bodies of the men that have rebelled against me; for their worm shall not die, their fire shall not be quenched, and to all flesh they shall be an object of abhorrence."

[56] *Interpreter's Bible,* V, 773.

CHAPTER IX

Blessings of the New Age
and Outbursts of Thanksgiving

IMMEDIATELY FOLLOWING THE THIRD ISAIAH THERE ARE ELEVEN ANONYMOUS SECTIONS OF PROPHETIC MATERIAL. IN THESE SECTIONS THERE IS IMPLICIT faith, passionate in its intensity, that those who are antagonistic to Israel will be defeated in their hope and the now scattered Israel will experience glad restoration to its former territory and to its Temple.

A. The Davidic Rootage of Judah

In 11:10 we have a brief oracle in itself messianic in nature. "Root of Jesse," father of king David, is a reference to the messiah, just as in Rev. 22:16 Jesus is represented as saying, "I am the root and the offspring of David, the bright morning star." Just like a flagstaff Judah will attract the nations. The date is *ca.* 450.

> 11:10 And it shall be in that day,
> The root of Jesse, which stands as an ensign to peoples,
> To him nations shall resort,
> And his dwellings shall be glorious.

B. The Mighty Hope of the Gathering Together of Now Scattered Israel

In 11:11-14, a second oracle, we have the utterance of a mighty hope that the Lord's people—now scattered over the Middle East including Assyria; Upper Egypt (Pathros); Elam, east of Babylonia, which is also called Shinar; Hamath in northern Syria; and the indented coastland and islands of the Aegean Sea[1]—will be gathered to their common homeland in Judah. No longer will there be rivalry between Judah and Ephraim, the Southern and Northern Kingdoms, respectively, of Israel. Together they will swoop down upon their common enemies, the Philistines in the west, and will

[1] Scott, *Interpreter's Bible*, V, 251.

recover the Lord's now scattered people from Assyria, Egypt, Pathros in Upper Egypt, Ethiopia, Elam east of Babylonia, and Shinar, which is Babylonia. Ephraim, the Northern Kingdom, and Judah, the Southern Kingdom, their former rivalry now a thing of the past, will together plunder "the sons of the east," Edom, Moab, and Ammon.

> 11:11 And in that day,
> The Lord will raise his hand a second time,
> So as to repossess the remnant of his people
> Which is left, from Assyria and from Egypt,
> And from Pathros, from Ethiopia and from Elam,
> And from Shinar and from Hamath.[2]
> 12 And he will raise up a signal to the nations,
> And will gather the banished of Israel,
> And he will assemble the dispersed of Judah
> From the four corners of the earth.
> 13 And the jealous rivalry of Ephraim shall come to an end,
> And those harassing Judah shall be cut off:
> Ephraim shall not be jealous of Judah,
> And Judah shall not show hostility to Ephraim.
> 14 But they shall swoop down upon the shoulders of the Philistines
> toward the west.
> Together they shall plunder the people of the east.
> Against Edom and Moab they shall stretch out their hand,
> And the Ammonites shall be subject to them.

C. THE LORD IS PREPARING THE WAY FOR THE RETURN OF EXILES FROM EGYPT AND ASSYRIA

In 11:15-16, a third oracle wherein, plain to sight, there are allusions to the Exodus, the Lord is represented as preparing the way for the return of the exiles from Egypt and Assyria. The tongue of the Egyptian Sea, which is the Gulf of Suez, will be dried up by the fierce breath of the Lord. The "river," the mighty Nile in Egypt, will be reduced to seven waterless wadies, the number seven suggesting completeness of such reduction to utterly dry water beds.

> 11:15 And the Lord will dry up
> The tongue of the Sea of Egypt;
> And he will wave his hand over the Nile,
> With his scorching wind,
> And he will smite it into seven streams,
> That men may cross with sandals.

---

[2] Omitting, with BH, "And from the islands of the Sea."

16 And there will be a highway from Assyria for the remnant
    Which is left of his people,
  Just as there was for Israel
    In the day when he came up from the land of Egypt.

D. THE OUTPOURING OF GOD'S SPIRIT ON JUDAH

In 32:15-20, a fourth oracle, we are in an entirely new mood. The prophet, not Isaiah, as a glance at 44:3 and 45:8 on the one hand, and 60:17 and 61:11 on the other will show, looks ahead in confidence to the transforming power of the spirit of God. The date is approximately 450 B.C. An anonymous prophet is speaking. The transition from disaster to the outpouring of the divine spirit is most marked. The outpouring of the spirit of God, the effect of justice and righteousness, peaceful living in quiet security, and the final picture of successful farmers who deal kindly with their animals, giving them freedom to graze in areas where water is plentiful, bring the chapter to a climactic close. Cheyne views the forest of vs. 19 as a symbol of the proud and scornful rulers of Judah to whose imminent judgment from the Lord the prophet refers under the figure of hail.

32:15 Until there be poured upon us a spirit from on high,
       And the wilderness becomes gardenland,
         And gardenland be accounted a forest.
16 And justice shall abide in the wilderness,
     And righteousness shall dwell in the gardenland,
17 And the product of righteousness will be peace,
     And the service of justice, security forever.
18 And my people will dwell in peaceful habitations
     And in secure dwelling places,
       And in resting places at ease.
19 And the forest will go down in hail,
     And the wooded height in humiliation will be laid low.
20 Happy are you who scatter seed beside all waters,
     And who send forth the feet of the ox and the ass.

E. THE DEAF SHALL HEAR, THE BLIND SHALL SEE

In 29:17-21 and 29:22-24 we have a fifth and a sixth oracle, two later supplements to the original work of Isaiah, which date after 450. The first supplementer ignores any moral basis of change in the spiritual attitude of the people and simply states that in "a very little while," by the initiative of God, Lebanon, famous for its forests of cedar and cypress, will be transformed into a fruit-bearing region. This physical transformation will be accompanied by a wonderful new epoch in the life of its people wherein the deaf and blind, the meek and poor, shall experience amazing blessings of healing and release. The ruthless evildoers, however, who are now harsh oppressors of the Jewish people, will become impotent.

> 29:17 Is it not yet but a very little while
>   Until Lebanon shall be turned into a gardenland,
>   And gardenland shall be esteemed as a forest?
> 18 And in that day the deaf
>   Shall hear the words of a book,
>   And instead of [spiritual] darkness
>   The eyes of the blind shall see.
> 19 And the blind shall again rejoice in the Lord,
>   And needy human beings will be glad in the Holy One
>   of Israel.
> 20 For the ruthless man will cease to be, and the scoffer
>   will perish;
>   And all who are alert doers of iniquity will be cut off.
> 21 Those who bring a man into condemnation,
>   And who lay bait for him who reproves in the gate,
>   The righteous will thrust aside into chaos.

F. The Sense of Awe and the Hunger for Instruction

The second supplementer is responsible for vss. 22-24. He represents the Lord, God of Jacob, who had ransomed Abraham, as assuring Jacob, father of Israel, that he will have no sense of shame when he sees what the Lord will do to his people. The Lord will awaken in that nation both the sense of awe toward him, and on the part of the erring and the fault-finding, the hunger for instruction.

> 29:22 Therefore, thus says the Lord, who redeemed Abraham, concerning
>   the house of Jacob:
>   "No more shall Jacob be put to shame,
>   And no more shall his face be abashed.
> 23 For when he sees his children,
>   The work of my hands, in his midst,
>   They will sanctify my name;
>   Aye, they will sanctify the Holy One of Jacob,
>   And will regard with awe the God of Israel,
> 24 And those who err in spirit will come to understanding,
>   And [rebellious] murmurers will learn instruction."

G. The Lord Waits to Be Gracious to You

Isa. 30:18-26 is later than the Third Isaiah and gives us a picture of blessings in the new age which are reserved for the people of God who are now in adversity. We are aware of a sharp contrast. There is here no rebellion on Israel's part. The Lord is a righteous and just God. Israel may rest in the expectancy that if they wait patiently in faith God knows and cares, and at the right moment, chosen by him, he will intervene. He will hear their cry of need, and although they will experience adversity and affliction, such experiences will lead to the recall of what their teachers had taught as to the way they should go for guidance when they face moments of uncertainty and of need. Says Isaiah:

> 30:18 Therefore the Lord waits to be gracious to you;
> And therefore he will arise to have compassion on you,
> For the Lord is a God of justice.
> Oh the happiness of all those who wait for him!

19 Yes, O people in Zion, who dwell in Jerusalem, you shall not weep any more. He will surely show favor to you at the voice of your cry; when he hears it he will answer you. 20 And although the Lord give to you bread of affliction and waters of oppression, your teachers will not any more be thrust into a corner, but your eyes shall keep seeing your teachers. 21 And your ears shall hear a word from behind you saying, "This is the way, walk in it," when you turn to the right hand or when you turn to the left. 22 And you shall defile the metal plating of your silver idols and the ephod of molten metal of your gold, and shall scatter them; as monstrous filth you shall call it. 23 And he will give rain for your seed with which you shall sow the ground, and bread from the yield of the soil, and there shall be fat and rich food. And your cattle he will tend in that day, lambs of roomy pasture; 24 And the oxen and the male asses, tillers of the soil, will eat seasoned fodder which the winnowing shovel winnows with a pitch fork. 25 And upon every high mountain and upon every lofty hill there shall be lifted up channels of streams of water in the day of great slaughter, when towers fall. 26 And the light of the moon shall be like the light of the sun, and the light of the sun sevenfold, like the light of seven days, in the day when the Lord binds up the fractures of his people and heals its severe wounds.

H. An Elegy Over Moab

1. The Historical Setting of the Elegy

The most likely historical setting of 15:1-16:14, an eighth oracle is the attack upon Moab by the Nabatean Arabs (Obad. 1:1 and Mal. 1:3), which probably occurred in the fifth century B.C. Characteristic of the hostile attitude of Nabateans toward viticulture is their destruction of the vines (16: 8-14). It is likely, as Bewer suggests, that a Moabite poet was the author of this section.[3] The poem is in the nature of an anonymous elegy over Moab—a lament over the destruction of the cities of Ar, a fortified city south of the Arnon River (Num. 21:15), and of Kir, also called Kir-heres (Isa. 16:11), or Kir Hareseth (Isa. 16:7; II Kings 3:25), and today designated El-Kerak, situated in the extreme southern section of Moab. As R. H. Pfeiffer says, "except for the 'Moabite Stone' commemorating the reign of Mesha about 850 B.C. . . . it is the only remnant of Moabitic literature now extant." It probably dates from *ca.* 450.[4]

2. Catastrophe in Moab

The first strophe of the poem (15:1-5a) states the nature of the disaster, the destruction of Moab, and its effect. It describes the lamentation thus occasioned which spread throughout that country. We note the characteristic Moabite mourning rites, such as the ascending of and the weeping on the high places (vs. 2), the shaving of the head (cf. Amos 8:10) and beard (cf. Jer. 41:5), and the girding on of sackcloth (cf. Jer. 48:37) on the part of the inhabitants of Nebo and Medeba to weep and wail.

The news of the catastrophe spreads north across the Arnon River to Dibon (Dhîban), thence to Nebo (Jebel Neba), ten miles east of the Dead Sea and four thousand feet above it, and from there to Medeba, fifteen miles northeast of Dibon.

> 15:1   An oracle concerning Moab.
>   Because in the night
>   Ar of Moab has been destroyed;
>   Because in the night
>   Kir of Moab has been destroyed;
>   2 The daughter of Dîbon has ascended
>   The high places to weep;
>   Over Nebo and over Medeba
>   Moab utters a wail;
>   Upon every head there is baldness,
>   Every beard is clipped;
>   3 In their streets they have girded on sackcloth;
>   Upon their housetops they make a wailing,
>   And in their plazas everyone wails,
>   Lying prostrate in tears.
>   4 And Heshbon cries out, and Elaleh;
>   As far as Jahaz, their voice is heard;

[3] *The Book of Isaiah,* p. 45.
[4] *Introduction to the Old Testament,* pp. 444-45.

> Therefore the loins of Moab tremble;
> His soul quivers within him.
> 5a My heart cries out for Moab,
> Fleeing unto Zoar.

3. Additional Catastrophe in Moab

The second strophe (15:5b-9; 16:2) vividly portrays the danger in which Moab finds itself in the flight to Zoar, a city situated near the southern end of the Dead Sea. Weeping lamenting tears the Moabites ascend Luhith, which, according to Eusebius, is located in southern Moab between Ar and Zoar. They go on the way to near-at-hand Horonaim (Jer. 48:5), probably in southern Moab[5] and as they ascend, raise a wail because of destruction. The waters of Nimrim (vs. 6) refer to the modern Wadi en-Numera, which lies east of Sodom and flows into the Dead Sea at its southern end.[6] The Wadi of the Willows (vs. 7) is the Wadi el-Hesa, which forms the boundary between Moab and Edom. Eglaim is probably the Moabite town—called, 'Aigaleim by Eusebius—which is situated nine miles south of Areopolis.[7] The location of Be'er Elim (vs. 8) is not known, but it must have been near Moab's southern boundary. "The waters of Dîbhan" (vs. 9)—thus correctly designated in the Vulgate, instead of Dîmon—refer to modern Dîbon, a city recently excavated by the American School of Oriental Research in Jerusalem. It is situated north of the Arnon River. The mood of lamentation characterizes this section. As Bewer has noted, 16:2 has been misplaced and rightly belongs after 15:9.[8] It pictures the daughters of Moab at the fords of the Arnon River as timid young birds in flight, inexperienced young nestlings suddenly sent out of the nest. We sense their peril and their fear that breathe in the prophet's words.

> 15:5b For the ascent of Luhith,
>   They will climb it with weeping:
>   For on the way to Horonaim
>   They shall raise a cry of destruction;[9]
>   6 For the waters of Nimrim
>   Shall become a desolate waste;
>   For herbage has dried up, grass is at an end,
>   There is nothing green.
>   7 Therefore, the abundance they have acquired
>   And their store

---

[5] See Bewer, *The Book of Isaiah*, p. 46.
[6] *Ibid.*
[7] So BDB, p. 8.
[8] *The Book of Isaiah*, p. 47.
[9] I.e., Shattering.

> Over the Wadi of the Willows[10]
> They will carry away.
>
> 8 For the cry has gone around
> The border of Moab;
> As far as Eglaim is its wailing,
> And its howling reaches as far as Be'er-Elim.[11]
> 9 For the waters of Dibon are full of blood;
> Yet will I bring upon Dibon additional calamities;
> A lion,[12] for the fugitives of Moab,
> And for those who have remained in the land.
> 16:2 And it shall be like a wandering bird,
> Whose nest has been scattered.
> Daughters of Moab will become
> Like birds in flight, like nestlings sent forth.[13]

4. Moab Fugitives Request Judean Protection

In 16:1, 3-5 the Moabite fugitives, after having arrived at Sela in Edom—which, as Bewer says, "is either Petra or a place near the southern end of the Dead Sea," [14] (Judg. 1:36)—sent messengers to the ruler of Judah in Jerusalem bearing Moab's customary annual tribute of lambs and the wool of rams (II Kings 3:4) and asking for Judean protection. Through their messengers the Moabites venture to give the flattering assurance that if the Judeans respond to them in generous kindness Judah's treasured hope for the dynasty of David will come to fulfilment. Says the narrator:

> 16:1 And they have sent lambs,
> Like creeping things upon the earth,
> From Sela of the wilderness
> To the Mount of the daughter of Zion.

Thus in vss. 3-5 the Moabites are represented as speaking to the Judeans seeking from them protection. Then on Mount Zion their hope for the stable and secure dynasty of David will actually be fulfilled if this protection is granted.

> 16:3 "Give counsel,
> Play the role of umpire;
> Make your shadow like the night
> In the midst of noonday;
> Shelter [the] outcasts,
> Do not betray the fugitives;

---

[10] Wadi el Hesa or Brook Zered, boundary between Edom and Moab.
[11] Near Moab's southern boundary.
[12] I.e., new invasion.
[13] Bewer, *The Book of Isaiah*, p. 47.
[14] *Ibid.*, p. 46.

    4 Let the Moabite fugitives
      Sojourn with you;
    Be a shelter to them
      From before the devastator,
    Until the tyrant is no more,[15]
      The despoiler shall have been finished.
        Tramplers shall have been destroyed from the land.
    5 Then a throne shall be established in loving kindness;
      And one shall sit upon it in faithfulness;
    A judge seeking justice,
      And prompt in righteousness."

5. The Arrogance and Pride of Moab

Judah knew all too well Moab's arrogant, bragging spirit, and was also familiar with its characteristic rites of lamentation, as well as with the eating of the raisin cakes at religious festivals and the culture of grapes, which also played a great part in the celebration of Moabite festivals such as were held at Kir Hareseth (modern El-Kerak) in the extreme south of Moab, a region famous for its viticulture. So Judah rejects the Moabite plea (cf. vss. 6-8). Sibmah (vs. 8) is located near Heshbon (modern Hesban), five miles northeast of Nebo, where, as Bewer says, "there is still much cultivation of the vine." [16]

    16:6 We have heard of the pride of Moab—
      Very proud!—
    Of his haughtiness and his majesty and his arrogance,
    But his boastings are unfounded.
    7 Therefore Moab shall howl for Moab,
      Everyone shall howl.
    For the raisin cakes of Qir Hareseth[17]
    They shall sigh, utterly stricken.
    8 For Heshbon has been devastated; withered
    Is the vine of Sibmah.[18]

6. The Failure of Vintage and Fruit Harvest

In 16:9-10 the lament over Moab's ruin comes to its climax. We sense the mood of intense grief. Vintage and fruit harvest—both have failed. Wine is lacking; gladness is gone; and Moabite prayer seems of no avail.

[15] *Ibid.*, p. 47.
[16] *Ibid.*
[17] BDB, 8.
[18] So read with Bewer, *The Book of Isaiah*, I, 47, instead of foundation.

16:9 Therefore I shall weep bitterly over Jazer,
     Vine of Sibmah;
  I will saturate you with my tears,
     O Heshbon, and Elealeh!
  For upon your summer fruits,
     And upon your vintage
  A devastation has fallen,
 10 And gladness and rejoicing have been taken away
     From the garden land;
  And in the vineyards no ringing cry shall be uttered;
   And wine in wine vats one shall not tread;
     Their vintage shouting is hushed.

7. The Imminent End of Moab

In vss. 11-14 the prophet mourns in his inner being over Moab. Its prayers, whether uttered on outer high place or in inner sanctuary, are of no avail, and the end of Moab as a national power is near at hand. Laments the prophet:

16:11 Therefore my heart mourns for Moab,
     Like the lyre, my inner being murmurs.
  12 And it shall be that when Moab appears on the high place, and goes into his sanctuary to pray, he will not prevail.
  13 This is the word which the Lord spoke to Moab in time past. 14 And now the Lord has spoken, saying, "In three years, like the years of an hireling[19] the glory of Moab shall be lightly esteemed by all the great multitude, and there shall be left a very few, not many."

I. OUTBURSTS OF PERSONAL AND CONGREGATIONAL THANKSGIVING

Isa. 12:1-6, a ninth oracle, presents two brief songs of thanksgiving which are of unknown origin and which date after 450, after the Third Isaiah. The first (12:1-2) is a song of personal thanksgiving. The second (12:4-6) is a song of praise for a festal day.

1. A Song of Personal Thanksgiving

In vss. 1-2 of this anonymous prophecy the author is sensitively aware that the anger of God has turned to salvation and comfort. The dread which the poet once had has been transformed to trust, and the realization of the Lord's saving power has inspired a song in his soul. Just as one draws water from a spring, so the poet draws blessings from the springs of God's saving grace (vs. 3).

---

[19] I.e., reckoned strictly.

12:1 And you will say in that day,
    "I will give thanks to thee, O Lord,
    For although thou wast angry with me,
        Thine anger will turn back and thou wilt comfort me.
  2 Behold, God is my salvation;
    I will trust and not be in dread,
    For the Lord is my strength and my song,
    And he has become my salvation."

2. The Beloved Rite of the New Year

By vs. 3 a song of personal thanksgiving and a hymn of congregational thanksgiving have been joined together, and their rendering accompanies the beloved and familiar rite of the New Year and the Feast of Tabernacles, the drawing of water.

12:3 And you will draw water with rejoicing
    From the springs of salvation.

3. A Congregational Hymn of Praise

In vss. 4-6 the poet utters a song of praise to the Lord, which will flow forth from the soul of Judeans on some festal day. It is not merely the utterance of Judah's praise, but a testimony to peoples other than Israel regarding the deeds of the Lord which they too experience, deeds such as have never before been known in human experience.

12:4 And you will say on that day,
    "Praise the Lord, call upon his name,
    Make known among the nations his deeds,
    Remember that his name is exalted.
  5 Make melody to the Lord, for he has done majestically.
    This is made known in all the earth.
  6 Cry for joy, yea, cry aloud,
    You who dwell in Zion,
    For great, in your midst,
    Is the Holy One of Israel."

This hymn (12:1-6) brings fittingly to a close the first major section of the book of Isaiah in its present arrangement. The two songs of thanksgiving form a concluding doxology.

J. The Doom of Tyre and Sidon

Isa. 23:1-14, a tenth oracle, is a poetic oracle of doom upon Tyre and Sidon. In the first strophe (vss. 1-4) the poet calls the Phoenician mariners to lamentation. The occasion for the lament was the fall of Tyre, which took place in 332 B.C., for as Bewer says: "It is only the capture by Alexander the Great in 332 that does justice to this description." [20] Scott summarily notes that "the general tenor of the oracle is clear enough if it is recognized that it is concerned with the Phoenician people under various designations —the **inhabitants of the coast** (vs. 2) and of **Canaan** (vs. 11), whose principal cities were **Tyre** and **Sidon,** whose trading colonies were **Tarshish** [Tartessus] and **Cyprus,** and who had a large trade also with Egypt." [21]

The Hebrew word for the uttering of an oracle means "to lift up," and the thing that is lifted up is not the voice, but the hand, in gesture of a solemn oath or curse. Thus the heading of this oracle, The Oracle Concerning Tyre, is the designation of a threat, a pronouncement of doom on a foreign people, in this particular instance, upon Phoenicia.

1. The News of the Fall of Tyre

In the first strophe (vss.1-3) the ships of Tarshish are the strong seafaring vessels of Tyre and Sidon that ply the Mediterranean in traffic with Tarshish, located on the southern coast of Spain, and with the isle of Cyprus, toward the eastern end of the Mediterranean. On the last stage of their homeward-bound journey the Phoenician sailors hear of the fall of Tyre, their famous commercial capital.

> 23:1 Oracle concerning Tyre
>> Wail, ye ships trading with Tarshish;
>>> For your fastness has been destroyed,
>>>> Entry from the land of Cyprus has been cut off.
>> 2 Wail, ye coastal dwellers,
>>> Merchants of Sidon,
>> Who ply the sea,
>>> Whose messengers are on great waters;
>> 3 Descendants of merchants,
>>> Its revenue, the Nile, gained from traffic,
>>> Its income, commerce of nations.

2. The Chagrin of Proud Tyre

In vss. 4-5 the prophet imaginatively speaks to Sidon, famed Phoenician city that is yet more ancient than, but not so strong as Tyre. In rhetorical exaggeration he portrays the chagrin of proud Tyre, the greatest

---

[20] *The Book of Isaiah,* 62.
[21] Scott, *Interpreter's Bible,* V, 294.

Phoenician seaport and stronghold. When the startling news of the fall of that famed city reaches Egypt the Egyptians will be moved to anguish. The poetical representation of the sea as the mother of children is most unusual, and there is no trace of anything like it in Hebrew mythology. As Bewer says: "It is Tyre who speaks disconsolately of the loss of her children as if she had never had any." [22]

> 23:4 Be thou ashamed, O Sidon, for the sea has spoken,
>   "I have not writhed in birth pangs, and I have not given birth,
> And I have not brought up choice young men,
>   Nor have I reared daughters."
> 5 When it is heard by Egypt,
>   They will writhe in anguish at the tidings about Tyre.

3. The Desecration of Earthly Pomp and Glory

In vss. 6-9, the second strophe, the prophet urges the Phoenicians to go, as wailing refugees, to their ancient colony of Tartessus (Tarshish), on the coast of southern Spain, because it is the Lord's intention to desecrate the pomp of all earthly glory and to humiliate the proud. Calls the prophet:

> 23:6 Cross over to Tarshish. Wail,
>   Inhabitants of the coastland.
> 7 Is this your jubilant city,
>   Whose antiquity is from days of old?
> Whose feet used to carry her
>   To a distance, to sojourn?
> 8 Who has counselled this,
>   Against Tyre, the crowned one,
> Whose traders are chieftains,
>   Her merchants distinguished men of earth?
> 9 The Lord of hosts has counselled it,
>   To dishonor splendor,
> To treat with contempt
>   All the honored of earth.

4. Exult No More, Virgin of Tyre

In vss. 10-14, the third strophe, Tyre is addressed, as Bewer rightly suggests. Enemies of Tyre have overflowed Phoenicia as the Nile overflows Egypt. The states of Phoenicia—i.e., Canaan—were under the power of kings, but the Lord has given a command against Phoenicia aimed at

[22] The Book of Isaiah, I, 60.

the destruction of its several strongholds. Tyre, the capital of a powerful commercial empire in Phoenicia, is addressed by the prophet:

> 23:10 They[23] have overflowed thy land like the Nile.
> Flee to Tarshish!
> There is no marketplace any more.
> 11 He stretched out his hand over the sea,
> He caused kingdoms to quake;
> The Lord has given commandment against Canaan[24]
> To annihilate its places of safety.
> 12 And he said, "Thou shalt not exult any more,
> Thou violated virgin,[25]
> Daughter of Tyre.[26]
> Cypriots arise, pass over!
> Even there you shall have no peace."

5. The Magnificence of Tyre's Products Is Doomed

In vss. 13-14 the prophet focuses attention upon the Kittiyyim (Chittim), the Cypriots, residents of the island of Cyprus, a colony founded by citizens of Sidon. This isle was famous for its well-known cities, with their siege towers and their brilliant palaces. All this magnificence is doomed to destruction, however.

23:13 Behold the land of Chittim!
[In explanatory words, which, as Bewer notes[27] are a later interpolation, the poet informs us as to who the Chittim are, saying, "this is the people that had not been one, that was founded by the Sidonians; they set up its siege towers, its cities and its palaces."]
He will make it a ruin.

All this is of no avail. The ships bound for Tarshish are summoned to wail over the destruction of Tyre.

6. Wail Over the Destruction of Tyre

> 23:14 Wail, ships of Tarshish,
> For your stronghold has been destroyed.

K. THE EVENTUAL RESTORATION OF TYRE

All of the verses of the eleventh oracle (23:15-18), with the exception of vs. 16, are in prose and are a later appendix which holds in prospect the

---

[23] I.e., the enemies.
[24] I.e., Phoenicia.
[25] Bewer, *The Book of Isaiah*, I, 61.
[26] Instead of Zidon, *ibid.*
[27] *Ibid.*

eventual restoration of Tyre. The seventy years (vss. 15, 17) are an implicit reference to the important words of Jer. 25:11-12 and 29:10 who definitely views the Chaldean domination of Judah as destined to last seventy years. This number seventy occurs again and again in similar contexts—Zech. 1:12; 7:5; Dan. 9:2 ff; II Chron. 36:21—and as Bewer says, "is a round figure." [28] The revival of Tyre did actually begin in 274 B.C.—that is, in exactly fifty-eight years, only twelve years less than the prediction of seventy. The author is anonymous. The most likely date is under the Seleucid kings following its destruction by Alexander in 332.

The songs of the harlot (Tyre), as Skinner says, are "the wiles by which a forgotten prostitute seeks to regain her influence." [29] The comparison of commerce to prostitution has an illuminating illustration in Rev. 18:3, where, speaking of Babylon, this New Testament apocalypse says:

for all nations have drunk the wine of her impure passion,
    and the kings of the earth have committed fornication with her,
        and the merchants of the earth have grown rich with the wealth of her wantonness.

Says this later appendix:

23:15 And it shall be that Tyre shall be forgotten for seventy years, as long as the reign of one king. At the end of seventy years, Tyre "shall fare like the harlot in the song." [30]
    16 "Take a lyre,
            Go around the city,
                Thou harlot who has been forgotten.
        Play beautifully,
            Sing many songs,
                So that you will be remembered."
    17 And it shall be at the end of seventy years, the Lord will graciously visit Tyre with favor and she shall return to her harlot's hire[31] and will act as a harlot with all the kingdoms of the earth upon the face of the ground. 18 And her merchandise and her harlot's hire shall be dedicated to the Lord. It shall not be stored up and it shall not be taken into possession,[32] but its gain from traffic shall be for those who are righteous before the Lord, to eat to satiety and to have as clothing choice attire.

[28] Ibid.
[29] Op. cit., pt. I, 191.
[30] Bewer, The Book of Isaiah, p. 61.
[31] I.e., revenues from her profitable business; ibid.
[32] I.e., for Tyre's own use.

CHAPTER X

An Apocalypse of Judgment
on the World
and a Prophetic Liturgy

T HE APOCALYPSE IS CHS. 24-27, AND CH. 33 IS A PROPHETIC LITURGY. THE
DATE OF THE FOUR CHAPTERS WHICH CONTAIN THE APOCALYPSE IS THE THIRD
century. The date of the chapter which composes the liturgy is the Maccabean era, either 162—when Lysias, the Syrian commander, violated the terms
of capitulation which, as we learn from I Macc. 6:51-62, Judas Maccabeus
had accepted—or the slaughter of the Hasidim, the pious ones, in 160 by
Alkimus and Bacchides in violation of their oath, and the subsequent struggle ending in the disastrous battle at Elasa (cf. I Macc. 7:5-20; 9:1-18).[1] This
is the latest portion of the book of Isaiah.

A. A REVELATION OF WORLD JUDGMENT AND OF THE ULTIMATE
REIGN OF THE LORD

Isa. 24-27 contains a significant apocalypse, by which term is meant revelation, disclosure. Three distinctively apocalyptic features are (1) the blowing
of the Lord's trumpet (27:13), intended to bring together from every direction those who are the elect of God; (2) the resurrection of the dead (26:
19), and (3) the divine judgment of angels (24:21a, 22f), "either fallen
. . . or . . . patrons of heathen nations."[2] As to the nature of apocalypse,
Bewer says: "The apocalypse is a development of the prophetic teaching
of the future. The beginnings of it are in Ezek. 38f, Joel 3, Zech. 14 and
especially in Daniel. It deals with the drama of the last things and the beginning of the reign of God on earth."[3] Three teachings of great significance
are to be found here. These are the hope of immortality, the universality
of salvation, and bodily resurrection from the grave. It is one of the unique

[1] Cf. Scott; *Interpreter's Bible*, V, 348.
[2] R. H. Pfeiffer, *Introduction to the Old Testament*, p. 442.
[3] *The Book of Isaiah*, p. 62.

portions of the book of Isaiah. G. B. Gray has finely entitled it "An Apocalypse of Judgment on the World, and of the Lord's Reign and Glory." [4]

As Pfeiffer says:

Theology and historical background, as well as the general characteristics of language and style, point to the third century as the period in which Is. 24-27 was written.

[This section] marks the transition from the nationalistic expectation of a revived kingdom of David to the apocalyptic visions of cosmic upheavals and rebirth of the whole world. . . . The apocalypse is concerned not merely with restoring the Jewish community in Jerusalem and protecting it from internal and external enemies, but with the whole world—mankind and the physical universe.[5]

George Adam Smith states the mood of these chapters as follows: "Despairing of the redemption of Israel in the present dispensation, and yet believing in the divine justice, certain ardent souls and schools of Israel predicted the sudden intervention of God himself with supernatural forces, resulting in the purgation of this world or even in its overthrow and replacement by new heavens and a new earth." [6]

Sheldon H. Blank, speaking of "Isaiah the apocalyptist," whose major work is the extended apocalyptic vision in chs. 24-27, says: "Stark terror is the apocalyptic mood; but it yields in the end to peace. Worlds clash and splinter. The wobbling earth grows dizzy, overturns and spills its load of corruption. But these somehow stay. In the calm that ensues they are there —the blessed." [7]

There are seventeen sections to this apocalypse. We shall translate each section afresh, giving the theme of each in every case.

1. The Lord's Imminent Destruction of the Land

I   24:1 Lo, the Lord
                Is about to empty out the land
            And make it a desert,
                And distort its surface,
                    And scatter its inhabitants.
             2 When the layman shall fare as the priest;
                The servant as his master;

---

[4] The Book of Isaiah.
[5] Pfeiffer, op. cit., pp. 441-42.
[6] The Book of Isaiah, p. 535.
[7] The Prophetic Faith in Isaiah, p. 165.

> The maidservant as her mistress;
> The owner as the seller;
> The lender as the borrower;
> The creditor as the debtor.
> 3 He will utterly lay waste,
> And take the earth as spoil;
> For the Lord has spoken.

2. Pollution of the Earth Because of the Violation of the Eternal Covenant

In imagination we see the polluted earth languishing under inhabitants who have violated the eternal covenant made by God with his people (Gen. 9:1-17). In 24:4-6 and 12-13 the author pictures the consequent wholesale destruction of the world, which has fallen under the curse of God.

> II 24:4 The earth mourns, it languishes,
> The world withers, it falls;
> The nobles of the earth grow feeble.
> 5 And the earth has become polluted
> Under its inhabitants;
> For they have overstepped [the] laws, they have transgressed the statutes,
> They have broken the eternal covenant.
> 6 As a consequence, a curse
> Consumes the earth,
> And the inhabitants of it are appalled,
> Therefore those dwelling on the earth
> Are diminished,
> And a mere remnant of men is left.
> 12 Appallment has been left in the city,
> And the gates are battered into ruins.
> 13 For so shall it be,
> In the midst of the earth,
> Among the nations,
> As at the beating of an olive tree,
> As at the gleaning,
> When the vintage is at an end.

3. All Joy Has Vanished from the Land

In 24:7-11 the vintage festivals, which were characterized primarily by the mood of happiness, have ceased. All evidence of mirth is absent. The city has become a desolate chaos, and joy has vanished from the land of Judah.

> III 24:7 The new wine mourns
> The vine languishes,

> All the joyous of heart sigh.
> 8 Exultation of tambourines is silenced.
> > The uproar of revelers has come to an end,
> > Exultation of the lyre has ceased.
> 9 They do not drink wine with songs;
> > Strong drink is bitter to those who drink it.
> 10 The city of wasteness[8] has been broken in pieces,
> > Shut up is every house so that none can enter.
> 11 Outcry for the wine is in the streets;
> > All joy has passed away,
> > > The mirth of the land has departed.

4. Songs That Give Glory to the Lord

In 24:14-16a we suddenly seem to hear songs glorifying God, songs which come from the ends of the earth and from the distant islands of the sea.

> IV   24:14   They lift up their voices,
> > They give a ringing cry,
> > > In exaltation of the Lord;
> > 15   Therefore in the east,
> > > Give glory to the Lord;
> > In the coastlands of the sea,
> > > To the name of the Lord,
> > > > The God of Israel.
> > 16a From the extremities of the earth
> > > We have heard songs
> > > > Of honor to the Righteous One.[9]

5. Israel Is Wasting Away

Israel, in spite of such songs which glorify her Lord, feels very weak. The "pit" of vs. 17 is figurative of calamity which will come upon the earth because of its sin.

> V   24:16cb But I said, I am wasting away,
> > I am wasting away,
> > > Woe is me!
> > The treacherous have dealt treacherously,
> > > Yea with treachery have the treacherous dealt treacherously!
> > 17   Dread and [the] pit and plot
> > > [Are] upon you, O inhabitants of the earth!
> > 18a And it will happen that he who flees
> > > From before disaster,
> > > > Shall fall into the pit.

[8] Possibly the capital of Moab; so Bewer, *The Book of Isaiah*, I, 63.
[9] I.e., the Lord.

18b And he who climbs up
    Out of the very mouth of the pit,
      Shall be caught in a trap.

6. The Divine Judgment Through Earthquake and Flood

Isa. 24:18c-23 floods from above and earthquake from beneath will so shake the earth's foundations that it will stagger as though drunken. Angelic princes and human kings fall under the divine judgment and will be imprisoned and eventually punished, to the shame of sun and moon. On Mount Zion, however, the Lord will be glorified before his people (vss. 18c-23).

VI   18c For the windows of the heavens
      Shall be broken open from on high,
        And the foundations of [the] earth shall quake.
    19 The earth is broken in pieces,
      Cracked through;
        The earth is greatly shaken.
    20 The earth staggers terribly,
      Like a drunkard,
        And it sways like a hut;
    For heavy upon it,
      Is its sin, and it shall fall,
        Never again to rise.
    21 And it will happen on that day,
      That the Lord shall punish
        The host of the high ones[10] in heaven,
    And the kings of the earth
      On the earth.
    22 And he shall forcibly remove them to the prison house,
      And they will be shut up in a dungeon,
        And after many days they will be punished.
    23 Then the moon will blush,
      And the sun will be ashamed;
        For the Lord of hosts will reign
    On Mount Zion,
      And in Jerusalem;
        And in the presence of his elders, he will be glorified.[11]

7. The Lord Receives Honor from Great Nations

In 25:1-3 the Lord, doer of mighty deeds, whose faithfulness to his people is perfect, receives the honor of great nations. In vss. 4-5 he is viewed as the

[10] I.e., angelic princes.
[11] Reading with BH יכבר.

protector of the weak and needy and the humbler of the proud boasters who
sing songs of hostility to his kingdom.

VII   25:1 O Lord, thou art my God;
               I will exalt thee, I will praise thy name;
               For thou hast done wonderful things,
               Of long standing is thy perfect faithfulness.
        2 For thou hast turned the city into a stone heap,
               A fortified city into a ruin;
               The citadel of the presumptuous is no more a city;
               It can never be rebuilt.
        3 Therefore mighty nations shall honor thee;
               Cities of terror-striking nations shall fear thee.
       4a For thou hast been a protector to the weak,
               A refuge to the needy in his distress,
       b A shelter from the rainstorm,
               A shade from the parching heat;
               For the breath of the ruthless
               Is like a downpour in winter,
       5a Like the parching heat in drought.
               The uproar of [victory] songs thou dost humble.
               The [hostile] song of those arousing terror
               Is stilled!

8. The Lord Will Wipe Away Tears from All Faces

In 25:6-8, as Gray says, "we have here one of the most catholic [i.e.,
universal] passages in the entire Old Testament, and one of the tenderest
presentations of Yahweh. . . . The writer . . . extended to the nations of the
world all that is tenderest in the Hebrew thought of Yahweh's relation to
Israel." [12] The Lord invites all nations to a feast on Mount Zion, a banquet
of rich food and well-matured wine refined upon the lees, which are the
grounds, the sediment. Here we sense the author's conception of the universality and immortality of God who "has swallowed up" and annihilated
death forever. Tenderly the Lord wipes the tears from the faces of all
human beings of all the nations of mankind.

VIII   25:6 And the Lord of hosts will make
               For all the peoples, on this mountain,
               A feast of fat things,
               A feast of wine [matured] on the lees,
               Full of marrow,
         7 And in this mountain he will annihilate

[12] *Op. cit.*, I, 429.

> The surface of the covering which covers
> All the peoples,
> And the mourning veil[13] that is woven
> Over all the nations.
> 8 He has swallowed up death forever,
> And the Lord God will wipe away tears
> From all faces,
> And the reproach of his people
> He will remove from all the earth;
> For the Lord has spoken.

9. Let Us Rejoice and Be Glad in His Salvation

In 25:9-12 it would seem, as T. K. Cheyne has suggested, that Moab (vs. 10) is "an imaginative type of all the proud enemies of Israel." [14] The tone of the prophet is contemptuous. Moab's end, as G. B. Gray says, is comparable to "that of a man drowned in dung-water," and "recalls the malignancy of the saga that told of Moab's birth (Gn 19³⁰⁻³⁷)." [15]

> IX 9 And one shall say in that day,
> "Behold our God,
> For whom we have waited,
> That he should save us.
> Let us rejoice and be glad
> In his salvation."
> 10 For the hand of the Lord will rest
> On this mountain,
> And Moab shall be trampled down under it,
> Like a trampled-down straw heap
> In waters of a dung pit.
> 11 And if he spread out his hands in the midst of it[16]
> Like the swimmer spreads forth his hands to swim,
> Then he will humiliate his pride[17]
> In spite of the skillful strokes of their hands.[18]
> 12 And the fortress of the high fort of thy walls,
> Shall he bring down, lay low,
> And bring to the ground, even to the dust.

[13] Literally, web.
[14] The Books of the Prophet, p. 151.
[15] The Book of Isaiah, I, 433.
[16] Bewer, The Book of Isaiah, I, 66.
[17] Cf. 16:6.
[18] Bewer, pp. 67 ff.

10. Praise Song to Jerusalem and Its God

In 26:1-6 Jerusalem's sole protection is its righteousness of life as expressed in its steadfast trust in God, the Rock of Ages. The Lord prostrates the haughty people dwelling in supposed security, using his own people as instruments of judgment. Says the prophet:

X   26:1 In that day this song will be sung in the land of Judah:
"A strong city have we;
    Salvation serves
        As walls and ramparts.
  2 Open [the] gates,
    That a righteous nation may enter,
    One which keeps faith,
  3 Whose steadfast purpose
    Is sustained in peace,
    Because he keeps trusting in thee.
  4 Trust in the Lord,
    Forever and aye;
  For the Lord
    Is the Rock of Ages.
  5 For he has prostrated those dwelling on high;
    The inaccessible city,
  He will lay it low,
    He will cause it to fall,
    He will bring it to the ground.
  6 The feet of the humble shall trample it;
    The feet of the poor,
    The steps of the helpless."

11. The Path of the Righteous

In 26:7-13, 14b uprightness of character and righteousness of conduct characterize the way of life of the Lord's people, whose God is just and whose justice, like light, penetrates his every judgment (vss. 7-8). The Lord, desirous of teaching his people, shows no consideration to those who are evil. Across the centuries of its history Israel has known many secular lords, but it regards the Lord alone as its true ruler. Annihilation and extermination—even of remembrance of the wicked—awaits them from the Lord (vss. 7-13, 14b).

XI   26:7 The path of the righteous is upright;
    The course of action of the righteous thou dost smooth,
  8 Yea, in the way of the Lord, Lord of justice,

We have waited upon thy name, and in remembrance of thee;[19]

9   With my soul have I desired thee in the night,
Yea, with my spirit will I longingly seek thee in the morning.
For like the light are thy judgments in the earth.

10   If the wicked be shown consideration,
They do not learn righteousness;
In a land of rectitude, they deviate from the right,
And do not fear
The majesty of the Lord.

11   Lord, thy uplifted hand
They do not behold.
Let them see [thine] anger against the nation,
Yea, let the fire against thine enemies
Consume them!

12   O Lord, mayest thou establish
Peace for us,
Even as, in accordance with all our deeds,
Thou hast dealt with us.

13   O Lord, other lords than thee have ruled over us,
But we do not know other than thee.
We keep thy name in remembrance.

14b   Therefore thou wilt punish and annihilate them,
And wilt exterminate all memory of them.

12. In Distress We Sought Thee

In 26:15-17 the poet acknowledges the increase of Israel as having been made possible by the Lord and as reflecting glory upon him. He likewise thinks of the hours of great distress when in desperate need the Israelite people cried out like a woman in birth pangs. He has now come to the realization that these painful experiences were the chastening of God. Thus he speaks:

XII   26:15   Thou didst increase the nation,
O Lord, thou didst increase the nation;
Thou didst get thyself glory,
Thou hast extended far all the boundaries of the land.

16   Lord, in distress we sought thee,
We cried out in distress when thy chastening was upon us,

17   Like a pregnant woman whom thou hast brought near to delivery
Cries out in her pangs,
So have we become
Before thee, O Lord.

[19] Reading with BH אַף ארח יי משפט קוינול שסך ולזכר, deleting with LXX as a gloss חאוח נפש.

13. The Resurrection of the Righteous Ones

In 26:14a, 14b, 19 we have one of the most unique utterances in the entire
Old Testament. It has to do with the resurrection of the dead. It limits
such resurrection to the Lord's righteous dead. No such hope is held out
for ruthless human rulers. Just as the dew and light fall upon plants and
quicken the life force latent in them, so the Lord's dew falls upon his righteous dead who are in the dust of the earth, and by resurrection he quickens
them into life. Thus it is that the Lord asserts his victory over the grave.

XIII 26:14a Their dead [20] will not live.
      They are ghosts, they will not arise.
    14b Therefore thou wilt punish and annihilate them,
      And wilt exterminate all memory of them.
    19 Thy dead shall live, their[21] bodies shall arise.
      They shall awake and sing,
       Those who dwell in the dust,
      For a dew of dawn is thy dew,
      And the earth shall bring to life the dead.

14. The Lord Comes in Judgment

In 26:20-27:1 the prophet, speaking to the Lord's people, calls upon
them to withdraw into privacy and consequent security while the Lord,
armed with his mighty sword, arises in judgment to destroy the iniquitous
inhabitants of the earth. The author here enters into the sphere of Semitic
mythology, according to which the Lord punishes Leviathan, the fleeing
serpent; and Leviathan, the coiled serpent; and the dragon, whose home
is in the sea. It is possible, as Hilgenfeld suggests, that the flying serpent
designates the Persian and the coiled serpent the Greek empire.[22] Cries the
prophet:

XIV 26:20 Go, my people, enter into your chamber,
      And shut your door after you;
      Withdraw for a brief moment,
      Until the indignation has passed.
    21 For lo, the Lord
      Is coming forth from his place,
       To punish the iniquity of the inhabitants of the earth,
      And the earth will lay bare its blood,
      And will no more cover up its slain.

[20] So read with BH.
[21] So read with BH.
[22] Owen C. Whitehouse, *Isaiah*, p. 286.

27:1 In that day the Lord will punish with his sword, relentless and great and strong, Leviathan the fleeing serpent, and Leviathan the twisted serpent, and will slay the dragon which is in the sea.

15. A Palestinian Vineyard Song

Isa. 27:2-5 is a delightful vineyard song. The vineyard represents Israel, and its keeper is the Lord, who guards it, yet at the same time is inclined to punish it even though he longs for his people to make their peace with him. Vs. 6, which is redactional, sounds a note of hope for the Lord's redeemed. The Lord's blossoming and productive people of the future will fill the earth with fruit,

XV   27:2 And he will say in that day,
         "A delightful vineyard, sing of it!
     3 I, the Lord, am guarding it;
         Moment by moment I will water it,
      Lest something be lacking regarding it,
      Night and day will I guard it.
      A wall I do not have.
     4 O that I had thorns and thistles,
      In battle would I march against it!
      And I would burn it up entirely.
     5 Or let them take hold of me as a refuge;
      Let them make peace with me,
      Peace let them make with me."
     6 In the coming days he will cause Jacob to take root,
      And Israel shall blossom and sprout,
      And shall fill the face of the earth with fruit.

16. The Ministry of Suffering

The theme of 27:7-11 is the meaning of suffering. The Lord takes no joy in the discipline of his people through suffering. If sinful Israel would but destroy its pagan altars and idol symbols of deity its iniquity would be rightly atoned for. Jerusalem is figuratively pictured as shattered, suffering for its sin, its branches, as it were, good only as fuel for fire. The people are destitute of discernment and of divine compassion.

Cries the prophet:

XVI   27:7 Has he[23] smitten him[24] with the blow of one smiting him?
        Or has he[25] been slain like the slaughter of one slaying him?

[23] God.
[24] Israel.
[25] Israel.

8 By driving her forth, by sending her away[26]
   Thou contendest with her.[27]
9 Not so! By this
   Shall the iniquity of Jacob[28] be atoned for,
      And this shall remove all the consequences of his sin:
   When he makes all the stones of the altar
      As pulverized stones of chalk;
         With no Asherim[29] and sun pillars remaining standing.
10 For a [once] fortified city is solitary;
   A residence expelled,
   And forsaken like the wilderness;
      There calves graze, and there
         Thorns and briers send forth branches,[30]
11 When its branches wither, they shall be broken off;
      Women, coming alone will make a fire of them.
   For a people of no understanding is it,
      Therefore he who created them will not have compassion on them,
      And he who formed them will not bestow favor upon them.

17. You Shall Be Picked Up One by One

In 27:12-13 the small apocalypse of the Book of Isaiah reaches its climax. In loving solicitude for his people, the unknown apocalyptist brings his unique work to a close. He is concerned with the whole people of Israel and with the entire biblical area. He contemplates a final harvest in which every individual that counts Israel his homeland is important. They will all be gathered—such is his expectancy—to Mount Zion. In imagination we hear the Lord's trumpet, and we see them return from the two pagan lands of Assyria and Egypt, whither they have been taken one by one to worship the Lord in the holiest place of which they can conceive.

XVII   27:12 And it shall be in that day that the Lord will thresh out from the flowing stream of the river[31] unto the river of Egypt,[32] and you shall be picked up one by one, sons of Israel. 13 and it shall be in that day a blast shall be given with a great trumpet; and they will come—those who are perishing in the land of Assyria, and those who are banished into the land of Egypt, and they shall worship the Lord on his holy mountain in Jerusalem.

[26] Jerusalem.
[27] Skinner, *The Book of the Prophet Isaiah*, pt. I, 215.
[28] Israel.
[29] Sacred poles.
[30] Duhm, *Das Buch Jesaja;* cf. Skinner, *op. cit.,* p. 215.
[31] Euphrates.
[32] Nile.

B. A Prophetic Liturgy

Isa. 33 is a prophetic liturgy which includes three movements of thought, (1) vss. 1-6, (2) vss. 7-16, and (3) vss. 17-24. We have here "a series of prophetic oracles related to the same situation . . . interspersed with prayers of entreaty (vs. 2) and lamentation (vss. 7-9), and (in vss. 14-16) with a liturgical dialogue" such as we meet with in Ps. 15 and Ps. 24:3-5. We are to think of these "alternating prayers and prophetic oracles" as "uttered at such a service of entreaty in the temple as is referred to in Jer. 14:12; 36:6; Joel 2:15-17; II Chr. 20:3-19." [33]

Calling attention to the more specific references (33:7-8) to envoys of peace and covenants that are broken, with good justification Scott connects this prophetic liturgy with the Maccabean struggle and views it as suitable to either of two episodes in it— (a) the destruction of the temple fortress in 162 by Lysias, the Syrian commander, or (b) the slaughter of the Hasidim, the pious or godly, in 160 by Alkimus and Bacchides.[34]

1. The First Movement of the Prophetic Liturgy

The first movement of this liturgy (33:1-6) is a prophetic reproach against the Syrian destroyer, immediately followed by a prayer for God's favor and his abiding, saving energy.

> 33:1 Ah, devastator, although you have not been devastated;
>> And treacherous one, although none have dealt treacherously with you!
> When you have finished as devastator, you will be devastated;
>> When you are done with dealing treacherously they will deal treacherously with you.
> 2 O Lord, show us favor;
>> We have waited for thee.
> Be thou our arm every morning,
>> And our salvation in time of distress.

(a) THE LORD OF JUSTICE AND RIGHTEOUSNESS WILL PROTECT ZION

In this section (33:3-6) the cultic prophet expresses his confidence in the Lord's protection of Zion. Zion's security depends upon the Lord's presence and power and the stability of Judah rests upon such basic elements of Judean character as the prophets Amos, Isaiah, and Micah had stressed as absolutely essential. It is the potent, living presence of the God of Isaiah's inaugural vision—"high and lifted up"—upon which Judah's future de-

---

[33] Scott, *Interpreter's Bible*, V, 348.
[34] *Ibid.*

pends, and it is only his presence filling the hearts and lives of Judeans that will guarantee stable equilibrium in the nation. We hear, in imagination, the roar of the Lord's voice that hurls into scattering flight the peoples from whom booty has been taken just as locusts devour. The prophet then pictures the exalted and triumphant Lord filling Zion with the qualities of his own being and granting it deliverance.

> 33:3 At the sound of uproar,
>   Peoples have fled;
>   At the exalting of thyself
>   Nations are scattered;
> 4 And spoil has been gathered,
>   As the locust devours
>   Like a running of locusts
>   Rushing upon it.
> 5 The Lord is exalted,
>   For he dwells on high;
>   He will fill Zion
>   With justice and righteousness;
> 6 And he will be the stability of your times,
>   Abundance of salvation, wisdom, and knowledge;
>   The fear of the Lord
>   Is his treasure.

2. The Second Movement of the Prophetic Liturgy

Vss. 7-16 form the second movement of the prophetic liturgy, which falls into two parts. Vss. 7-9 are a congregational lament. Heroic Judeans who are for peace weep bitter tears; highways are deserted. As Scott says, there has likely taken place "some definite betrayal by the enemy." [35] Honest witnesses are despicably ignored and the dignity of man is disregarded. The very earth languishes. Glorious Lebanon is ashamed; the lovely plain of Sharon, noted for its fertility, has become a desert. The stately oaks of Bashan, east of the Jordan, extending from the Jabbok River to Mount Hermon, and the fertile slopes of the mountain promontory of Carmel on the Mediterranean Sea are pictured as utterly leafless and barren.

A. THE PRIESTS CRY OUT

> 33:7 Lo, the priests of the altar[36] cry out;
>   Envoys of peace weep bitterly.
> 8 Highways are desolated,
>   Travelers on the road have ceased.

[35] Interpreter's Bible, V, 350
[36] Ibid,

> Covenants are broken,
> Witnesses[37] are despised.
> Man is not held in esteem.
> 9 The land mourns, it languishes;
> Lebanon moulders, displays shame;
> Sharon has become like a desert;
> And Bashan and Carmel shake off their leaves.

B. THE LAMENT OF THE CONGREGATION MEETS THE EAR OF THE LORD

Isa. 33:10-13, the second part of the liturgy, forms a congregational lament which reaches the ear of the Lord. The desperate need of man, whom God himself had called into being, now arouses the divine initiative. The God of international judgment intervenes in mighty strength to overthrow the peoples of the pagan world—in the first instance, the Syrians, the immediate enemy of Judah. In vs. 13 the entire world is called upon to acknowledge what has already been accomplished in the divine counsels, as Scott says, "although to his own people it lay still in the future." [38] The prophet represents God as arising for action and utterance. We hear his rebuke as it comes to pagan nations near and far demanding the acknowledgment of his might.

> 33:10 "Now will I arise,"
> Says the Lord.
> "Now I will exalt myself,
> Now I will rise up.
> 11 You conceive chaff,
> You bring forth stubble;
> My spirit is like fire,[39]
> It will consume you.
> 12 And nations will be as if burned to lime,
> They will be set on fire like thorn bushes.
> 13 Far distant lands will hear what I have done;
> And you that are near, acknowledge my might."

C. SINNERS IN ZION ARE AFRAID

Among the Israelites themselves were some unto whom, as I Macc. 6:21 informs us, were joined ungodly men who had been afraid and had sided with the Syrians against Judas Maccabeus, Israel's deliverer. These are designated "sinners in Zion," who, in this time which calls for heroic loyalty, were concerned merely for their own safety. In 33:15-16 the prophet answers

---

[37] So read with DSS.
[38] *Interpreter's Bible*, V, 351.
[39] So read with Targum רוחי כמו.

the question asked in vs. 14*b*—a question which betrays their lack of courage
—with a challenge. He summons them to that manner of conduct which
alone will guarantee the Lord's protection of Judah in these hours of crisis.

> 33:14 Sinners in Zion are afraid;
> I see trembling of godless men.
> "Who among us can dwell in devouring fire?
> Who of us can dwell amid everlasting burnings?"
> 15 He who walks righteously,
> And speaks habitually what is right;
> Who rejects unjust gain of extortioners,
> Who shakes off his hands,
> From taking a bribe,
> Who shuts his ears
> From hearing a plot to murder,
> And shuts his eyes
> From looking upon evil.
> 16 He shall dwell on high;
> A stronghold of cliffs shall be his secure retreat;
> His bread shall be provided him,
> His water shall be dependable.

3. The Third Movement of the Prophetic Liturgy

This closing movement of the prophetic liturgy (vss. 17-24) falls into two
parts (a) 33:17-20 and (b) 33:21-24.

(a) THE PROSPECT OF A NEW ERA FOR JUDAH

Vss. 17-20 paint before our eyes a beautiful prospect of a new era for
Judah which will be under the reign of a messianic king. All terror at the
ruthless and powerful domination of a foreign power is gone. A new king,
divinely anointed, a messianic ruler, will reign in Zion. Upon him the Lord,
the divine monarch of Judah, has placed his authority (vs. 17). The Judeans
then, in great relief, will ponder the terror which they had earlier experienced at the remorseless demands of that foreign power when it was at the
point of carrying the Judeans into exile.

> 33:17 Your eyes will behold
> The king in perfection of beauty,[40]
> You shall see a land of broad extent.
> 18 Your mind will muse upon [past] terror.
> "Where is the scribe?

[40] Reading ‏וּפִי מְכַלֵּל‎.

> Where is the weigher of tribute?
> Where is he who counts the captives?"

19 You shall see no more a people talking unintelligibly[41]
> A people of unfathomable speech which you cannot under-
> stand.

20 Look upon Zion,
> City of our sacred seasons.
> Your eyes shall see Jerusalem,
> A place of secure abode,
> A tent which cannot be removed,
> Whose tent pegs will never be pulled up,
> And none of whose tent ropes will be snapped.

(b) JUDAH'S PROTECTION BY THE UNSEEN PRESENCE OF GOD

In vss. 21-24 the prophet compares Jerusalem to a mighty, world-famed fortress of history such as that of Nineveh or Babylon or Thebes, the latter being such a one as Nah. 3:8 had described:

> that sat by the Nile,
> With water around her,
> Her rampart a sea,
> and water her wall.

While Jerusalem had no such material protection, far more effective than securely driven tent pegs and strong ropes is the protection of "the Name"—that is, the majestic, though unseen presence of the Lord, the God of Judah, her judge, commander, and king. This potent spiritual presence Jerusalem will abundantly experience, and best of all, Judah's iniquity will be removed and her sickness cured.

33:21 For a glorious abode shall be ours[42]
> A place of rivers, of broad canals.
> Vessels assuming authority shall not sail on it,
> And stately ships cannot pass through it.

23a They have loosened its tent ropes,
> So it cannot hold their mast firm in place.
> They have not spread out the sail.

22 But the Lord is our judge,
> The Lord is our commander,
> The Lord is our king,
> He will save us.

23b Then he will apportion to the blind, prey and spoil in
> abundance,

[41] Reading לועז with BH.
[42] Read כי מושב אדיר יהיה לגו with Kissane, *Isaiah*, I, 371-73.

> To the lame, even, he will multiply booty.
> 24 And no inhabitant will say, "I am sick."
> As for the nation that dwells in it,
> Iniquity will be taken away.

4. A History of Spiritual Triumph

It is of great consequence, as we come to the end of those phases of Old Testament religion which we meet in the Book of Isaiah, to realize the importance of the redactional work of the prophetic books in the period following 400. The late Robert H. Pfeiffer said in the last book that came from his pen:

"The purpose of it was to adapt the ancient oracles to the needs and tastes of Judaism. . . . In Isaiah, Jeremiah and the pre-exilic prophets, the oracles of doom have been systematically softened, if not actually neutralized, through promises of restoration and salvation.

Nevertheless, the history of Old Testament religion is a history of spiritual triumph. . . . For the God of Israel forever reveals himself and offers salvation and healing to his people.

From that single stem of biblical religion there grew rabbinic Judaism and Christianity and, at a later time, Islam—the three great monotheistic faiths which together proclaim to the world that God lives. He demands righteousness and justice, yet his judgments are tempered by mercy for he is a God who judges, yet who loves. Here, indeed, is the continuing story of a spiritual triumph." [43]

[43] R. H. Pfeiffer, *Religion in the Old Testament*, p. 224.

BIBLIOGRAPHY

Albright, William F. "The Biblical Period." *The Jews: Their History, Culture, and Religion.* Edited by Louis Finkelstein. 3rd edition. New York: Harper & Row, Publishers, 1960.

Anderson, Bernhard W. *Understanding the Old Testament.* Englewood Cliffs, N. J.: Prentice-Hall, 1957.

Barnes, William E. *The Two Books of Kings.* New York: Cambridge University Press, 1908.

Barton, George A. *Archaeology and the Bible.* 6th edition. Philadelphia: American Sunday School Union, 1933.

Begrich, Joachim. *Studien zu Deuterojesaja.* Stuttgart: W. Kohlhammer.

Bewer, Julius A. *The Literature of the Old Testament.* 3rd edition. New York: Columbia University Press, 1960.

———, editor. *The Book of Isaiah.* 2 vols. New York: Harper & Brothers, 1950.

Blank, Sheldon. *The Prophetic Faith in Isaiah.* New York: Harper & Brothers, 1958.

Breasted, James H. *A History of Egypt.* New York: Charles Scribner's Sons, 1909.

———. *Ancient Records of Egypt.* 5 vols. (In preparation.) New York: Russell & Russell, Inc.

Brown, Francis; Driver, S. R.; and Briggs, C. A. *Hebrew and English Lexicon of the Old Testament.* London: Oxford University Press, 1955.

Burrows, Millar. *The Dead Sea Scrolls.* New York: The Viking Press, 1955.

———. *More Light on the Dead Sea Scrolls.* New York: The Viking Press, 1958.

Bury, J. B.; Cook, S. A.; and Adcock, F. E. *Cambridge Ancient History.* Vol. III.

Buttenwieser, Moses. *The Prophets of Israel.* New York: The Macmillan Company, 1914.

Cary, Henry, editor. *The History of Herodotus.* Book II.

Cheyne, T. K. *The Book of the Prophet Isaiah.* Leipzig: J. Hinrichs, 1898.

———. *The Prophecies of Isaiah.* 3rd edition, revised. Vols. I and II. New York: Whitaker, Ray & Wiggin, 1884.

———. *The Prophets.* 2nd edition. Vol. I. London: Routledge & Kegan Paul, Ltd.

Coffin, Henry Sloane. Exposition of Isa. 40-66. *The Interpreter's Bible.* Vol. V. Nashville: Abingdon Press, 1956.

Creelman, Harlan. *An Introduction to the Old Testament.* Grand Rapids, Mich.: Zondervan Publishing House, 1917.

Davidson, A. B. *The Called of God.* Edited by J. A. Peterson. Edinburgh: T. and T. Clark, 1902.

Driver, G. R. "Difficult Words in the Hebrew Prophets." *Studies in Old Testament Prophecy.* Edited by H. H. Rowley. New York: Charles Scribner's Sons, 1950.

Duhm, Bernhard. *Das Buch Jesaja.* 4th edition. Göttingen: Vandenhoeck and Ruprecht, 1922.

Eissfeldt, Otto. *Variae Lectiones of Dead Sea Scroll.* New Haven, Conn.: American Schools of Oriental Research, 1950.

Elliger, K. "Der Prophet Tritojesaja," *Zeitschrift für die Alttestamentliche Wissenschaft,* XLIX (1931).

Elmslie, William A. L., editor. *The Book of Chronicles.* New York: Cambridge University Press, 1916.

Fisher, Willis W. *Isaiah and the Nature Cults.* Chicago: University of Chicago Press, 1938.

Frost, S. B. *Old Testament Apocalyptic.* London: The Epworth Press, 1952.

Ginsberg, H. L. "Some Emendations in Isaiah," *Journal of Biblical Literature,* LXIX (1950).

Glueck, Nelson. *The Other Side of the Jordan.* New Haven, Conn.: American Schools of Oriental Research, 1940.

Gray, George Buchanan. *A Critical Introduction to the Old Testament.* New York: Charles Scribner's Sons, 1913.

————. *The Book of Isaiah.* Chs. 1-39. (*International Critical Commentary.*) New York: Charles Scribner's Sons, 1912.

Gunkel, H. *Die Propheten.* Göttingen: Vandenhoeck and Ruprecht, 1917.

Haller, Max. *Das Judentum.* Göttingen: Vandenhoeck and Ruprecht, 1925.

Herberg, Will. *Four Existential Theologians.* Garden City, N. Y.: Doubleday & Company, 1958.

Hooker, Morna A. *Jesus and the Servant.* London: Society for Promoting Christian Knowledge, 1959.

Hyatt, J. Philip. *Prophetic Religion.* Nashville: Abingdon Press, 1947.

Kissane, Edward J., editor. *The Book of Isaiah.* Vols. 1 and 2. Dublin: Browne and Nolan, Ltd., 1941 and 1943.

Kittel, R. *Biblia Hebraica.* Edited by A. Alt, O. Eissfeldt, and P. Kahle. 7th edition. Stuttgart: Privilegierte Wurttembergische Bibelanstalt, 1951.

————. *Great Men and Movements in Israel.* New York: The Macmillan Company, 1929.

Knudson, Albert C. *The Religious Teaching of the Old Testament.* Nashville: Abingdon Press, 1918.

————. *The Beacon Lights of Prophecy.* New York: The Abingdon Press, 1914.

Leslie, Elmer A. *Old Testament Religion in the Light of Its Canaanite Background.* New York: The Abingdon Press, 1936.

————. *The Prophets Tell Their Own Story.* Nashville: Abingdon Press, 1939.

Lods, Adolphe. *The Prophets and the Rise of Judaism.* New York: E. P. Dutton & Company, 1937.

Luckenbill, D. D. *Ancient Records of Assyria.* 2 vols. Chicago: University of Chicago Press, 1927.

Marti, Karl. *Das Buch Jesaja: Strack-Zochler Kurzgefasster Kommentar.* Tübingen: J. C. B. Mohr, 1900.

Milley, C. Ross. *The Prophets of Israel.* New York: Philosophical Library, Inc., 1959.

Moore, George Foot, and Brockington, L. H. *The Literature of the Old Testament.* 2nd edition. New York: Oxford University Press, 1948.

Mowinckel, Sigmund. "Neuere Forschungen zu Deuterojesaja." *Acta Orientalia* I, 1937.

Muilenburg, James. "Isa. 34," *Journal of Biblical Literature,* LIX (1949).

————. Introduction and exegesis of Isa. 40-66. *The Interpreter's Bible.* Vol. V. Nashville: Abingdon Press, 1956.

Peake, A. S., editor. *The People and the Book.* London: Oxford University Press, 1925.

————. *A Commentary on the Bible.* New York: Thomas Nelson & Sons, 1957.

Pedersen, J. *Israel: Its Life and Culture.* 2 vols. New York: Oxford University Press, 1926, 1940.

Pfeiffer, Robert H. *Introduction to the Old Testament.* Revised edition. New York: Harper & Row, Publishers, 1948.

————. *Religion in the Old Testament.* Edited after his death by Charles Conrad Forman. New York: Harper & Row, Publishers, 1961.

Prichard, James B. *Ancient Near Eastern Texts Relating to the Old Testament.* Princeton, N. J.: Princeton University Press, 1950.

Procksch, Otto. "Jesaja." *Kommentar zum Alten Testament.* Leipzig: A. Deichart, 1930.

Robinson, H. Wheeler, editor. *Record and Revelation.* New York: Oxford University Press, 1938.

————. *The Religious Ideas of the Old Testament.* New York: Charles Scribner's Sons, 1913.

Robinson, T. H. *Prophecy and the Prophets in Ancient Israel.* New York: Charles Scribner's Sons, 1923.

Rowley, H. H. *The Growth of the Old Testament.* New York: Longmans, Green & Company, 1950.

————. *The Old Testament and Modern Study.* New York: Oxford University Press, 1952.

Rogers, Robert W. "Isaiah." *The Abingdon Bible Commentary.* Edited by Frederick C. Eiselen, Edwin Lewis, and David G. Downey. Nashville: Abingdon Press, 1929.

Rudolph, W. "Jesaja 24-27." *Beiträge zur Wissenschaft.*

Sanders, J. A. *Suffering and Discipline in the Old Testament and Post-Biblical Judaism.* Rochester, N. Y.: Colgate-Rochester Divinity School.

Scott, R. B. Y. Introduction and exegesis of Isa. 1-39. *The Interpreter's Bible.* Vol. V. Nashville: Abingdon Press, 1956.

Skinner, John. *The Book of the Prophet Isaiah.* (*Cambridge Bible.*) Revised edition. 2 vols. New York: Cambridge University Press, 1915.

Smart, James D. *A New Approach to Isa. 40-66.* Toronto: University of Toronto, 1931.

————. "A New Interpretation of Isa. 66: 1-6," *Expository Times* (London), XLVI (1934-35).

Smith, George Adam. *The Book of Isaiah.* Revised edition. 2 vols. London: Hodder & Stoughton, 1921.

Smith, Sidney. *Isaiah: Chaps. XL-LV.* New York: Oxford University Press, 1944.

Smith, W. Robertson. *The Prophets of Israel.* New York: D. Appleton & Company, 1882.

Torrey, G. C. *The Second Isaiah.* New York: Charles Scribner's Sons, 1928.

Volz, Paul. "Jesaja." *Kommentar zum Alten Testament.* Vol. II. Leipzig: A. Deichart, 1932.

Whitehouse, Owen C. *Isaiah.* (*New Century Bible.*) 12 vols. New York: Frowde, 1905-9.

LIST OF ABBREVIATIONS

ASOR   American School of Oriental Research

BDB   Brown, Driver, and Briggs, *Hebrew and English Lexicon of the Old Testament*

BH   Kittel, *Biblia Hebraica*

HBD   Hastings, *Bible Dictionary*

IB   *The Interpreter's Bible*

JBL   *Journal of Biblical Literature*

LXX   Septuagint

SPCK   Society for the Promotion of Christian Knowledge

INDEX TO BIBLICAL REFERENCES

284

INDEX TO PERSONS AND SUBJECTS